Guidance and Counselling for Children and Adolescents in Schools

Thank you for choosing a SAGE product!
If you have any comment, observation or feedback,
I would like to personally hear from you.

Please write to me at **contactceo@sagepub.in**

Vivek Mehra, Managing Director and CEO, SAGE India.

Bulk Sales

SAGE India offers special discounts
for bulk institutional purchases.

For queries/orders/inspection copy requests,
write to **textbooksales@sagepub.in**

Publishing

Would you like to publish a textbook with SAGE?
Please send your proposal to **publishtextbook@sagepub.in**

Subscribe to our mailing list

Write to **marketing@sagepub.in**

Guidance and Counselling for Children and Adolescents in Schools

Namita Ranganathan

Professor, Central Institute of Education,
University of Delhi

Toolika Wadhwa

Assistant Professor, Department of Education,
Shyama Prasad Mukherji College,
University of Delhi

Los Angeles I London I New Delhi
Singapore I Washington DC I Melbourne

First published in 2017 by

SAGE Publications India Pvt Ltd
B1/I-1 Mohan Cooperative Industrial Area
Mathura Road, New Delhi 110 044, India
www.sagepub.in

SAGE Publications Inc
2455 Teller Road
Thousand Oaks, California 91320, USA

SAGE Publications Ltd
1 Oliver's Yard, 55 City Road
London EC1Y 1SP, United Kingdom

SAGE Publications Asia-Pacific Pte Ltd
3 Church Street
#10-04 Samsung Hub
Singapore 049483

Published by Vivek Mehra for SAGE Publications India Pvt Ltd, typeset in 10/12 Times New Roman by Zaza Eunice, Hosur, Tamil Nadu, India.

Library of Congress Cataloging-in-Publication Data Available

ISBN: 978-93-860-6291-8 (PB)

SAGE Team: Amit Kumar, Indrani Dutta, Apoorva Mathur, Suhag Dave and Ritu Chopra

BRIEF CONTENTS

DETAILED CONTENTS

Section 3: Psychotherapy and Mental Health

AN OVERVIEW OF THE BOOK

Mental Health concerns have been a focal area since the turn of the century. Reports in print and electronic media have emphasised the need to live a healthy life. Health is now increasingly being looked at not just in physical but also in psychological terms. Psychological well-being has, in fact, become an important theme for discussion in popular discourse. This interest in psychological well-being has two implications. On the one hand, it shows an increasing awareness of the need for living a healthy life. On the other, it indicates that there is an increase of stress in everyday life, which merits attention. Emphasis on competition and success has brought about lifestyle changes and added to the complexity in relationships, maintaining balance, and finding space, freedom and meaning in life. All of these highlight the need to address mental health concerns in contemporary times. Nowhere is this need to address mental health concerns felt more acutely than in school settings.

Media reports on violence and aggression in school settings have been received with feelings of anxiety as well as awe. Violence and aggression are manifested in many forms. They range from simple, verbal bullying, attitudes of indifference and defiance towards school and social norms to more serious forms of assault and attack. In some cases, physical violence towards students and teachers has also been reported. These incidents indicate the direction of impending change towards a society that is marked by greater intolerance, impatience and often a complete disregard for others. While there is no denying that there is an urgent need to curb such a trend, teachers and parents alike have expressed helplessness in being able to deal with it. Many helping professionals while expressing their concern about this growing trend, at the same time acknowledge that this is often a reflection of the feelings of being ignored, not receiving love and acceptance and not finding an outlet for cathartic expression, often experienced by children and adolescents.

To take this further, it is also important to recognise that the years that children and adolescents spend in school are usually marked by long hours of studies, heavy school bags and frequent examinations. Academicians and educationists have long indicated this growing social trend of valuing academic meritocracy over holistic development. Growing children are thus left with little free space to think, explore and develop as individuals. Instead, they are forced to learn to compete, compare and value success. The past decade has witnessed changes in the education system in the country. Many private schools now emphasise multifarious exposure and attempt to create opportunities for new experiences across different scholastic and co-scholastic domains. Unfortunately, participation in co-scholastic activities has become as much a matter of competition as in the scholastic domain. As a consequence, children are not just required to excel in academics but also in a variety of other activities. With the increased involvement of children in multifarious activities, characteristics of a natural childhood that are manifested through desires, interests and a carefree attitude, are no longer visible in them. This is also evident in reality television shows that provide quick and wide exposure to many children who wish to participate. The need for instant, albeit short lived, fame is evident in both adults and children who are participants in such shows. In turn, this phenomenon has led to mushrooming of music, dance and sports institutions, along with the overgrowth of tuition centres that focus on performance-based studies. Children attending schools are often left alone to grapple with the mounting, unchecked and often unrecognised pressure that may have arisen from what maybe well-intentioned advice by significant others at home and school.

The concerns are more complex during the adolescent years. Sex education is still a taboo in most schools despite national bodies advocating its need. Likewise, although it has been recommended that curricular spaces be provided for sexuality and adolescence education programmes in schools, in effect, they have not received serious attention from most schools. While on paper most schools are expected to conduct activities and workshops for developing and promoting life skills, these often remain only on paper, especially when teachers are themselves not well prepared to address the relevant concerns. Likewise, most parents experience inhibitions in discussing issues related to sexuality with children. Adolescents then turn to peers and media to satisfy their curiosities. These may or may not be adequate and accurate sources of information. The result is misinformation, half-baked notions and ideas and persistent curiosity.

The concerns listed above are only a few common, pertinent aspects of the lives of school-going children. Children and adolescents, in fact, experience a lot more. Life in contemporary, urban India is marked by independence at home, often with little family time spent together. Nuclear family structures, all members of the family being employed in jobs involving long hours and increasing engagement with technological gadgets are a few of the reasons which account for adolescents not being able to find a listening ear at home. Schools are focused on completing courses and other curricular requirements on time and they expect that all children will adjust to this. For the child who is lost, facing difficulties or is unable to keep pace, schools at best employ a single psychologist or counsellor who would have no time to lend an empathetic ear to every child. She/he would be completely preoccupied with referrals and individual cases. There seems to be neither scope nor space for the promotion of psychological well-being in most children. What usually transpires in schools is that only when everyday concerns become deep-seated problems, they get reported and addressed. As a result, the mental health of children remains a dimension requiring cure rather than promotion and maintenance.

At the outset, it is important to highlight here that school mental health needs to be looked at from a preventive, promotive and conservative perspective rather than one based on cure. Along with family, the school serves as an important institution that provides space for promoting mental health of the school-going children. By providing support and guidance to children, the school can provide a healthy space to grow, hone one's talents and discover oneself. The teachers, the school environment and the activities organised in the classroom and the school have the potential to promote physical and psychological well-being in children and adolescents. The school must work in tandem with the home towards building a healthy, loving, caring and supportive environment.

This book is an attempt to address the concerns discussed in the earlier paragraphs. It presents an understanding of mental health not as a medical or cure intensive model but as one aimed at promoting healthy living. The idea is to help parents, teachers and significant others involved in caregiving functions towards children and to understand the needs, dilemmas, issues and concerns that children and adolescents experience. The book focuses on two intertwining threads that provide the linkage across the various themes addressed. First, it works on the premise that parents and teachers are joint stake-holders working towards a common goal of providing a healthy environment for the growth of children. Any attempt at preventing, promoting, conserving or curing mental health issues for school-going children will be incomplete if it is one-sided. In other words, the school and home need to collaborate together towards achieving this goal. Second, it is important to understand the experiences of children. The experiences of school-going children need to be understood from their perspective, to get deeper insights into their world view.

The book has accordingly been divided into three sections. The first section builds a perspective on the mental health of children and the various dimensions of well-being that arise at home and school. The second section serves as a practical handbook that provides direction and suggestions for what can be done to engage proactively with children and adolescents. The third section focuses on the theories that form the basis of psychotherapy and mental health practices.

The first section discusses the perspectives on mental health at home and school. It begins by describing the historical evolution of the concept of mental health and highlights the nature and need for focusing on mental health in schools. Chapter 2 addresses the policy perspectives in mental health. It aims at enabling caregivers to understand policy initiatives and build appropriate environments for children and adolescents to grow and function. Chapter 3 focuses on understanding the world from the perspective of children and so attempts to bridge the gap between adults and children. Chapter 4 is specifically located in the school context. It aims at identifying existing spaces in the school system that provide opportunities for addressing issues and challenges in the domain of school mental health. Chapter 5 is focused on understanding the context in which children live and grow. Often, children in school are understood as a homogeneous group with similar needs, interests, potentials, capabilities and concerns. The chapter goes beyond this myth to uncover the complexities and uniqueness of the world of each child. This includes concerns at the personal as well as social level, including families, peers and societies. The section concludes with a chapter on the importance of taking a proactive stance, that is, Chapter 6. This chapter provides broad guidelines for building a school environment that addresses the concerns raised in the earlier chapters.

The second section uses the perspective built in the first section to provide specific suggestions. The framework provided in Section 1 is used to address specific age-related concerns. Chapter 7 discusses some of the behavioural problems that are manifested in school-going children. The focus is on both identification and management of behavioural problems. The next chapter, that is, Chapter 8, addresses addiction and abuse that are commonly seen in school-going children. It challenges the myth that addiction and abuse are adult problems, not visible in young children. Chapter 9 focuses on addressing inter-personal conflicts. School is an important place for social adjustment. This chapter focuses on helping children understand the perspective of others, particularly elders. It therefore addresses inter-generational conflicts and how to resolve them. The chapter also addresses the need to build skills of expression and articulation, thereby strengthening communication. Chapter 10 addresses a major concern in school education. Sex education is an important aspect for school-going children. In the light of changing policies and perspectives, teachers often feel inept in addressing these issues in school. This chapter provides suggestions for age-appropriate activities that can be organised in schools. Chapter 11 addresses the overarching theme of self and identity. In this chapter, the focus is on providing specific strategies that would help children develop self-confidence, understand themselves better and develop a sense of identity that would form the base for their place in society in adult years. Chapter 12 focuses on stress and anxiety. *Tension, pressure, frustration, anxiety* and *stress* are commonly used terms by school-going children. This chapter attempts to enable teachers and parents to demystify stress and anxiety, identify the causes of stress and enable children to cope with them effectively. In the final chapter of this section, that is, Chapter 13, the focus is on parents and teachers as counsellors. Caregivers have to play an important role in helping children to deal with academic, social, emotional and personal challenges. They, thus, need to develop the skills and techniques for counselling, which have been discussed at length in this chapter.

The third section focuses on the theories and therapies that underlie mental health practices. The first three chapters in this section present the evolution of theories in psychology. These are represented in the psychotherapeutic traditions of psychoanalysis, behaviourism and cognitive behaviourism, and humanism. Chapter 17 provides an overview of alternative therapeutic practices that are commonly used by therapists and counsellors across the world. The final chapter in the book, that is, Chapter 18, presents an understanding of human nature, informed by the theories and therapies previously discussed. Against this backdrop, the conceptualisation of a mentally healthy personality is also discussed.

Besides sourcing theories, statistics and existing research literature, the book also draws heavily from the real life engagements of school counsellors, teachers, researchers and experts in the field. These have been presented in the form of case vignettes, narratives and dialogues. The purpose is to illustrate key areas and highlight the roots of various experiences of children and adolescents at home and school. Most cases presented in the book are based on real life events and experiences. Names of the persons involved have been changed wherever necessary in order to maintain privacy and confidentiality.

It must be remembered that the Indian sociocultural milieu presents great heterogeneity. Culture, context and geographical variations across regions abound. The lives and experiences of children and families from urban, tribal, rural and sub-urban backgrounds are usually quite different. Yet, the boundaries between rural and urban are no longer as clearly defined as earlier, owing to the advent of modernization and access to technology. Recognising the plurality that exists, while the contents of the present book have an urban thrust and setting, it is hoped that professionals would be able to adapt the points and issues raised to rural contexts and settings as well.

Throughout the book, the readers may remember that the notions of mental health and well-being go beyond the curative perspective. In fact, the book will serve to highlight the need and processes involved in maintaining mental and emotional well-being by going beyond the prevention and cure model, focusing on the promotional one instead.

ABOUT THE AUTHORS

Namita Ranganathan is a Professor at the Department of Education, Central Institute of Education, University of Delhi. She has over thirty years of teaching experience in teacher education programmes. Her specialisations are in the area of developmental psychology, personality psychology and education for mental health. She has been extensively engaged with schools across the country through various projects with The United Nations Population Fund (UNFPA), CARE India, Aga Khan Foundation and Save the Children, among others. She has also been on several management bodies of Kendriya Vidyalayas and several private schools.

Toolika Wadhwa has been working as an Assistant Professor at the Department of Education, Shyama Prasad Mukherji College, University of Delhi, since 2009. Her doctoral research was in the area of identity development and religion in the context of families and schools. Her work as a teacher educator as well as her research work with Aga Khan Foundation and UNFPA have enriched her exposure and understanding of schools.

Some Perspectives on Mental Health

The first section of the book attempts to build an understanding of the notion of mental health. The chapters in this section work towards helping readers develop a background in the theoretical underpinnings of Psychology in which an understanding of mental health concerns can be couched. The discussion in this section is broad based and develops a sociocultural perspective towards understanding mental health and its relevance in everyday life.

The theory-building exercise has been used to cover issues of normality and deviance, concepts of guidance and counselling, common challenges and myths associated with school mental health, and the social context of mental health of children. The chapter ends with highlighting the need to shift from a curative model of mental health to one that is preventive and promotive. This is followed by a discussion of policies that are relevant for providing a just and empathetic environment for children. While the discussion in this section is theoretical and revolves around issues that are relevant to schools, case examples and narratives have been interwoven to bring to fore the manner in which these issues surface in everyday life. Further, a common thread in the book is in the social contextualization of the child. Thus, wherever relevant, illustrations from contemporary social issues have been raised to discuss their relevance to the lives of children.

The first section forms the base on which the practical framework suggested in the second section of the book rests.

Understanding Mental Health

1

HISTORICAL EVOLUTION AND CONTEMPORARY NOTIONS OF MENTAL HEALTH

Work in the area of mental health started with a focus on mental hygiene. The term *mental hygiene* was first used by William Sweetzer in the fifteenth century. The mental hygiene point of view works on the assumption that any psychological ill health, when it occurs, has to be dealt with like any other physical illness. Focus has to be on its treatment and on removing its causes and symptoms. This may be termed as the 'illness perspective in mental health'. Here the emphasis is on cure rather than on maintaining good health. This perspective dominated the studies in mental health until the last quarter of the twentieth century.

School-going children regularly face difficulties in adjusting to the changing environment at home and school. Developing friendship bonds, handling academic pressures, sibling relationships, understanding self and changing dynamics in family relationships are some of the many concerns they face. Any of these areas can become a cause of distress. If unmanaged, this distress can lead to vulnerability to disturbances in a person's mental health. Any form of disturbance in mental health, even if it appears very minor, can affect the overall functioning of an individual and thus merits attention.

The shortcoming of the curative perspective is that mental health becomes a concern only when something goes wrong! This is somewhat similar to taking medicines when one's body manifests symptoms of discomfort, such as a headache or fever. In school settings, this translates into an ignorance of students' needs till the time they convey the same through their words or actions. Thus, a violent child would be complained about, taken to the counsellor or given therapy. However, till the time a disturbed child does not express his discomfort, he/she may be left unattended. Quiet children, who are not trouble makers, thus, often go unnoticed in class. Their behaviour does not show any overt signs of discomfort and therefore, does not demand attention. This is equally true for children at home. Parents tend to direct attention towards the more demanding child. Consider the following case:

Seven-year-old Smita went for a family holiday during her school summer vacations. On the return journey, their car met with an accident. She was sitting in the back seat with her mother. Both of them escaped unhurt but her father was admitted to the hospital with the help of some local residents. He was later shifted to a hospital close to their home. Although her mother and grandparents attempted to keep her insulated from the turmoil at home; hospital, medicines, death, money and prayers in hushed, urgent tones were the words that she heard every day. During this time, Smita was hardly allowed to meet her father. The only time she went to the hospital, she saw various tubes connected to his body and he was barely able to smile at her. The card that she had made for him was quietly placed by his bed. Her father eventually recovered after spending a month in the hospital. Her vacation was just getting over and she finally resumed school. In school, she did not discuss this accident. Her class teacher noticed that she had become quieter and withdrawn. But her work continued to be undisturbed and she did not show any trouble. The image of her father's tired, ill and pale face continued to haunt her for many nights.

Schools often do not recognise their role in helping children cope with stress. Where teachers willingly take on the role of counsellors, they are often clueless about what they can do. It is usually seen that the teacher often only steps in when the situation goes out of hand and the child's behaviour becomes a source of disruption to classroom processes. In Smita's case, for instance, the teacher is quite likely to not take any action since she is a regular student, completes her work on time and does nothing that disrupts the classroom. From Smita's perspective, in the absence of conversation about the accident, at home or at school, she is left to grapple with the chaos, bewilderment and sense of insecurity that she is experiencing in her life, all by herself. The relevant questions to ask are: What could be the possible long term consequences of her experience? Would she have coped better had she been able to talk about it? Was the family's approach of insulating her a healthy way of dealing with the situation? Should the school at all play a role in helping her deal with the stress that she may have experienced? In such situations, parents, siblings and often members of the extended family would have to show greater sensitivity. Conversations in hushed tones and the apparent attempt at keeping children insulated from disturbing family incidents or impending disturbances can sometimes be counterproductive. The child may not be expressive but may end up feeling lost and disconnected. Care should be taken to ensure that the child is emotionally ready to face the family situation through engaging in conversations with the child and allowing him/her to share concerns, fears and insecurities, if any.

The school's role becomes all the more significant if we look at the same situation from a mental health rather than a mental hygiene perspective. The mental health perspective not only focuses on dealing with illness but encompasses healthy functioning, social adjustment, emotional balance and also an ability to enjoy one's life. The term is often used interchangeably with behaviour health, with some psychologists looking at mental health only from a biological perspective, thus focusing only on prevention and cure of pathological mental illnesses such as clinical depression, schizophrenia, bipolar disorders and the like. Behaviour health is seen to include behavioural problems such as substance abuse, violence and aggression, conduct disorders associated with anger and so on. For the purpose of this book, the term mental health is understood to include not just mental illnesses and behavioural problems, but also maintaining psychological and emotional well-being. It includes conceptualisations of self and identity, self-esteem, coping with developmental changes and social pressures. WHO provides a holistic perspective on mental health, describing it as a state of well-being in which an individual realises his/her own abilities and is able to cope with the stresses of everyday life. Further, the person puts in productive work and contributes to the community.

Thus, the term mental health has both individual as well as social dimensions. As mentioned earlier, it encompasses social adjustment. At the same time, it also includes how people perceive themselves. Further, mental health is conceptualised as a continuum with illness and wellness on opposite sides. Each individual has the potential to move along the continuum towards illness or wellness depending on his/her experiences and sense of psychological resilience. In other words, the status of one's mental health is not static. Each person has the potential for improving mental health or lapsing into states of mental ill-health, even if temporarily.

Let us pause here and revisit Smita's case that we discussed earlier. If we look at the same case from a mental health perspective, the teacher would probably not wait for signs of distress in a student's behaviour. For instance, an informal discussion about the vacations in class or a simple class task asking students to write or speak about their experiences during the vacations may have initiated a conversation for Smita. The more important aspect here is for parents and teachers to develop personal bonds with students so that they feel comfortable in approaching them to share and discuss important events and experiences in their lives, their fears, anxieties and emotional states. Creating spaces for the same is a significant first step in this direction. We will discuss how to do this in greater detail in subsequent chapters.

If we closely examine the central idea addressed in both the mental hygiene and mental health perspectives, we would see that the emphasis is on understanding what is considered 'normal'. Let us explore this notion of 'normality' a little more.

Let us look at who is considered to be mentally healthy. We would see that the emphasis is on social adjustment. In simpler words, people who behave and live within socially acceptable norms are considered to be normal. Any deviation from social norms is considered 'abnormal' or away from normal. For instance, in most locales in India, boys are not expected to have long hair. In schools, in particular, length of hair is seen as an indicator of hygiene as well as disciplinary norms. There are, of course, exceptions to this norm for people from particular religious and cultural backgrounds. But, by and large, a young boy, an adolescent or a man will not be expected to have long hair or even be accepted if he chooses to wear his hair long. Similar notions are also associated with the choice of clothes where it is seen that girls/women experiment more with colours and prints than boys/men. It is not uncommon for people to stop on the streets of India to stare at individuals who have defied social norms. These norms extend to notions of dressing, eating, behaving, interacting, sexuality and so on. Other examples of normality, which an individual is expected to have, include well-defined and often predetermined ways of coping, demonstrating emotions and behaving in specific settings and occasions. Any digression from the social norms with respect to these evokes labels of being odd, abnormal, peculiar, non-conformist, maladjusted and so on, from the lens of the society.

The notion of mental health also includes the dimension of personal adjustment within it. Emotional and psychological well-being, thus, are also subsumed in the concept of normality. It is expected that in addition to being socially well-adjusted, a 'normal' person would be able to live in comfort and peace with oneself. This means that besides maintaining an outward persona to meet social norms, the person should be able to live an honest and fulfilling life. Look at the following case.

Samuel studies in class ten and is popular among his friends. He is considered a star student in the school as he is well behaved and excels in all fields, including academics, sports, debate and theatre. He is particularly good at mathematics and science and holds a school record of always scoring above 95 per cent in both subjects. His teachers and peers often attribute it to his family lineage. Both his parents are renowned scientists. His teachers and family have never doubted that he would take up science post class ten and make a career in the field.

Samuel is happy with the appreciation he gets. But he has never been interested in science. He wants to take up humanities and study history. He is fascinated by ancient civilisations and reads avidly about them. His social science teacher is aware of his interest but has never encouraged him to take up humanities in senior classes. In a way, his career path has been pre-decided even without asking him. Torn between personal and social desires, Samuel has developed a friends' circle away from home and school. He meets them on the pretext of having all night study groups and engages in alcohol and mild recreational drugs. He feels happier with his new friends than with his family and friends from school.

Do you think Samuel would be happy studying science in senior classes? What could be the possible reasons for which he is not able to voice his interest in humanities? What will be the consequences if he is not able to study humanities? These are some of the concerns that emerge from Samuel's case. Part of the stress that Samuel is experiencing is due to the pressure created by parents and teachers for performing well. On the outside, Samuel is a well-adjusted teenage boy. However, his own thoughts would reveal some serious dilemmas that he would be dealing with, often with little help from his social circle. He lives a dual life where his school teachers, peers and family are yet unaware of his coping through substance misuse. Looking at all aspects of his case, we can see that Samuel is using unhealthy coping mechanisms to deal with his struggles. Would we consider Samuel, who appears socially well adjusted, to be normal? The answer is no. A healthy, normal person would be able to accept his concerns and express them to and address them with the help of family and friends. He would thus not need to lead a secret life that serves as an escape mechanism and can lead to serious mental and physical consequences in the long run. Thus, normality would include both personal as well as social adjustment.

MODELS OF NORMALITY

The discipline of mental health draws heavily upon psychology. With the changing perspectives that have marked the evolution of the discipline of psychology, there have been parallel shifts in mental health as well. Here, we will discuss how these transitions in perspectives, along with new advancements, have changed the notion of what is considered normal over a period of time. However it is important to understand that with the advent of new notions, older conceptualisations only get added to and enriched. None of the notions are entirely wrong, nor have they died down with age. Instead, new additions and understandings have helped to broaden the field. At present, the notion of normality can be understood from three main perspectives: biomedical, statistical and sociocultural.

The biomedical model of normality is akin to the mental hygiene perspective. It identifies a person to be normal when the person is physically fit and does not show symptoms of illness. An absence of clinical psychological illnesses, such as depression, bipolar disorders, etc., and physical ailments is considered to be a sign of good health. In this model, a person diagnosed with illness can move to normality after 'cure' through medicines and therapy. Cure would refer to absence of behavioural manifestation of abnormality.

In the statistical model, individual behaviour which is in consonance with the behaviour of the majority of the population is considered to be normal. It works on the concept of the normal probability curve (NPC). Nearly 70 per cent of the population lie within one standard deviation from the mean under the NPC. Behaviour that is akin to the behaviour of the population in this range is considered normal. The greater the deviation from this standard, the greater would be the abnormality. Persons who are two standard deviations away from the mean are considered to be mentally unhealthy. The simplest example of this is a study of intelligence. On a standardised test of intelligence, people who score significantly lower or higher than the average intelligence level of the population are considered to be abnormal. Those scoring lower than 70 on a standardised IQ test are considered to be intellectually deficient. Those scoring above 130, likewise, would also be considered as possessing higher ability since their score is also significantly at deviation from the normal.

The biomedical and statistical models work on predefined definitions that apply to all universally. The sociocultural model locates normality within the context of the person being studied. Thus, normality would be defined according to the context. In other words, what is considered normal in a particular time and place may not be considered normal in another social and temporal context. Clothes, hairstyles, colours, eating habits, rituals and religious practices are some of the examples of culture-specific behaviour. An example of this is the practice of dowry. For centuries, India was unique in considering the practice of dowry as normal. Although it is illegal now, asking and giving gifts as dowry at the time of the daughter's wedding is not an uncommon practice in India. It is seen as culturally acceptable. The same would not be considered normal in other social settings. When people from abroad visit India, they try to adapt to local settings in terms of clothes and eating habits so that they do not stand out and are well accepted in the cultural setting. The same is true for Indians travelling abroad.

Key Debates in Mental Health

The discussion of the different models of normality raises some interesting debates in mental health. If we believe that normality is rooted in cultural settings, then there will be no universal definition of what is considered normal, as against the statistical and biomedical models. This raises the universalism versus cultural relativism debate in mental health. Do we believe that there is one universally applicable definition of a mentally healthy person that is valid across cultures and social settings, or, do we believe that notions of mental illness will vary across time and place? The debate was initiated in the early 1950s when social cognition theorists challenged the biomedical model of mental illness that likened mental illnesses to physical illnesses. Subsequently, sociological and anthropological definitions significantly contributed to the study of human societies and cultures, highlighting similarities and differences across cultural practices. Cultural relativism provides the freedom to each culture to practice what is relevant to that society without an imposition of what may be relevant to the dominant, outside culture. Here all cultural beliefs are equally well respected. Universalists, in contrast, argue that biological similarity and unity among all human beings supersedes cultural differences.

Universalism, as discussed above, puts forth the view that concerns and notions in the area of mental health are applicable across the world, irrespective of cultures. Understanding the notion of normality through this perspective gives rise to the statistical perspective. The statistical perspective to mental health understands normality on the basis of averages that may be found through research studies that analyse data, generally collected through large samples that transcend boundaries of space or time or both. Results from such research are considered valid if they apply to large populations and hold true in most settings. Findings from these researches are considered generalisable. While such researches serve an important function in themselves, they take away the focus from individual contexts and situations. Mental health is as much personal and subjective as it is social and warrants that each individual be understood in his/her context. So, while generalised research studies may apply to large populations, an ideological perspective would, in contrast, focus on understanding the concerns within specific local contexts. The focus would be on understanding particular cultures, family types, schools or individuals.

This debate is also addressed as the idiographic versus nomothetic perspective. The nomothetic perspective attempts to understand large groups of people to arrive at general laws of behaviour that apply to all. As against this, the idiographic perspective attempts to understand individuals' personal stories and do an in-depth analysis of their lives to arrive at a detailed understanding of the same. The nomothetic perspective can thus be seen as an extension of universalism, where general laws are seen to apply to large groups of people. The bottom line in this approach is that a common set of mental health issues, concerns and dilemmas will be seen to apply to all human beings. As against this, the idiographic approach celebrates the uniqueness of each individual. Each of these approaches has its basis in different schools of thought and carries its own sets of advantages and disadvantages.

The nomothetic approach is more suitable when arriving at generalisations about behaviour through scientifically valid experiments. It is rooted in behaviourism, social cognition and psychiatric approaches. It is helpful when studying, for example, discrimination and prejudices against particular communities, religions, castes, classes or other groups of people. Where behavioural modification or control is the target, such approaches work best. The disadvantage of this approach is that it does not celebrate or even acknowledge the identity of each individual.

In the idiographic approach, the focus is on studying a person or a small group of individuals to arrive at a holistic understanding of that person or group. Findings from such studies are usually localised to specific groups or individuals with specific sociocultural contexts. They are not used for generalisations about large groups. However, they sometimes serve as initiating points for further large group studies. The works of Piaget and Freud are prominent examples of such approaches. Universal theories were generated on the basis of their studies on a small, select group. Case-based longitudinal approaches work well in such studies.

While both approaches have their own merits, and theories based on either of the two approaches are important, when it comes to school settings, wherein teachers are expected to understand each individual student, probably an idiographic approach would prove to be more useful. In this, the teacher would interact with every individual and try to make sense of his/her point of view and experiences. This will serve to provide a contextual dimension to the teacher-student interaction and generate knowledge that is specifically useful to that particular student, school, class and situation.

NEED FOR FOCUSING ON MENTAL HEALTH IN SCHOOLS

Although not an emerging area, mental health still warrants more attention than it enjoys at present. The Overview section of this book highlighted some issues of contemporary relevance that highlighted the need to give greater attention to mental health concerns in school settings. To reiterate briefly, growing violence and aggression in schools, changing family structures and home dynamics, urbanisation, prevalence of sexual crimes, and the influence of media and technology on growing children demand immediate attention. Schools and teachers have often expressed a sense of helplessness in helping children and adolescents deal with these issues. Against this backdrop, mental health of children and adolescents becomes an area of immediate concern for schools.

Almost everyone is aware of the utility of over-the-counter medications for headaches, common colds, muscle sprains, cuts and bruises and so on. But do we pay as much attention to managing our mental health on an everyday basis? Do children and adolescents need help, support and encouragement to handle mental health concerns? Psychiatrists and clinical psychologists are contacted only when the behavioural manifestations of problems become excessive and demand professional attention. There are many physical illnesses that medical practitioners are unable to locate in bodily malfunctioning. The causes are diagnosed by them to be psychosomatic in nature. What may be inferred from this is that psychological distress often manifests itself in the form of physiological symptoms like diminished appetite, frequent unexplained headaches, general weakness and immunity loss and so on.

GOALS OF MENTAL HEALTH

The next crucial question then is: What should be the goals of mental health? The overall goal of mental health is to live a happy, well-adjusted and fulfilling life. Let us briefly discuss what such a life would entail.

Although happiness is a relative term, it is quite obvious that it is of primary importance in mental health. Being happy does not mean not experiencing sadness or bouts of feeling low. Mental health would, in fact, mean openness to experiencing all emotions. Happiness, then, is not a finite goal to achieve. It is not an unchanging state of mind but depends on the perception of an individual in looking at various events and situations. It is a subjective state of mind. Of particular significance is the fact that happiness is often contagious. Happy parents and teachers lead to happy children, who often reflect this happiness in their enthusiasm and confidence.

Personal and Social Adjustment

Adjustment refers to having a harmonious existence. It permeates both personal and social life. A very significant component of personal and social adjustment is emotional intelligence. The term refers to individual's capability to refer to one's own and others' emotions and identify different kinds of emotions (Goleman 1995). It helps to guide individual behaviour appropriately and engage with others better. People with higher emotional intelligence, in other words, have better interpersonal relations and performance. This view has also been supported by Gardner's work on multiple intelligences (Gardner 1983). Thus, being personally well-adjusted involves being aware of one's preferences, making choices and being confident of decisions made. At the same time, it also includes being aware of one's weaknesses and accepting them. A well-adjusted person should feel worthy and loved. In terms of social adjustment, it refers to harmonious relationships with those around us. While a person should not feel compelled to act according to social pressures, yet a socially well-adjusted person would not behave in a manner that disrupts relationships, is hurtful and antithetical to well-being of others. Instead a socially well-adjusted person would behave with an attitude of acceptance towards social norms.

Living a Fulfilling Life

A fulfilling life refers to working efficiently, achieving one's capacities and feeling good about it. While different psychological theorists have used different terms to define what a fulfilling life is, in simplest terms, it refers to working to one's potential and evincing a sense of joy from it. A person who does a lot of work by breaking social contact, or falls ill due to overwork, would not be considered mentally healthy. Instead, an efficient work attitude would be where one is able to live a balanced life while fulfilling personal, professional and social commitments.

GUIDANCE, COUNSELLING AND MENTAL HEALTH

The three terms addressed here are important functions that parents and school teachers perform to help students move towards the goals of mental health that have been discussed above. Teachers often feel overburdened with teaching and tend to look at guidance and counselling as additional tasks that they are required to do. On the contrary, teachers who are focused on developing sound mental health in their students would find improvements in behaviour and learning of students when they accept the tasks of guidance and counselling as part of their everyday school experience and subsume it in their role profile. In this scenario, mental wellness would lead to better adjusted students who would, in turn, be able to learn better. Further, students and teachers would share a good rapport with each other, making communication easier and better.

At the heart of guidance lies the basic aim of promoting wellness among students. Teachers and parents alike have to act as guides in helping the children make appropriate choices in life. These choices may relate to career, body image concerns, peers, lifestyle, engagement with family, participation in school life and so on. As a guide, a teacher or a parent is required to act as a mentor, helping children and adolescents find appropriate information and make informed decisions. The process of counselling also works on the same principle, with one or more person/s seeking help in finding solutions to a problem they may be facing. Depending on the situation and the nature of counselling undertaken, a counsellor may choose to actively listen, facilitating the counselee arrive at a decision he/she may find best for him/her. Or else, the counsellor may use a directive approach, telling the counselee how to act and solve the problem at hand. Guidance is given on more generic issues and counselling when specific problems are being faced, which require some intervention or psychological support.

Guidance and counselling are not always restricted to individuals. Groups of students share some common concerns and school teachers may often find it appropriate to initiate group sessions on these. For instance, the sessions may include: understanding good touch and bad touch, learning social behaviour, sharing, controlling emotions and so on, during the primary school years; handling peer pressure, time management, gender sensitisation, respecting others and so on, during early adolescence; and creating awareness about substance misuse, addressing concerns of body image and identity, awareness and acceptance of sexuality, career alternatives and so on, during adolescence. The common aspect across these sessions is to identify the concerns of school students over the course of their developmental years. Guidance and counselling are thus helping activities that promote and conserve mental wellness and prevent and cure mental illness.

Here, it is important to highlight the need to develop an attitude of mutual respect. Parents and teachers act as role models for students and children. By modelling relationships that are based on respect for each other's lifestyles, opinions and personal space, teachers and parents can ensure that children also learn to accept divergent views. This in turn builds an attitude of openness and a willingness to learn. One must remember that respect has to be mutual. Often parents do not demonstrate respect but 'command' it from children. In a school and home environment, where adults show respect for each other as well as towards children, children will develop self-confidence, express their thoughts better and learn to appreciate multiple perspectives.

ON A CONCLUDING NOTE

This chapter provides an overview of the concept of mental health and spells out key debates in the area. The need for understanding mental health in school settings and what it aims to achieve have also been discussed. Against this backdrop, the subsequent chapters would focus on specific issues of contemporary relevance. The overarching concern is to aid school children and adolescents to lead relatively stress-free and fulfilling lives. Finally, guidance and counselling are important functions that parents and teachers must engage with, for which a comprehensive understanding of the psychosocial world of children and adolescents in school is essential.

Mental Health Policies and Implications for Schools

2

The previous chapter presented a theoretical perspective to understanding mental health. It provides an important backdrop against which school mental health services need to be designed. Therapeutic approaches to mental health of school-going children are equally important in ensuring that educational practitioners and caregivers are able to effectively work towards providing a better environment for the growth and development of children and adolescents.

At the same time, it is equally important to understand policy perspectives towards mental health. They provide the basis for many decisions taken at the school level. Educational policies, albeit with their limited focus on mental health, are the frameworks in which educational institutions function. Decisions with far reaching implications about age-appropriate curricula, admissions, examinations, everyday school activities, provisions for facilities and the like are based on policy recommendations and mandates. It is thus important for all who are engaged with education to be well aware of policies in the areas of education and mental health.

The present chapter begins with a discussion on four key policy perspectives: National Mental Health Policy of India of 2014, Right to Education (RTE) Act of 2009, Protection of Children from Sexual Offences (POCSO) Act of 2012, and the Rights of Persons with Disabilities (PwD) Act of 2016. These four policies have been selected for detailed discussion since they have important implications for understanding guidance, counselling and mental health issues related to children, adolescents and schooling. They will be discussed in relation to the main recommendations that they make and the implications of the recommendations for schools. The chapter ends with a consolidation of important recommendations for schools to effectively implement these policy provisions.

KEY POLICY INITIATIVES

In this section, a brief discussion on the vision as well as recommendations of the policies relevant to mental health of children in educational settings has been presented. In the last 10 years, the government has undertaken several initiatives to promote education across the country. This has led to expansion in the facilities provided for education, particularly in schools. In addition, several schemes aimed at enhancing access to education, providing better quality education and ensuring that education is provided in a safe and healthy environment have been launched. Among the many initiatives, the RTE has been undoubtedly the most significant. While it focuses specifically on educational settings, it is implicit that the need for providing a safe environment does not rest with schools alone, or ends there. The child continuously engages with the society and the larger world. Therefore, it is important that his/her safety and well-being are protected and provided for. The long pending National Mental Health Policy of India, 2014 and the POCSO Act, 2012 are the two other key initiatives in this direction. They aim at building a secure ethos in which children can live and grow. Since education is concerned with all children, it includes in its ambit children with disabilities and those from marginalised contexts as well. The PwD Act, 1995 is also thus deeply significant, along with its expanded and modified Rights of PwD Act, 2016. Mental health practitioners deal with children with disabilities and schools must become inclusive spaces. Knowing about provisions and the schemes for persons with disabilities is, thus, important for parents, teachers and all other helping professionals. Each of the policies has been briefly discussed in the sections that follow.

Right to Education Act, 2009

The RTE Act provides for free and compulsory education for all children in the age group of 6 to 14 years, till the completion of elementary education. The Act provides for admission of children in age-appropriate classes so that they are at par with others in the classroom. Special training and bridge courses have been made available to help out-of-school children to make up and reach the desired level of the class in which they are placed. Providing access to a neighbourhood school for the successful implementation of this Act has been made the responsibility of the state. The Act prevents discrimination against children belonging to disadvantaged groups in pursuing and completing elementary education. There is a prohibition on capitation fee and for any kind of screening procedure while admitting a child. Thus, the Act lays down specific guidelines that pave the way for universal access to education to all children, irrespective of their economic and social backgrounds. This is further supported by ensuring that three-fourth members of the School Management Committee are parents or guardians of children admitted to the school.

Another important aspect of the Act is the no detention policy that prevents a school from expelling or holding a child back in any class till the completion of class 8, the culmination of elementary education. Further protection to the child is provided by the Act by explicitly banning all forms of physical punishment and mental harassment. While detailing out the curriculum and evaluation processes, the Act emphasises on the all-round development of the child, and 'development of physical and mental abilities to fullest extent'. It further emphasises 'making the child free of fear, trauma and anxiety and helping the child to express views freely' (RTE 2009). In other words, the Act provides for free space to learn, explore and grow. Continuous and comprehensive evaluation, as against year-end final examinations, is a forward looking step in this direction.

Protection of Children from Sexual Offences Act, 2012

The POCSO Act, 2012, at the very outset itself, states that the privacy and confidentiality of the child must be maintained in order to ensure his/her proper development. Further, the judicial processes involved in the implementation of the law must keep the interest and well-being of the child at the forefront, with focus on aspects such as physical, emotional, intellectual and social development. The Act specifically applies to the involvement of the child, through coercion or otherwise, in any unlawful sexual activity, including pornography and prostitution. It includes in its ambit all children and adolescents below the age of 18 years. It details out the extent of the activities that are considered offensive and also spells out the extent of punishment that can be lawfully meted out to the offender. Further, it also provides for legal persecution of persons who abet similar offenses against children.

The Act specifies that the media reports will not disclose the name or other details of the child, including photographs, family details, school and neighbourhood that may lead to the identification of the child. In ensuring that the child feels comfortable should any untoward incident happen with him/her and have to be reported, the Act spells out that the child may be interacted within a place that he/she feels comfortable in. Further, the police personnel may not be in uniform when the statement is being recorded. The police are required to take adequate steps to ensure that the victim does not come in contact with the offender. The Act also provides that parents, guardians or any other person that the child reposes trust in will be allowed to be present in the special court during the course of the trial.

Significantly, the Act provides for involvement of NGOs, mental health professionals, social workers, psychologists and child development experts at the pre-trial and trial phase in order to assist the child.

National Mental Health Policy of India, 2014

The policy takes a proactive stance while defining mental health. It reiterates the view of the World Health Organisation in defining mental health as not 'just the absence of mental disorders'. It defines mental health as a state of well-being, focusing on:

- Realisation of one's own abilities.
- Coping with normal stressors of life.
- Working productively and fruitfully.
- Making positive contributions to society.

As can be seen from the discussion above, the policy focuses on both the personal and social dimensions of mental health. It also places emphasis on prevention, promotion and curative aspects of mental health. In doing so, it significantly brings to light the difference between mental health problems, mental illness and mental disability. Mental health problems refer to a range of psychological and social conditions that are likely to influence a large number of people. Mental illness and disability are specific and more serious conditions that would influence fewer people. The notion of disability associated with mental illness is as much a social construct as it is a medical construct. Thus, not everyone who suffers from mental illness will experience the barriers that hinder complete social participation.

Another very important aspect highlighted by the policy is in creating a distinction between a person with mental illness and/or disorder and the illness/disorder itself. Quite often, a person with mental illness is reduced to being identified with the mental illness itself. Here, the policy emphasises the need to separate the illness/problem from the person's identity.

The policy comes to the forefront at a time when mental illnesses are considered to be on a rapid increase worldwide. The policy projects that by 2020, depression will be the leading cause of disability worldwide. In view of this, the policy has identified strategic areas including effective governance and accountability, promotion of mental health and prevention of mental disorders, and universal access to mental health services. The policy also emphasises community participation, research, monitoring and evaluation.

Persons with Disabilities Act, 1995 and Rights of Persons with Disabilities Act, 2016

School plays a major role in building inclusive spaces that develop attitudes of acceptance that spread into the larger social system. In many ways, school is the microcosm of society. The PwD Act, 1995 was the first step in policy making that aimed at developing an inclusive social system. It covers seven disability areas, namely: blindness, low vision, leprosy-cured, hearing impairment, loco-motor disability, mental retardation and mental illness. The Act further details out each of the disabilities for purposes of identification and categorisation. It proposes provision of facilities of education and employment, including extra study time, special facilities through open schools, non-formal education and the use of technology and providing scholarships and free books. It further provides for filling up of 3 per cent vacancies with persons with disability, where 1 per cent each is reserved for people with visual challenge, hearing challenge and loco-motor disability, including cerebral palsy. Similar provision is also made in institutions of higher education. The Act also advocates barrier free access and modified curricula to suit the needs of children with special needs.

In replacing the PwD Act of 1995, the Rights of PwD Act of 2016 broaden its scope by increasing the number of disabilities that are included in its ambit and also specified the details of provisions made for PwD to ensure support through access to resources, adequate funding from the government and continuing with benefits such as reservation. The Rights of PwD Act includes nineteen disabilities instead of the seven that were earlier covered, including learning difficulties. Instead of focusing only on PwD, it specifically provides for building spaces for inclusive education where 'inclusive education means a system of education wherein students with and without disability learn together and the system of teaching and learning is suitably adapted to meet the learning needs of different types of students with disabilities'. The Rights of PwD Act is in line with the recommendations of the United Nations Convention 2006, where the focus is on empowerment and marks a shift from an attitude of sympathy and service to one of dignity, respecting diversity and participation as equals. Significantly, the Rights of PwD Act not only talks of categories of physical and mental disabilities but also recognises that social categories such as gender can also be grounds of discrimination and, thus, be disabling.

It continues to provide for benefits of reservation in education and employment to persons with 'benchmark disability' or disability over 40 per cent. Chapter 3 of the Rights of PwD Act specifically addresses the duties and responsibilities of educational institutions. This focuses on providing equal opportunities for access without discrimination, making provisions for accessible infrastructure, diagnosing, monitoring and addressing learning difficulties and creating a discrimination free atmosphere. Further, it also emphasises provision of trained special educators and support staff. This also implies that the district, state and central government should provide for adequate teacher education institutions to meet the needs of trained educators in various educational institutions. In addition, the Rights of PwD Act provides for scholarships and modifications in curriculum as required.

Besides education, the Rights of PwD Act also addresses issues of discrimination in employment and protects the rights of persons with disabilities in work conditions. It also talks of the need for creating awareness through print and visual media, providing medical facilities and addressing concerns of sexual and reproductive health. Overall, the Rights of PwD Act focuses on providing for a right to life with dignity for persons with disability.

What is significant in it is the expressed change towards attitudinal empowerment, through building a cohesive and enabling environment that provides for minimising restrictions in availing opportunities and facilities.

IMPLICATIONS FOR SCHOOLS

The discussion on the policies brings to the fore two key considerations. First, policy recommendations recognise the importance of a safe and secure environment for children. Second, all four policies work from a rights perspective and advocate providing an environment that is conducive for the all-round growth and development of the child. The implications for schools are thus immense.

Rights Approach

What is common across the four acts and policies discussed above is that the focus has shifted from one of sympathy and pity to that of a person's rights. Provision of facilities and opportunities, thus, does not involve charity or service. In fact, there is a recognition for an equal right to life of respect and dignity. This, in turn, shifts the focus from disabilities to abilities. Impairments are looked upon as challenges and the potentials and abilities of persons with disabilities become the prime concerns. Schools must recognise that implementing these laws is a significant step towards developing empowered citizens. Thus, children must learn to fight for their rights, be aware of provisions that they are entitled to and learn about the redressal mechanisms. In children without disabilities, schools must work towards building acceptance of diversity and attitudes of fairness. These will, in turn, contribute towards building a society where citizens can look after themselves and support others around them.

Providing a Safe Environment

The recommendations go beyond architectural changes in providing barrier free access. They focus quite emphatically on psychological safety and security of persons with disabilities. This is a welcome change as it is not just physical access that prevents persons with disabilities from participating in social activities. In fact, it is the attitude of rejection, discrimination and, sometimes, bullying and harassment that leads to a life of isolation and deprivation for persons with disabilities. In addition, it also points to the fact that disability is not a physical but a socio-psychological phenomenon. Implicit in this recognition is the move towards bringing about attitudinal changes that are foremost in ensuring a life of dignity and self-respect.

Go Beyond Academics

For decades, persons with physical, mental or socio-emotional disabilities—stemming from visual, hearing and loco-motor impairments, mental illnesses and disorders, and social challenges related to gender, caste and tribal backgrounds—were not allowed access to schools. While the scenario in India has improved somewhat in terms of providing some categories of children with disabilities access to schools, yet access alone does not ensure their full participation. Often they are seen in pull out classes and their inclusion is very limited. By specifying a focus on all-round development, the provisions imply that schools must ensure participation in various activities of school life including sports, debating, performing arts and the like. So schools have to make extra provisions for equipment and infrastructure that would facilitate such inclusion and ensure the readiness of teachers for seamless inclusion attitudinally and in terms of strategies and practices that are adopted.

Provide Comfort

Social exclusion resulting from disability creates an atmosphere of discomfort. This does not only result in imposing restrictions in social interaction but also impacts self-esteem and identity. When schools are exclusive spaces, children without disabilities also miss out on one dimension of empathy and appreciation of abilities. In their lack of exposure, they lack an understanding of an alternative lifestyle, stemming out of different needs. Later in life, in higher education and employment, persons without disabilities feel hesitant in talking to persons with disabilities for fear of disrespecting their space and being unknowingly offensive. This further enlarges the existing gulf in relationships. Instead, schools should work towards building relationships of mutual trust, respect and comfortable dependence between teachers and students, as well as between peers. In addition, school environment needs to provide comfort and security that fosters free expression, exploration and development. This necessitates a complete ban on corporal punishment and efforts towards prevention of situations of stress, trauma and psychological harassment.

Home School Continuity

The RTE Act, specifically, and other acts and policies also recommend a continuity between home and school. In other words, schools should understand home and family contexts and provide conditions of education that are suited to students' needs. Families in turn need to understand the needs of the school and experiences that their child has at school. This will help in providing a continuity of experiences and a safe and secure environment. Parents also need to be aware of the peer group of their child and the kind of engagement he/she has with others around him. The teacher plays a pivotal role in this direction. It is through this continuity that children can feel loved and free from stress and trauma, stemming out of a conflict of ideologies and environs.

Proactive Stance

Another distinctive feature of recent policy developments is the need to take a proactive stance. Rather than providing for cure, the policies advocate an approach of prevention of experiences of conflict, distress and disharmony. Recognising the importance of childhood experiences and the significant role of school and family at this stage, the policies recommend measures that would develop attitudes of kindness and regard, and eventually empathy, early in life. Besides infrastructural facilities and other similar tangible provisions, the policies also provide for conducting awareness drives, ensuring comfort and psychological security. A rights approach provides protection from discrimination and harassment.

Training of Teachers

The RTE Act provides for ensuring that there will be trained teachers to teach in schools. The National Mental Health Policy and PwD Act also make provision for trained personnel to ensure that the needs of children with special needs are met. Schools are also required to ensure that teachers are regularly provided in-service programmes that help them to refresh pedagogies, communication techniques and relationship-building skills. While teachers need to be thorough with the knowledge of content, they also need to be aware of policies and provisions that relate to children in school settings. All teachers would require to be equipped with counselling skills to engage with students and develop a bond of faith and comfort with them.

RECOMMENDATIONS FOR SCHOOLS THAT FLOW FROM POLICY PROVISIONS

The implications discussed in the previous section provide the broad framework that would help schools and teachers to work in sync with policy provisions. The discussion in subsequent paragraphs presents a set of concrete measures that schools may work with.

Train Teachers Regularly

Schools that recognise the need to regularly provide in-service training opportunities to teachers are often able to provide better quality education. In-service training on various issues provides two benefits. On the one hand, it provides a freshness of perspective to teachers who are able to learn about developments and advancements in the field of education. On the other, it benefits the school by ensuring that teachers have the skills to meet policy guidelines in providing quality education to students. This includes skills of counselling, attitude of compassion and pedagogies for addressing the diversity in the classroom.

Hire Trained Counsellors

A major drawback plaguing schools is the dearth of trained school counsellors. Schools that do not have a full time counsellor tend to miss out on addressing the mental health needs of their students. Teachers often do not have time to listen to every student in their class on a regular basis and it is only when something out of the ordinary occurs that teachers' attention is captured. This is even more relevant for classes where class size is large and the student–teacher ratio is more that 30:1. A trained counsellor can address the concerns of students in both group and individual settings. Further, counsellors are better equipped to handle behavioural and psychological problems that children may be facing. It must also be kept in mind that in large schools housing 800–900 children, one counsellor would probably not be able to address the needs of all children. Counsellors for each level of education—primary, middle and secondary—may be needed to ensure that all children feel welcome to share their thoughts, dilemmas, concerns and problems. Moreover, the issues vary with age groups as do the strategies to deal with them.

Awareness Programmes for Students

As has been discussed earlier, the policies now recommend a proactive approach. In this, it is important that not just teachers, but students as well, become sensitive towards others around them. Workshops and lecture–discussion sessions that focus on building life skills of acceptance, empathy, collaboration and compassion would work towards capable, just and responsible citizens. Awareness programmes can also focus on removing the stigma around mental health concerns and disabilities. In addition, students can also be helped to recognise signs of concern and indicators of distress and be encouraged to reach out to their peers.

Community Outreach Programmes

Schools must recognise the significance they hold in society. In many places, parents and community members turn to teachers for advice and help even for non-academic matters, particularly those that relate to their children. Schools are seen as nurturant places where children are safe and well protected. Initiatives taken by the school in reaching out to the community can go a long way in building a healthy living space. Community outreach programmes also benefit students in connecting to the concerns of the world outside the school, thereby building sensitivity towards social causes. Street plays, awareness drives in and around school premises, special sessions for parents, walks and marathons are some of the ways in which schools can connect with the community and address mental health concerns.

Avoiding Labels

Students are often stereotyped as too studious, undisciplined, hyperactive, all-rounder, low achieving, incapable, lazy, irregular and so on. Such labels usually prevent teachers, and resultantly students, from looking at the student as anything other than the label. Such a singular vision can never do justice to a student in his/her entire range of potentialities. Further, beliefs, biases and pre-judgements often become akin to a self-fulfilling prophecy. For instance, it is not uncommon to walk into a noisy class in a school and hear students narrate stories of how their class is infamous for being the most unruly class of the school. When students know that they have been labelled as unruly, they stop trying to be anything but 'unruly'. This prevents them from recognising themselves. Such labels can cause trauma and have a negative impact on children's identity development.

Mentorship Programmes

Mentorship programmes help children to engage with issues that may not be a part of the curriculum but are important and relevant for them. Although all teachers, and in particular the class teacher, should be available to students to discuss their concerns, organising a special class once a week or once a fortnight, in which one teacher engages with a small group of ten to twelve students, can help build a strong bond in a close-knit group. Further, the teacher can engage with individual students in informal spaces throughout the school day. Peer bonding and focused guidance that is tailored to the needs of the individual student can ensure that every child feels loved and cared for. In smaller groups, students may also feel less hesitant in sharing their thoughts that cannot be voiced in larger classrooms. Informal spaces of interaction allow the teacher to talk about things that are relevant to the child but cannot be addressed in the structured curriculum, subject to the confines of the classroom. Having a mentor in school also translates into availability of an elder for guidance and venting out for the child. The teacher is also able to monitor the child's academic and non-academic engagement and progress more closely through the mentorship programme.

Bridge Courses for Academic Support

Right to education provides for admission in age-appropriate classrooms. This ensures that a child studies with children who have similar socio-emotional needs, even though he/she may have started school late. In addition, students in a classroom will be at varying levels of learning. This would also require additional academic inputs. In both scenarios, the school should make provision for conducting bridge courses, extra classes and providing academic support wherever possible to students who need extra help. In most cases, this additional support will be required on a temporary basis. Peer learning can also be encouraged to ensure that children learn to help each other in academics in informal settings and also identify that learning sources can be many and varied. It is important here to mention that additional support should be part of the routine life of school. Any association of incapability, stigma or shame with attending academic support groups during or after-school hours can further dip the academic performance of the student.

Develop Communication Channels

Besides mentorship programmes, the school can work towards building communication channels so that students know that they can approach teachers at various platforms. Forming committees for specific needs such as transportation, cleanliness, health, counselling, academic support and the like are important, so that students can seek help when desired. The school can also choose to involve students from various classes in these committees so that a group of students feel comfortable in sharing their concerns with other students in the school. In addition, the school can also develop a grievance redressal mechanism. This may be done through frequent open discussion sessions within classroom or in houses, having a drop box where students can put in feedback and concerns anonymously or an email account and the like. What is important is that whichever method is adopted, it has to be feasible for students and should be regularly monitored and followed up.

Build Sensitivities, Prevent Discrimination

Discrimination in schools can be on account of physical impairments, social categories of caste, class, region, religion, gender and academic performance and learning achievements. While teachers themselves need to be sensitive towards students' experiences and embrace diversity across students, the same also needs to be developed in students. Through workshops and seminars, teachers need to be prepared to reflect on their own thoughts, identify biases and sources of potential discrimination. They may also wish to reflect on existing school practices that may be discriminatory and thus restrictive in participation of particular students and teachers in school activities. Building sensitivities in students can be challenging because they may not be aware of the biases and prejudices that they may be carrying from outside school. Young children are also sometimes unable to take into account the perspective of others and may not realise that their words and actions can be hurtful. Teachers will have to take the lead in helping children be tolerant and embrace peers from diverse backgrounds and ability levels. They must also be observant and identify any signs of discriminatory behaviour within the classroom and address it at the individual and group level to ensure that such practices are not taken lightly. Perspectives and attitudes developed at this stage can actually help children grow up to become sensitive adults, thus leading to a ripple change in society.

Building Safe Spaces

The school must provide protection from injury and physical harm. Schools that are under construction or renovation must ensure that children are away from the places of harm. There should be an active mechanism of ensuring that children are accounted for at all times during school. Schools often keep a watchful eye on students who are unnecessarily outside classes. In preventing sexual harassment in schools, they also ensure that students do not engage with teachers, staff and older children in secluded spaces. In addition, schools where the junior and senior wings are separated, older children are often not allowed access to junior wings to prevent bullying and harassment.

In addition, schools should be spaces that are free from trauma and stress. In nuclear families, and where often both parents are working, parents often tend to think of the school as a safe space for children to go to when they are at work. Reports of incidents of mental and physical harassment in schools are thus often unnerving. A place that is characterised by fear and anxiety cannot provide a positive learning environment. The school authorities must implement a policy of zero tolerance for punishment. This includes punishment of both physical as well as psychological nature. It is significant that children learn freely and explore without stress and trauma.

Recognise Signs of Sexual Offences

Given the increase in sexual crimes over the past few years, it is pertinent that school teachers and students both be aware and vigilant. In the paragraphs above, it has been discussed why schools need to be free from fear and trauma. At the same time, it is important to recognise that sexual harassment in school settings has also become fairly common. This may involve a person in authority, such as a teacher or a non-teaching staff member, or older school students or even peers. Sexual offences include forcefully establishing physical contact and/or recording such engagement. It may also take the form of remarks in public or private platforms, gestures or forced reading or viewing of content of sexual nature. Children may also become victims of sexual abuse in home settings, in the neighbourhood and during travel to school. It is also a common perception that sexual offenses are only meted out against girls by boys and men. This is not true. Young boys can also be victims of sexual offenses and, in fact, these most often go unreported. While the forms can be many, children may often not be able to recognise what is sexually offensive. At other times, fear, guilt and shame may prevent them from voicing their trauma. It is thus important that teachers be prepared to keep a watchful eye on students and recognise any signs of sexual offence. This may manifest itself through a heightened curiosity about sexuality, increased isolation, aggression, emotional imbalance and underachievement in schools. It would be helpful to conduct regular sessions with students, parents and teachers to recognise signs of sexual offense and tell students what to do if they themselves or see someone else become a victim of sexual offense. In addition, healthy attitudes towards sexuality must be developed to ensure that children themselves do not become sexual offenders. Schools must also form an anti-sexual harassment committee to address any reported cases of sexual offences.

Promote Healthy Gender Relations

Healthy relationships with peers go a long way in building self-esteem and identity. Healthy relations with peers from other genders are also helpful in understanding each other's concerns and pressures and thus in developing empathetic attitudes towards each other. Children grow up together and are able to develop sensitivities towards each other and also learn to appreciate each other for abilities and are not bogged down by stereotypes. It is also important that schools develop attitudes of acceptance towards the third gender and help students learn to accept it as a diversity in society. If there exists gender diversity in a classroom, teachers should ensure that there is no discrimination against children belonging to the minority and healthy relations are promoted. Sitting with the opposite gender is often prohibited in senior classes, while it is used as a disciplining tool in junior classes. These are examples of practices that promote an unhealthy attitude and create distance between peers. Students learn to look at each other in the singular dimension of gender and do not develop attitudes of friendship, comradery and learning together.

Rethinking Authority

Teachers should be encouraged to think about their roles in the classroom and revisit the nature of their relationship with students. Can students learn only when they look at teachers as persons in positions of authority? Or can teachers envision their roles as facilitators who are helping children to learn and grow together?

Authority is also often used as a disciplining tool that ensures that children sit straight backed in neat rows, come in prescribed uniform and obey school rules completely. Experimentation with looks is seen as disobedience and digression rather than as a means of expressing themselves. Teachers need to think about providing spaces to children to express themselves and develop relationships that are based on comfort. This need not translate into an atmosphere of chaos. In fact, freedom with responsibility from an early age can actually help children develop the value of discipline intrinsically without the need for resorting to authoritative measures. Decisions can be taken jointly through discussion between teachers and students. This in turn teaches the valuable skill of negotiation and understanding. In other words, authority need not form the fulcrum of school engagement.

Envisioning Comprehensive Evaluation Practices

All policies have focused on all-round development of children and embracing diversity. While curriculum modification and using resource material can ensure teaching to address diverse needs, if evaluation practices remain unchanged, schooling would continue to focus on marks rather than potentials. Contemporary times have shown that schooling is focused on marks more than learning. Students often end up studying subjects that they may have no interest in and that they do not wish to pursue further. In addition, paper and pencil tests at the end of the year create unnecessary pressure of evaluating a whole year's work on the basis of a three-hour performance. It is also restricted to acknowledging the achievement of those with good memory and writing skills. Continuous Comprehensive Evaluation (CCE) was a welcome step in moving away from dogmatic evaluation mechanisms. However, if not implemented in its true spirit, CCE can also act as a tool of marking achievement in terms of marks and evaluating only one kind of skills. It then becomes a burden for both students and teachers rather than an opportunity to present diverse opportunities to students. CCE can, in fact, help a teacher to tailor-make evaluation systems that allow for the use of technology, project work, performing and creative arts, presentations and written assignments as evaluative exercises. Flexibility in time frames and a focus on the learning of the individual student over time, rather than in comparison to other students, can also be organised to help build a stress-free environment in which students look at evaluation as ways of monitoring their own progress rather than as tests that are meant to form judgements about them.

ON A CONCLUDING NOTE

Policy perspectives are significant in ensuring that children grow up in a safe and secure environment. However, a policy will remain mere words on paper without teachers developing attitudes and sensitivities in children that the policies recommend. While acts and resolutions can provide legal recourse, the aim of schools should be to work towards building a society that does not need to take recourse to law for living a stress-free life of dignity and respect.

Understanding Children and Adolescents in School

3

The first chapter focused on the conceptualisation of mental health and the historical evolution of the concept. The need for addressing the mental health concerns and issues faced by school students was also discussed, followed by discussion of policy perspectives in the next chapter. In the present chapter, the focus will be on understanding the needs of school children and adolescents and the psychosocial world in which they live.

As a starting point, let us look at Table 3.1

Table 3.1   Understanding the Children's World from their Perspective

Age Range of Children	What Parents Say	What Children Hear	What Children Think and Feel
5–7 years	'Don't climb on that tree. You will fall.'	'You are not capable of climbing the tree. You don't know anything.'	'Everyone does it. I will climb the tree and show my parents how capable I am.'
10–12 years	'No I will not buy you an iPhone to take to school. School is a place to study and not show off to your friends. We don't work so hard to waste money only for buying fancy gadgets for you.'	'Your friends' parents waste money on them. You should focus on studies. We don't love you so much to waste our money on you.'	'All my friends bring expensive phones and iPads to school. Why can't my parents understand how humiliated I feel? They just don't love me like other parents love their children. It is as if I am not even their child!'
13–15 years	'We don't think you should attend the party. We don't know what sort of people will be attending it. We want you to be safe.'	'We don't trust your judgment with people. You are too young to take care of yourself. You need us around everywhere. We don't like your friends anyway.'	'My parents never liked my friends. They just don't want me to be happy. They think I am still a child and can't take decisions for myself.'
16–18 years	'Don't take Science in class eleven just because your sister did. I think you have a greater aptitude for Humanities.'	'You are not as intelligent as your sister. There is no point wasting money and time on studying Science.'	'My mother never encouraged me. She thinks I am incapable. She always loved my sister more than she loves me.'

Source: Authors.

These are a few examples of how children see the world around them. Similar instances can be seen in school settings where rules related to examinations, uniforms and dressing styles, late coming, hairstyles and so on, may not appeal to students. Where children are given the space and freedom to question, they will voice their concerns. Where authority and/or punishment is used to silence children into obedience, they often grow up with a sense of being stifled, misunderstood and shunned. This can at times lead to resentment, low self-esteem and sour family relationships and, at times, hostility towards parents and siblings. What Table 3.1 also highlights is that the perspectives of children and adults often vary greatly. Thus, even when parents and teachers have their best interests at heart, children and adolescents will interpret it from their own viewpoint and may not arrive at the same understanding as the parents. It is therefore very important to understand the world of children from their own perspective.

UNDERSTANDING THE NEEDS OF CHILDREN AND ADOLESCENTS

It would be incorrect to think of needs, concerns and dilemmas of children as universal. Each child lives in a context specific only to him or her and thus deserves to be understood within that context specificity. Nevertheless, psychologists provide us with some universal dimensions that are applicable to all children. Let us look at some of these theories before we move on to exploring the uniqueness of children's contexts.

Maslow's seminal work on understanding needs can act as a guide to understand children's needs. He advocated that people's actions are need driven and that these needs present themselves in an orderly fashion. He organised needs into a pyramid and presented the basic physiological needs, at the base of the pyramid (Figure 3.1). These are followed by the need for safety and security, love and belongingness, esteem and finally self-actualisation.

Figure 3.1   Role of Home and School in Fulfilling Children's Needs: Maslow's Need Hierarchy

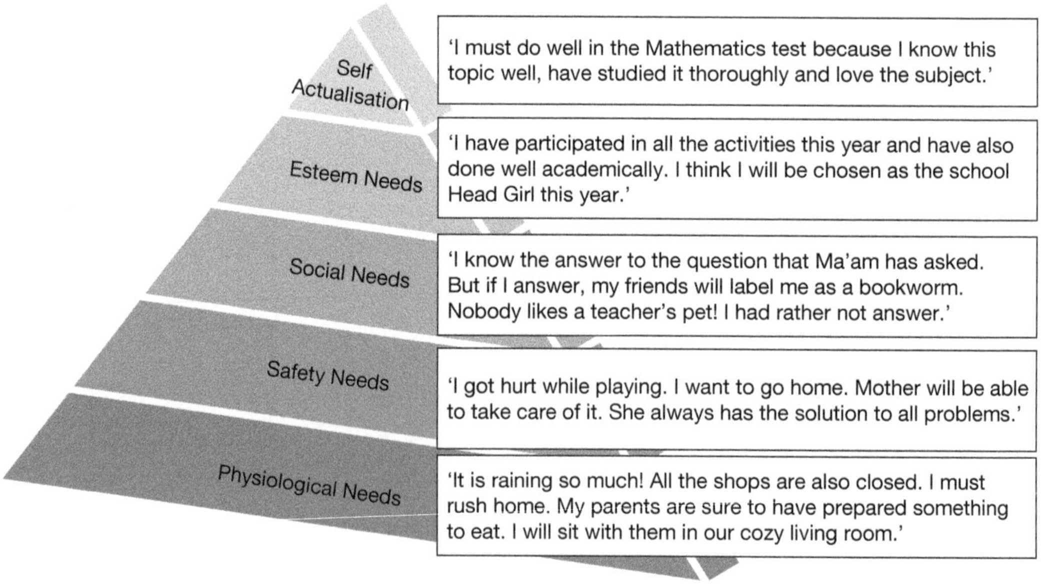

Self Actualisation — 'I must do well in the Mathematics test because I know this topic well, have studied it thoroughly and love the subject.'

Esteem Needs — 'I have participated in all the activities this year and have also done well academically. I think I will be chosen as the school Head Girl this year.'

Social Needs — 'I know the answer to the question that Ma'am has asked. But if I answer, my friends will label me as a bookworm. Nobody likes a teacher's pet! I had rather not answer.'

Safety Needs — 'I got hurt while playing. I want to go home. Mother will be able to take care of it. She always has the solution to all problems.'

Physiological Needs — 'It is raining so much! All the shops are also closed. I must rush home. My parents are sure to have prepared something to eat. I will sit with them in our cozy living room.'

Source: Authors.

Each of these needs have been arranged in a hierarchical order. As has been explained above, a lower order need arises first, followed by the higher order needs at the top. Maslow argued that very few people in society reach the highest level of self-actualisation needs as most people remain struggling in fulfilling the lower order needs. Later researchers have argued for a parallel experience of needs of various levels. In other words, school-going children will experience various needs together and work towards fulfilling all of these. The diagram above provides some examples of how these needs influence school-going children. You would notice that these needs arise and get fulfilled within the familial and social context in which children live. Significant others play a pivotal role in fulfilling the needs of children. Providing love, security and appreciation are vital to promote the development of children along the hierarchy of needs. The examples above also serve the important purpose of highlighting the role of the family and school in children's development of self and identity. Infancy and early childhood are marked by dependence on the family for the fulfilment of physiological needs and safety of food, shelter, clothing and so on. Here safety refers to both physical protection as well as emotional and social security. The child finds comfort in the emotional anchorage provided by his/her parents or other family members. This is followed by social needs in which peers, besides the family, assume a dominant role. During late childhood and adolescence, school-going children increasingly turn towards their peers for love and acceptance. At the next level, the need for the recognition for hard work, abilities and potential becomes important. This includes self-appreciation as well as appreciation from others. At the highest level, there is a need felt to achieve and perform to the best of one's potential and abilities.

There is little doubt that young children tend to get irritable and throw tantrums when they feel hungry, sleepy or insecure. Research has also shown that children who are nurtured in a loving, caring and secure environment at home and school, are more likely to have better school adjustment, establish better relationships and are happier (National Scientific Council on the Developing Child 2004; Repetti, Flook and Sperling 2011). This is also in consonance with the work of Erikson, a developmental psychoanalyst, who holds that the inability to establish trust in relationships during infancy can lead to development of a sense of fear that may, subsequently, result in anxieties, insecurities and mistrust of the world around him or her. We will revisit Erikson's theory in the subsequent sections of this chapter. Here, it is important to give due credence to the role played by relationships in the healthy development of self. In this regard, the person-centred approach, developed by Carl Rogers is particularly relevant for the emphasis that it gave to the role of caregivers. Rogers' approach highlights the need for positive regard and self-actualisation as the two basic needs which impact the development of self of an individual. He looks at positive regard as the basic human need for acceptance, respect and affection from others. Positive regard often comes with a set of 'conditions of worth'. In return for positive regard, parents, teachers and significant others attach value to behaviour that is acceptable and thus 'worthy' of being loved. Children must meet these expectations of others to 'get' positive regard from them.

'If you excel in this exam, I will buy you a bicycle.'

'If you win the school dance competition, your name will be announced in the school assembly.'

'You must not talk back to your elders. Aren't you a good boy?'

'Good girls do not climb on trees.'

The statements in the box given on the left are all examples of how simple rewards can impose conditions of worth on children. Here, tangible rewards such as a bicycle, or intangible ones, such as being a good boy or good girl, can impose conditions of worth. On the one hand, these conditions can serve the purpose of directing children towards appropriate behaviour, on the other, they can pose restrictions in helping children realise their full potential, thus inhibiting their actualising tendency. Socialisation processes can lead these conditions of worth to become conditions of self-worth. As they grow, children slowly start to evaluate themselves by the parameters set by others to judge them. Body image consciousness, underachievement in studies and dissatisfaction with one's performance are some of the issues that might emerge from conditions of worth. Consider the following case:

> Reshma is 15 years old. She was still in primary school when her parents and extended family started talking about collecting money for her marriage. She often heard her aunts remarking that her parents would need extra money as she is dark complexioned and it would be difficult to find a boy who would agree to marry her. Although she is doing well academically, she is aware that she will not be allowed to continue education after her schooling. She has accepted that she needs to be good at housework a lot more than her examinations. She knows she is dark and thinks that she is not beautiful. Being apt at housework is the only way that she can save her family's reputation and marry well. Although she doesn't like it, she spends a lot of time in the kitchen every day. All her friends are fair and beautiful. She doesn't feel like meeting them. She has stopped looking at herself in the mirror.

The case study of Reshma above highlights how young girls undergo stress and anxiety on an everyday basis. Society imposes its own standards of beauty and good looks on children. Young boys feel the need to exercise to build muscles and wear clothes of a certain kind so that they are loved and admired by others. This also leads them to develop a self-concept that is disconnected with their real self. Self-concept can be defined as a set of characteristics that we assign to ourselves. These characteristics may or may not be an accurate representation of who we are. In the case discussed above, Reshma, with repeated reinforcement from family and friends has started to believe that she is not beautiful based on the notion that only fair people are beautiful. She may be a beautiful person but she has stopped believing in herself. This false sense of self can lead to a low self-esteem which in turn can affect an individual's performance in other areas as well. In this case, Reshma's social life is also affected as she no longer wishes to interact with her friends. She has learnt to value only those aspects of herself that others value in her. In contrast, if she had been encouraged by her parents and teachers to focus on her abilities in academics or other domains, she may have been able to develop a positive sense of self, have faith in her ability to live her life more confidently and take her own decisions.

All significant others, which include teachers, parents and peers, should attempt to value people for who they really are. In the simplest of terms, this can be done by providing unconditional positive regard to each other. This does not mean, however, that each behaviour needs to be appreciated or that children should be allowed to do whatever they wish to do. Rather, it means that they should not be judged for their mistakes or lack of success. Also, if and when they have to be reprimanded, the manner in which it is done should be inoffensive and not damaging to their sense of self. Most importantly they should not be judged for being born in a certain way. The box below presents the real life story of Sohaila Abdulali.

> Sohaila Abdulali is a writer and activist of Indian origin. She completed her schooling from Bombay, India in the seventies. When she was 20 years old, she wrote about being raped as a 17-year-old and how she and her family dealt with it. She wrote an op-ed about the incident again in the *New York Times* after the Nirbhaya incident in December 2012.

In her article, she talks about how her family and friends did not let the sexual assault become the central focal point of her life. She instead continued to study and explore the world. While she took time to overcome her personal trauma, it did not become a social trauma for her and she was able to find her calling in writing and journalism.

Sohaila subsequently married and now lives with her husband and daughter in New York.

Her complete article can be found at:

http://www.nytimes.com/2013/01/08/opinion/after-being-raped-i-was-wounded-my-honor-wasnt.html?_r=0

Sohaila's story clearly illustrates how a strong and supportive family can help build confidence in one-self and provide courage to overcome trauma. While Sohaila herself has shown exemplary strength in moving on from an experience that could have broken her spirit, it is important to recognise that this may not be true for other rape survivors, who do not necessarily find a supportive familial and social context. Newspapers are replete with reports of young girls who were traumatised and unaccepted at home and school on account of similar incidents. In cases of sexual assault, the victim–offender dyad is quite evident. Schools, particularly in urban contexts, have also witnessed a surge in the reported incidents of sexual experimentation. Such reports often bring about shame to the student, his/her home, as well as school. Many a times, students tend to change schools, or sometimes are stopped by their parents from continuing their education. It is important for schools to note that students involved in such incidents need to be addressed with great sensitivity and care. They need to be helped and counselled rather than made to feel guilty. While it is important that parents stay aware of the activities of their children and adolescents and help them to stay safe, they also need to provide appropriate personal space to them. Yet, if an untoward incident happens, parents and schools should engage in active counselling to help the child or adolescent to feel supported and loved. They should help him/her to share thoughts and feelings, as well as overcome any sense of shame or guilt by reiterating that it is not the victim's fault. Support may also be required in helping the person to face society, peers and undergo medical and legal processes. Further, peers may also be sensitised in helping the victim to deal with the trauma by engaging sensitively and not sensationalising the incident. The specific issue of sexuality and related concerns has been addressed in Chapter 10.

CONCERNS AND DILEMMAS OF CHILDREN AND ADOLESCENTS

The previous sections highlighted the needs of children and adolescents and the significant influence of family in addressing these needs. This section will highlight some of the common concerns and dilemmas that children and adolescents face. To begin with, it is important to highlight that each child is unique and therefore the nature of concerns and dilemmas need to be understood within his/her psychosocial context. An attempt is being made in the text that follows to address some of the concerns and dilemmas that are commonly visible in children and adolescents of school-going age.

Peer Relationships

One of the primary concerns that school-going children face are those related to peers. Peer relationships can prove to be both positive as well as detrimental. The influence of peers is evident in children as young as three years. Conversations of young children at pre-school revolve around their possessions including water bottles, pencil boxes, erasers and so on. Who has the latest lunch box with the cartoon character in vogue printed on it? Whose birthday party was attended by the maximum number of friends? How fancy was the birthday cake? Who wears the prettiest dresses? These are some of the questions that are significant in the lives of young children. They often percolate to conversations with parents where they get translated into demands for new possessions that they can show off to their friends.

In older children, being popular in class is a coveted position. This relates both to being accepted by teachers as well as by peers. A common urban trend these days is to give very expensive return presents during birthday parties. Also, a new trend to have a theme-based party with fancy games and eats has been observed. Some children arrange their birthday parties in restaurants and malls. All these create pressures of their own. Children are also seen to compete not just in their academic achievements but also in having the most number of friends, the movies watched, places visited, economic status of the family, toys, gizmos and gadgets owned, number of games played and so on.

With the onset of puberty, these concerns may shift to body image issues, love relationships, academic and co-curricular achievements and popularity amongst peers. Adolescents, in fact, probably are the most vulnerable in succumbing to peer pressure. At a time when they are struggling to find their own identities, they are also simultaneously striving to fit in with the crowd, be recognised and be appreciated. In this quest for acceptance, they experience the pressure to experiment with alternative ideas and behaviours that may not be congruent with their lifestyle. This may result in experimentation with sexuality, substance misuse, aggression and so on. Since risk, danger and adventure needs are very strong during adolescence, a number of behaviours and actions seen in them stem from these.

Each child/adolescent can be the victim or perpetrator of peer pressure. Through peer pressure, children/adolescents are expected to fit into normative categories of appearance and behaviour. This acts as a strong socialising agent on the one hand, and a strong hindrance to one's identity on the other. Undue pressure to fit in can lead a person to be confused, repressed, have feelings of self-doubt and inferiority and poor self-acceptance. This can be understood in tandem with Rogers' notion of 'conditions of positive self-regard,' wherein the person starts to judge himself/herself, along the same criteria on which others judge him/her. On the other hand, peer pressure may also lead a child/adolescent to be better behaved, get better grades in school and develop social skills of adjustment and acceptance.

Further, both parents and teachers should accept the need and role of peers as important socialising agents. Instead of looking at peers as a threat to the well-being of the child, parents should attempt to know their children's friends and encourage interpersonal interaction and strong friendship bonds. Often peers help children to deal with stress and anxiety and are their confidantes on issues that children are unable to discuss with adults. Parents may accept this as part of the normal course of growing up.

Family Life

The most significant and long lasting relationships that an individual has, are probably those with the family. Family fulfils the important roles of caregiving, building bonds and socialising a child for the subsequent adult roles to be played in society. The structure, interaction patterns and interpersonal dynamics within a family are rooted in the cultural settings within which the family is situated. Chaudhary (2004) illustrates the cultural rootedness of family life and processes. She elaborates that verbal interaction is more prevalent in western families whereas families that are based in agrarian cultures rely more on tactile interaction. In India, family is accorded greater importance in comparison to other countries, particularly those in the West which have more individualistic cultures. Indian families support a culture of togetherness, bonding and collectivism and so children grow up valuing the protection and insulation that the family provides. They learn to make decisions that are not just based on their own needs and wishes, but also respect and value the wishes and sentiments of others in the family. Further, like the Indian society, families in India are also characterised by hierarchies of age, gender and kinship relationships. 'In such a hierarchical structure, the concepts of equality and personal freedom are alien…. Members share feelings of family solidarity or familism and strive to uphold family dignity and status in society' (Bharat 2003). In a study by Larson, Verma and Dworkin (2003), adolescents reported family members as the first preference for spending time with. This indicated that they had internalised the cultural value that is promoted by Indian society in placing family at the centre of their lives.

The family pattern, parenting styles, interpersonal relationships among various members of the family and the home environment are thus important influences on the child's experience of family.

FAMILY PATTERNS

Indian families are traditionally patterned on a joint family system. A young child lives in a home built not just by parents and grandparents, but also several uncles and aunts. The relationship boundaries often blur between parents and relatives, siblings and cousins. The child may experience the home filled with many children of his/her own age. In the presence of many adults, there is always someone to provide love and protection when another is disapproving or angry. Happiness also exists in abundance. On the other hand, the great Indian joint family may also be characterised by somewhat strained interpersonal relations. These may be due to an attempt by parents to provide the best for their own children. Expressing this desire for their own children, however, may not be considered appropriate as it can be interpreted as discriminatory towards other children in the family (Kakar 2005). This may then lead to covert, competitive feelings between families, parents and children and may start the process of psychological nuclearisation within the joint family system (Kakar 2007). In this scenario, while living as one big family, each family unit looks at itself as a nuclear one, prioritising the needs of the immediate family over those in the extended family. This may lead to greater individualisation of the child even while living with a large family.

With growing urbanisation and resultant trends of migration, Indian society in the last two decades has seen a rise in nuclear families. These are typically characterised by parents and one or two children. Grandparents tend to visit or are visited during school vacations or when their help is required. Children find the time and space with their parents, which is somewhat missing in the joint family system. Trends in recent years however show that this may not hold true when both parents are working. Also the long work hours that urban jobs entail, particularly in the private sector, leave little time for parents to interact with their children. A nuclear family often does not provide the closeness available in an extended family. Moreover, the opportunity for a child to learn through oral family history and culture and likewise, early lessons in social adjustment may be missing. Parents these days are conscious of this and try hard to compensate for this vacuum. It is not uncommon to see many present day young adults reminiscing about their childhood and growing up years being marked with annual family vacations to their hometown, typically their grandparents' home.

Kakar (2007) highlights the growing urban trend reversal as the most recent phenomenon in urban areas. Here families are increasingly working towards living in joint families. In the absence of state support to the elderly, young couples also encourage parents to live with them and meet their medical, emotional and social needs. This trend has also arisen out of the significant contribution of grandparents in sharing responsibilities of caregiving for children. Chaudhary (2004) cites the work of Kapoor, who highlighted the different ways in which children of working mothers were perceived. Paternal grandparents saw the child as an 'heir of the family', as 'an adorable companion but not my own' by the domestic help for the child or as the 'product of parents who do not care enough' by the crèche incharge. Thus, caregiving facilities for the child are dependent on the family structure and working status of parents. This in turn significantly influences interpersonal relations of the child with others in the family.

Researches also show that it is no longer possible to categorise families into two neat categories of nuclear and joint families. There are many different patterns visible in families, particularly in urban India (Sharma 1990). In fact, complexity across families is visible in increasingly fluid family structures. With rising number of divorces, it is not uncommon for children to grow up with one parent and the other parent visiting occasionally. Children could also be growing up with step-parents and siblings. Work requirements also might require at least one parent to travel or live in a different city.

What this highlights is that there are as many different family patterns as there are families, including same gender couples and live-in partners. Even within the joint family system, variations are visible from the traditional pattern of several family units sharing the same space and a common kitchen. Now, family units may have clearly demarcated spaces, with separate kitchens. Some families also decide to stay separately but in close proximity for the sake of convenience (Ranganathan 2008). Verma and Saraswathi (2002) in their work on adolescence in India have also highlighted that although there is a lot of variation in family setups in India, families have retained their character of interdependence. 'While composition and living arrangements within families are rapidly changing in India, the joint-ness in terms of interdependence in major family decisions, remains for a majority of families' (Khatri 1972 cited in Verma and Saraswathi 2002). Larson, Verma and Dworkin (2003), cited Mistry and Saraswathi (2003) to highlight that middle class families have become more 'materially independent, but emotional interdependence persists' (p. 282).

PARENTING STYLES

Traditionally, parenting styles are categorised into authoritarian, authoritative and permissive, as per Baumrind's original classification. Parenting styles are more popularly classified in authoritarian, authoritative, democratic and laissez faire. In the Indian context, some of the features of authoritative parenting may be seen as overlapping with indulgent and overprotective parenting. Likewise, democratic parenting may be understood as benevolent parenting and laissez faire both as indifferent and neglectful parenting. Figure 3.2 presents an understanding of how parents following different parenting styles would react to the same situation.

Figure 3.2 is indicative of a typical family situation of intergenerational conflict. However, family experiences are rarely ever so simple. Children and adolescents seldom accept parental decisions that do not suit them without resistance. Disagreements and arguments are more a norm of family life rather than a rare occurrence. Yet, authoritarian parents are less likely to meet with resistance due to early socialisation of children into acceptance of the disciplinary norms of the family and, in some instances, threat of physical punishment. In such families, children learn to follow and obey their parents blindly, from very early in life. In subsequent years, they are more likely to face difficulty in decision-making since they have never been given this opportunity.

In an authoritative family, or an overprotective family, parents play a dominant role in decision-making. Although their children may find space for voicing their opinions, ultimate decision-making

Figure 3.2   Baumrind's Classification of Parenting Styles: A Case Study

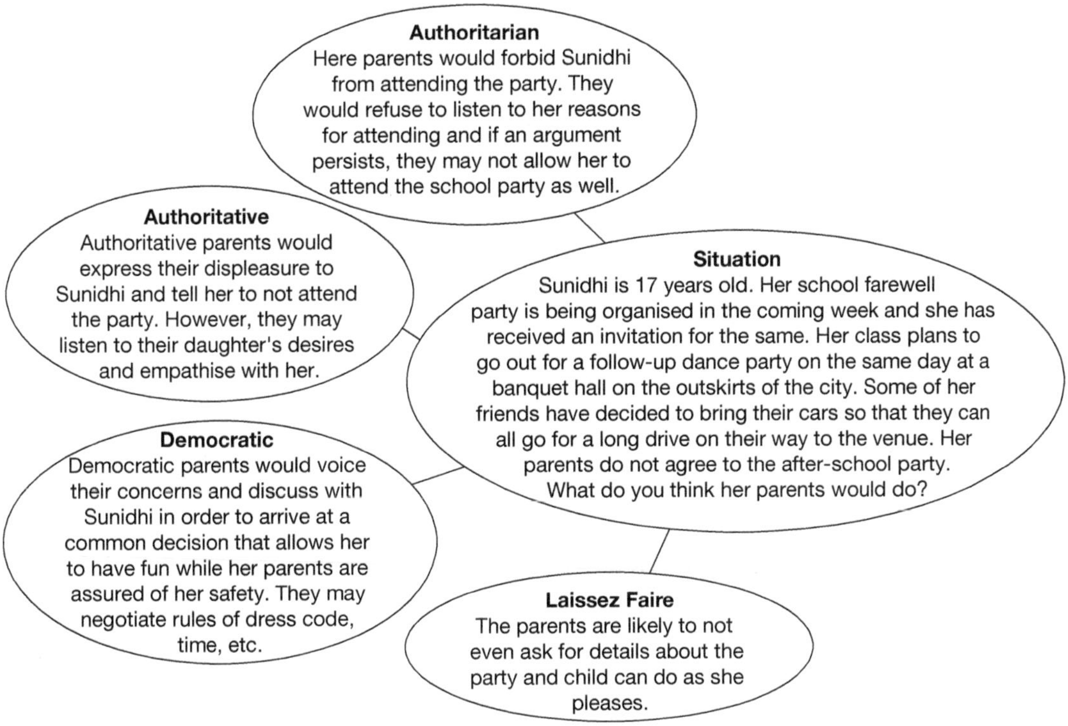

Authoritarian
Here parents would forbid Sunidhi from attending the party. They would refuse to listen to her reasons for attending and if an argument persists, they may not allow her to attend the school party as well.

Authoritative
Authoritative parents would express their displeasure to Sunidhi and tell her to not attend the party. However, they may listen to their daughter's desires and empathise with her.

Situation
Sunidhi is 17 years old. Her school farewell party is being organised in the coming week and she has received an invitation for the same. Her class plans to go out for a follow-up dance party on the same day at a banquet hall on the outskirts of the city. Some of her friends have decided to bring their cars so that they can all go for a long drive on their way to the venue. Her parents do not agree to the after-school party. What do you think her parents would do?

Democratic
Democratic parents would voice their concerns and discuss with Sunidhi in order to arrive at a common decision that allows her to have fun while her parents are assured of her safety. They may negotiate rules of dress code, time, etc.

Laissez Faire
The parents are likely to not even ask for details about the party and child can do as she pleases.

Source: Authors.

will be by the parents, probably with little regard to children's perspectives. Parents legitimise their stand by saying that it is in the best interest of their children. Overprotected children are cosseted and kept insulated from what parents perceive as impending harm and often precluded from a number of life experiences that other children might have. They thus develop a dependence function. In both cases, children may grow up feeling unworthy and may lack confidence in their thoughts and opinions.

In a democratic family set up, decision-making is usually a joint effort of parents and one or more children. Family members typically use discussion as a mode of listening to each other, clarifying doubts, presenting alternatives and express love, concern and acceptance of each other. This does not mean that the family is free from conflict or that parents are not in a decision-making position. It is just that children are likely to feel more valued, capable and worthy of thinking. Even when decisions go against the better judgement or wishes of either children or parents, more often than not, they would understand the others' reasoning and perspective, thus building better relationships and stronger inter-personal bonds.

In a laissez faire family, characterised by indifferent parenting, parents tend to have little control over their children, child holds the power. There is usually poor communication between parents and children, leaving little space for discussion, or taking collective decisions. Here, with very little support, guidance and care, children are left to their own resources. As a result, they may either become reckless or pleasure driven, or overly grown-up and responsible very early in life. There is usually an early adultification of these children.

In Indian families, parental beliefs regarding parenting values tend to reflect traditional emphasis on interdependence and respect for elders. 'In practice, one observes a relaxation in the patriarchal hierarchy, especially among the educated middle class, professional families. Marked gender differences however, continue to prevail' (Verma and Saraswathi 2002, 109). In general, girls experience greater parental control in social as well as household activities. Greater academic expectations and career aspirations are expressed from boys. This trend has also seen some change in recent decades. Another significant trend in the urban middle class is that fathers are becoming more involved with parenting and interactions with children of both genders. High parental control has been seen to have some implications for mate selection and responsibility taking in jobs, later in life (Verma and Saraswathi 2002).

It is important to point out here, that parenting styles vary across families and there is no style that can be considered best for all families and situations. In other words, parents may resort to different parenting styles depending on their family structure and specific situation. At present, more and more styles of parenting are emerging, especially in metropolitan cities. The bottom line is that every parent will use what he/she deems suitable and worthwhile to bring up his/her children. Further, it would be inappropriate to assume that even in the most authoritarian families, parents do not love their children. In fact, they believe that they know what is best for their children and attempt to provide the same to them. Thus their intention is to give their child the best.

Contemporary times also see some new parenting styles that have emerged out of changing lifestyles and family patterns. In families where both parents are working, for example, children may grow up with their grandparents. This increases the gap between the primary caregivers and their children and may lead to greater conflicts and misunderstandings between family members. This is because decision-making for children rests with their parents who return late from work and have little time for negotiation with their children or their own parents. In other families, where both parents are working and dependent on hired care services for their children, a new style of parenting which may be referred to as 'remote control parenting' can be seen. In this style, parents may be away from home for a substantial part of the day, leaving their children at crèches or with domestic help. Older children and adolescents may stay alone at home. Whatever be the case, parents keep a check on their children's activities through the use of technology. Use of webcams that they can access from their work places and the use of phones, are common to monitor the activities of their children and stay updated with their safety and care. Modern workspaces are also increasingly providing choices of working at home to allow parents to maintain work–life balance. Here, family life is complicated further as children are expected to learn early when parents are not available to them, despite their being 'available' at home. The demarcations between time allotted to work and home are less clear and cause greater confusion to impulse driven children. This may often result in impatience and frustration for parents as well.

HOME ENVIRONMENT AND INTERPERSONAL RELATIONSHIPS

Parenting styles directly influence the relationship between parents and children. The relationships that family members have with each other are also equally influential in shaping the family experiences of children. Children observe and experience interactions between parents, and in joint family systems, and between parents and other members of the family. Everyday routines serve as important sources of linguistic and cultural messages, serving important socialisation functions. 'Rhymes, rhythmic movements, and verbal games are particularly important in Indian parent–child interaction. Conversations within the family are thus a powerful source of cultural and psychological information' (Chaudhary 2004, 76). These verbal and non-verbal interactions often act as socialisation processes, teaching children how to behave in social situations. They are also the basis on which children form relationships with members of the extended family.

Financial strains, differences in opinions, disputes over family inheritance and physical and psychological abuse are some of the reasons that can lead to an unhealthy home environment. While parents may try hard to insulate their children from the 'real' context, children are able to sense the home situation based on tone of a parent's voice, presence of a particular family member and also by the absence of communication between certain members in the family. Research studies have shown that children as young as six months are able to sense tensions in the home environment, in times of stress and strife (Graham, Fisher and Pfeifer 2013). Infants may be able to capture the stressful home environment, but they will not be able to understand the causes behind it. This may in turn lead them to continuously seek a secure environment and develop attention seeking behaviour from the caregiver who they feel most comfortable with.

Taking care of a child is a full time responsibility that is physically and mentally demanding. In urban contexts, there are also financial demands, stemming from the rising costs of crèches, day care centres, domestic helps and schooling. This in turn requires people to be more committed to their work places and generate substantial incomes. Sometimes, work pressures and the effort required in meeting the demands of family life may lead young couples to develop irritability and have frequent outbursts on children. A common tendency is to find fault in the child, whenever he/she commits a mistake. The focus is on the child rather than on the environment in which the child is growing up.

The economic background of the family is an important factor in building the home environment. Children growing up in underprivileged backgrounds struggle with basic necessities, including food, clean water and basic healthcare. In somewhat better households, that do not struggle to make ends meet and have relatively more stable family incomes, but at subsistence level, children are still less likely to have access to early childhood care and education. In middle and upper class families, children's pre-schooling is considered a necessity and not a luxury. This contrast is evident when children from heterogeneous backgrounds enter schools.

Another aspect of the home environment is the behaviour and interaction of parents and other family members with each other. Children look up to their family members as role models. Children in the eight to fifteen years' age group usually learn and follow the same kind of behaviour that they see at home. If, for instance, a child has grown-up observing his father hit his mother, he would also learn to disrespect women in similar ways. Similarly, young girls would learn to tolerate violence against them because they have always seen men at home engage in violent behaviour with the women in the family. It may also be emphasised that violence and aggression are not only gender based. Flaring tempers, raised voices and violent behaviour at home teach children that they do not need to control their emotions and that is okay to express their anger and frustration by harming the person in front of them. It also indicates that raising one's voice can help one to get whatever he/she wants and that it is okay to be inconsiderate towards the feelings of others. All of this gets learnt even when the caregiver is not violent towards his/her child!

Raising a child as a single parent is a difficult task in itself. However, the most difficult experience for the child is the process of separation between parents. Couples who are still undecided about continuing their relationship, or those in the process of seeking divorce, often end up dragging their children into their personal battles. Although unwittingly, parents often force their children to take sides and support them in legal custody battles. Young children are often unaware of the magnitude of the problem and are in most cases, left to deal with their own conflicting emotions themselves. These experiences can have long lasting effects on not just the relationship of the child with his/her parents, but also on his sense of emotional and psychological well-being.

It would appear that it is only young children who are most affected by conflicts and strife at home, and older children are able to deal with the situations in a better manner. While this may be somewhat true, it would be incorrect to underplay the magnitude of the effect of an unhealthy home environment on older children and adolescents. Whether it is due to constant strife and tension, or due to separation, or family disputes, older children are often expected to understand the difficulties at home and behave with maturity when engaging with them. At the same time, they are not considered old or mature enough to have a say in family matters. Thus, while they are expected to be empathetic, they are also expected to be silent witnesses. This can be emotionally very draining for a pre-teen or an adolescent, who is well aware of the gravity of the situation at home, is also able to form an opinion, but is expected to watch silently and also guard family secrets. The young adolescent is left with no place to share his/her concerns, feelings, thoughts and dilemmas.

It must also be highlighted that arguments and conflicts are not always degenerative for the child at home. No relationship is devoid of arguments. They are a necessary form of negotiating and arriving at decisions. They also teach children to be assertive and voice their opinions where necessary. The nature and content of the argument, along with frequency and the consequences for the family, are important aspects that decide the effects on the child witnessing them.

Social and Familial Expectations

The importance attached to respecting the family's wishes and maintaining family honour in India has become evident in recent years through the rise in the reported incidents of 'honour killings' of young men and women who had decided to marry against cultural norms of caste and religion. While these may be exaggerated incidents, Indian children grow up constantly attempting to please their parents and maintain their social image. Contrary to their own wishes, they often base their decisions on their family's expectations from them.

Socialisation processes in the family, neighbourhood and community prepare a child to fit into pre-scribed social roles. It would be worthwhile to take a deeper look at how gender is constructed in the Indian setting. The world over, gender differences are made evident in choice of clothes and hairstyles for infants and toddlers. The styles and colours of clothes clearly demarcate children on the basis of gender. Boys and girls are also provided and encouraged to play with gender-specific toys. Most parents and relatives tend to buy toys representing outdoor orientation, high energy and aggression like guns, police cars, remote controlled devices and mechanical construction games for boys. Girls are provided with dolls, doll houses, kitchen sets, jewellery-making sets and other craft-based activities that can be played within the confines of the home and are more gentle and engaging. This is however changing in the urban space, where the gender divide is not so acute, and more girls are seen playing outdoor games and wearing unisex clothes. Despite this, some gender-based distinctions are still observable. It is important to understand that these distinctions are not limited to homes. Schools are equally respon-sible in creating gender dividing spaces. A casual look at a senior secondary science classroom in any urban school would explode the myth that girls and boys share equal study spaces in urban settings. The number of boys is even greater in non-medical stream classrooms. The trend is reversed in home science classrooms, or for that matter in the humanities group. Similar differences are also seen in participation in sports. Girls are often discouraged to participate in sports, as is also evident at the national level with women's teams across sports, receiving lesser funding and support. In many families, lesser importance is given to the education of girls than that of boys in the same family. Girls are expected to partake in household chores in most families. Even where children in the family receive the same upbringing, adolescent and young adult women are expected to take responsibility of the household and prepare for marriage.

The influence of media can also not be ignored. Children as young as six years are inspired by what they see their heroes wear on screen. Clothes of fantasy characters depicted in animated movies as well as Bollywood actors and actresses are often available in children's sizes in the market and are in great demand. Young girls can be seen wearing heeled shoes at parties and wearing hair accessories and jewellery. There is little distinction in the cuts and styles of clothes between children and adults. All this again points to the early adultification of children. Children and adolescents participating in reality shows on television, are appreciated for adultlike performances and conversations. This pushes them and the thousands of children watching television at home towards adultlike behaviour themselves, even when it is not true to their nature. A growing trend that is also visible is encouraging very young children to participate in competitions in school and community, as well as reality shows on television. This not only encourages competitiveness, but also demands that children learn a number of different kind of activities. Mothers often exchange notes about the nature and number of classes that their children are attending. Along with school work, this leaves children with little time to engage in activities that they are themselves interested in. Somewhere the natural and spontaneous child gets lost in the parents' quest to make him/her a 'social object.'

The socio-economic background of the family has a strong role to play in the socialisation of a child. As has been discussed earlier, the family's financial status is likely to have a bearing on the facilities available and the exposure of the child to the world. This in turn, also affects the aspiration structure, career goals and life style that are carved out. Further, children are also seen to befriend children of similar socio-economic backgrounds. A heterogeneous peer group in school and college increases the possibility of befriending across socio-economic groups but parents often choose to exercise control over who their children interact with. Where interaction with children from diverse backgrounds is visible, hierarchies based on the socio-economic status of the two children also become evident. For instance, in a game of cricket, the employer's son is always seen to be batting, while the helper's son is bowling and fielding. Such hierarchies are maintained in all the games they play, as are the tone and language that they use in interacting with each other.

The discussion above points out that children and adolescents are presented with certain role models by the family and society. These role models may be presented through ideals, or through prescribed codes of behaviour appropriateness, which affect a whole set of choices including interaction patterns, career aspirations, interests, lifestyle choices and preferences of sexuality, among others.

Academic Stress

The earlier sections have already discussed how family background and social expectations influence the preferences and choices of children. Besides family expectations, children also face academic stress from a very young age. In a world marked by cutting edge competition, parents want their children to succeed, which seems to be only possible through academic excellence. Advertisements in newspapers and television highlight how parents tend to cherish children who do well in studies and are able to secure a place in the best colleges. This leaves little space for mediocrity and every child is left dreaming of being the class topper.

While the system of continuous and comprehensive evaluation was introduced to reduce the pressure of year-end examinations, it has introduced a series of assessment practices throughout the year. Many teachers, parents and school students complain that this has increased the academic stress because of the frequency and nature of activities introduced in school. Without a curiosity and a love for the subject, children feel distanced from studies and find them to be a burden. In such scenarios, textbooks and home tasks fail to inspire children to learn. Yet, they feel pressurised to not just study but to learn to score well.

In higher classes, since studies require more time and engagement, children are often required to join coaching classes for specific subjects. A school day leaves little time for the child to eat in peace, let alone engage in recreational activities. From here on, begins the rigmarole of non-stop drill and long hours of coaching classes for preparing for competitive examinations at the end of schooling. This is particularly true for students in the science stream. All of this adds to academic stress. Coupled with family's expectations, students worry about the options available to them in the future, in case they are not able to clear the entrance examinations. The matter of living up to the expectations of the family, justifying the expenditure on coaching classes and fulfilling the dreams and aspirations of their parents also add to the stress. An increasing number of children are falling prey to excessive anxiety, stress and depression that requires professional counselling.

Parents can play a particularly important role in helping children to cope with academic stress. The first step begins during early years of schooling. Instead of overemphasising scoring high marks and winning competitions, parents need to work towards an attitude of experiencing joy in the process of learning. At the same time, parents must express faith in children's capabilities and encourage them to aspire for more. The child should feel confident in his/her abilities and engage in active discussion about pursuing life goals.

DEVELOPING A SENSE OF IDENTITY

The childhood and adolescent experiences that an individual has, majorly influence the development of his/her sense of self and identity. Both the home and the school play a significant role in this regard. In fact, one of the main aims of schooling is to enable every child to emerge with a sense of self and identity. The experiences that a school sets up for its students are always influenced by this aim. Juxtaposed against this is the stage of adolescence in which, developmentally, adolescents are on a journey to find meaning in their life and commit to a set of values, an ideology and a focused set of life goals. They basically search for answers to the question: 'Who am I?' They have to be assisted in this quest by significant others around them, which include family, friends, peers and teachers. In fact, the need to be accepted, loved and appreciated are dominant in this phase, as also the need to understand oneself. Identity development thus is not just a personal but also a social phenomenon. In this section, a discussion on the need and process for developing identity will be taken up in light of the works of some identity theorists. Throughout the discussion, the psychosocial experiences of young adolescents who are on an identity quest should be kept in mind.

Erikson was one of the pioneering theorists on identity. He propounded an eight-stage approach to understand the search for identity by an individual, which starts at birth and finishes only with the end of his/her life. The eight stages follow the developmental course of the human development life span. He proposed that at each stage, the individual goes through a developmental crisis, which he called an ego conflict, that he/she must resolve before moving on to the next stage. A successful resolution of the conflict influences the individual positively. The inability to successfully resolve the conflict will impact the subsequent stage and how the individual deals with it. The eight psychosocial stages are discussed in Table 3.2.

Table 3.2   The Eight Psychosocial Stages Developed by Erikson

Stage 1	
Infancy	
Trust Versus Mistrust	
Infants are dependent on others for need fulfilment.	
TRUST	**MISTRUST**
Children learn to trust others while growing up in a warm, nurturing environment where their needs are fulfilled.	Infants develop mistrust if their needs are ignored and they grow up in an insecure environment marked by discomfort and fear.
Stage 2	
Late Infancy to Toddler Years	
Autonomy Versus Shame and Doubt	
Children start expressing their independence through their behaviour.	
AUTONOMY	**SHAME AND DOUBT**
Children develop a sense of autonomy if caregivers show confidence in their abilities to work independently.	A child who is discouraged from working independently, or is frequently punished may feel restrained in behaviour and develop feelings of self-doubt and shame.
Stage 3	
Early Childhood	
Initiative Versus Guilt	
Children go out to explore the world with greater independence in the school, neighbourhood and peer group. A greater interaction with the social world throws many challenges towards the children.	
INITIATIVE	**GUILT**
Children feel positive if they are able to take initiative to meet challenges and engage with the social world. For this, they need to be encouraged, guided and supported by their caregivers.	If children are made to feel uncomfortable or are laughed at in social settings, they can develop feelings of guilt at not being able to engage effectively with the social world. Caregivers may also make them overly anxious in social settings which would prevent healthy social adjustment.
Stage 4	
Late Childhood to Pre-teen Years	
Industry Versus Inferiority	
Primary school years require children to develop skills for learning and building knowledge.	
INDUSTRY	**INFERIORITY**
Children develop confidence if they are able to work hard and meet the challenges that schooling puts forth. Caregivers play a significant role in encouraging them to meet these challenges and appreciating their efforts and achievements.	An inability to meet the challenges of schooling may result in feelings of inferiority stemming out of being left behind in comparison to peers.

(Continued)

(Continued)

Stage 5
Adolescence

Identity Versus Identity Confusion
This stage is characterised by an attempt at finding one's identity and embarking on a quest to answer the questions: Who am I? What am I all about? Where am I going in life?

IDENTITY	IDENTITY CONFUSION
To develop a healthy identity, adolescents need to engage in a period of psychosocial moratorium and explore different personal and professional paths before committing to a role.	If adolescents are not allowed to adequately explore different choices or choose a particular path to follow, they are likely to remain confused about their identity.

Stage 6
Young Adulthood

Intimacy Versus Isolation
The early adulthood years are marked by an attempt to develop close bonds and relationships with friends and significant others.

INTIMACY	ISOLATION
An adult who has settled on an identity role would now attempt to develop close relationships and intimacy with a life partner or close friends.	An inability to develop close personal relationships can lead to feelings of social isolation.

Stage 7
Middle Adulthood Years

Generativity Versus Stagnation
The developmental task at this stage involves making significant contribution to the next generation.

GENERATIVITY	STAGNATION
Middle aged adults would share their experiences to provide positive guidance to the next generation. This may be done through parenting or other mentoring roles such as social workers, teachers, etc.	A feeling of stagnation can develop if one feels worthless at not having achieved and contributed something positive to the next generation.

Stage 8
Old Age

Ego Integrity Versus Despair
Older adults, settling into a retired life, would reflect on how they have lived their lives.

EGO INTEGRITY	DESPAIR
A positive evaluation of one's life would lead one to develop a sense of integrity and consider one's life as a life lived well.	If one looks back at life and finds mostly negative associations, he or she may experience despair at having lived a worthless life with no positive contribution.

Source: Adaptation of table based on Woolfolk (2006, 100).

Each of these stages is interrelated and so it is difficult to look at development of independence, identity and intimacy, for example, as disconnected processes. Significantly, Erikson's work highlights that school-going children during late childhood and adolescents are likely to face many psychosocial challenges and so require very sensitive and careful handling by parents, school and society. They are very important stages for fostering mental health.

Drawing on Erikson, James Marcia's (1966) work provides four identity statuses that mark the possibilities in the search for identity during the adolescent stage. In his view, an adolescent who is still exploring alternatives before making a commitment to any one choice would be experiencing **identity moratorium**. An adolescent who has committed to a specific life path without examining meaningful alternatives would have a **foreclosed identity**. A **diffused identity** would be experienced by someone who has neither made a commitment, nor is exploring alternatives. An individual who has explored alternatives, committed to a set of values, goals and an ideology by finding answers to the question *Who am I?* would be **identity achieved**.

A crucial aspect of the process of identity development is that it occurs within a social context. Bronfenbrenner's socioecological perspective highlights the important role played by family in developing a sense of self. His theory places the person at the centre of five concentric circles that represent his/her proximity to different environmental systems: microsystem, mesosystem, exosystem, macrosystem and chronosystem. Each of these systems influences the development of self. The microsystem is closest to the person and therefore has the most direct bearing on the individual. This system includes close interpersonal relationships like those with the family, peers, school, immediate neighbourhood and so on. The mesosystem represents the context of interaction of the various elements of the microsystem with each other as well as with the person in the centre. An example of the mesosystem is the interaction between the home and school. Bronfenbrenner asserted that the most important link in developing and maintaining the well-being of children and adolescents is between the home, the peer group and the school (Bronfenbrenner 1990).

The individual may not have a direct interaction with elements in the exosystem, yet the elements within this system have a strong influence on the individual, for instance, the legal system, the friends of family, media, technology and so on. An outer layer represents the influence of the socio-economic and cultural setting within which the individual lives. Living in a political state that does not promote or support the education of girls had a strong role to play in the life of Malala Yousafzai, who was shot at the age of fifteen for being vocal about the right of girls to school education in Swat valley, Pakistan. Such settings are represented in the macrosystem. Being born in a particular historical time also influences the social settings within which the individual functions. This is represented by the chronosystem. The five systems, represented through concentric circles thus represent the context within which the 'self' unfolds.

Georgass (1988, 1993) developed Bronfenbrenner's concentric circles approach further. He emphasised that the radius of each concentric circle also represents the significance of each element and the degree of its influence (cited in Dasen 2003). It may also be noted that the framework discussed above provides a static understanding of the social context of self. In contemporary psychology, the self is not seen as achieved but as dynamic and evolving. On similar lines, the context is also not static, but is continually changing. Different elements of different systems would also vary in terms of their influence on the person, depending on their developmental life stage and settings. Further, experiences during each life stage would also influence experiences in subsequent years. Bronfenbrenner's work may be reinterpreted in the form of a spiral rather than that of concentric circles.

The following spiral (Figure 3.3) is an illustrative example of the life story of Sohraab (Wadhwa 2013). Sohraab was born to a Zoroastrian (Parsi) father and Christian mother in 1982. The family

Figure 3.3 What Statistics do not Reveal: Experiences of Children and Adolescents

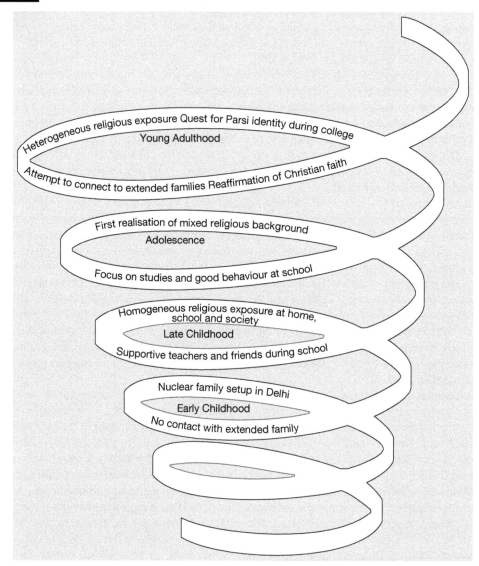

Heterogeneous religious exposure Quest for Parsi identity during college

Young Adulthood

Attempt to connect to extended families Reaffirmation of Christian faith

First realisation of mixed religious background

Adolescence

Focus on studies and good behaviour at school

Homogeneous religious exposure at home, school and society

Late Childhood

Supportive teachers and friends during school

Nuclear family setup in Delhi

Early Childhood

No contact with extended family

Source: Authors.

shifted to Delhi from Gujarat due to opposition from the extended family to the inter-religious marriage. He is an only child and was raised in Delhi with Christian beliefs. He is a post graduate in Business Administration and works with a multinational company.

The spiral indicates that Sohraab's early childhood years were influenced by growing up in a nuclear family. He also had no contact with the extended family. During his late childhood years, he had a homogeneous exposure to Christianity at home, at school and in the neighbourhood. In the absence of contact with the extended family, he received support from teachers and friends. He had little realisation of his mixed religious background till his adolescent years. However, this time was spent in concentrating on studies and maintaining a good reputation at school. His young adulthood years, when he was in college, took him on a quest to understand his Parsi roots. He attempted to reconnect with his extended family in Gujarat, albeit unsuccessfully. This, along with a heterogeneous religious exposure for the first time, led him to reaffirm his Christian beliefs.

Each layer of the upward moving spiral indicates a life stage. The significant external influences in the specific life stage are represented within the spiral. During early childhood, for example, the family and immediate caregivers may have a significant role to play. The neighbourhood and school may be more significant during early childhood and subsequent stages. Further, the significance attached to a particular factor, such as family, neighbourhood, society, culture, laws and so on, would also vary from individual to individual. The increasing width of each subsequent spiral indicates increase in the number of external influences as well as the development of self through life experiences. The spiral framework allows for a generic representation as well as developing a unique spiral for each individual.

GROWING UP IN A CHANGING WORLD

The previous section highlighted how identity development is not just a personal but also a social process. In a fast changing world, each one of us tries to keep pace with the changes, by making suitable adjustments to our lifestyle, values, beliefs and behaviour. Children and adolescents also struggle to keep pace with the changes around them to survive in a competitive world and be accepted in their peer group.

Discussions in children's groups often revolve around the latest Bollywood and pop songs, the movies watched, places visited and games downloaded on often their parents' cell phones and tablets. They compete with each other in having access to and being most conversant with the latest gadgets. The urban middle class and elite children learn to work on some of these gadgets in school and use the Internet to enrich their home tasks and projects.

During late childhood, children struggle towards gaining access to their own cell phones. In urban areas, having a cell phone is no longer a privilege. Most schools are struggling with restricting the usage of cell phones in schools. By this age, children increasingly start using technology independently. However, excessive use of technology can have many dire consequences for children. In most immediate and direct terms, technology addiction in terms of watching television, videos, playing games and so on can make a child unhealthy by increasing the hours of sitting in the same place and lessening the time spent in fresh air and in playing outdoor games. The child becomes a 'couch potato.' This can lead to health-related consequences including obesity and early onset of diabetes. Increased time in front of screens/monitors also negatively affects the eyes, and reduces concentration.

During adolescence, a fast-paced world is not just about frequently changing technology, but by the changes in education patterns and access and opportunities that characterise it. In an increasingly shrinking world, there is greater exposure to and a wide range of possibilities to a variety of experiences. Making choices and developing identity is even more complicated in such a world. It has already been discussed in the earlier section that the process of identity development is a social and not just a personal phenomenon. The work of Jenkins (2008) also highlights that it is not just our perception of self that determines our identity. Our sense of self is also influenced by what others perceive us to be. Identity is not just constructed in individuals but is also developed in identification with 'collectivities.' He emphasised that it is meaningless to understand identity in isolation from society. While each individual is unique, it is also important to understand him or her in terms of similarities and differences with groups. It is in these similarities and differences that individuals choose to form affiliations and develop group identities.

ON A CONCLUDING NOTE

This chapter provided an overview of how children relate to the world around them. It is important to reiterate that children can be understood well only if they are allowed to share their own perspectives and thoughts. This requires caregivers, including parents and teachers, to engage in active listening and respecting children for who they are. It is in this context that the next chapter will discuss the mental health needs, concerns and dilemmas of school children.

Issues and Challenges in School Mental Health

4

In the previous chapter, the importance of understanding the world of children from their perspective was discussed. It was also highlighted that a changing world throws up many challenges for school-going children and adolescents. These range from keeping pace with technology and changes in lifestyle, to the influences of changing family patterns. What this brings to light is that the school years and the time spent in school are crucial for meeting these challenges and maintaining and developing sound mental health. On an average, a child spends close to six hours a day in school in sustained conversation and engagement. This is at times more than the average waking time spent with the family. Schools thus act as important educational and mental health institutions.

The bonds developed with school teachers and peers can be used to meet the mental health needs of school children. Besides helping in developing close relationships in school, the school also provides the space for finding and developing one's potential, nurturing capabilities and exploring alternatives. In addition to teaching, school teachers fulfil caregiving roles. With an increase in the number of families with both parents working, teachers take on the role of primary agents of socialisation. Young children increasingly share their thoughts, wishes and everyday lives with teachers and school counsellors in classrooms and other spaces within the school.

STATISTICAL TRENDS, POLICY PERSPECTIVES AND CONTEMPORARY REALITIES

The discussion above emphasises that the school has the potential for addressing the mental health concerns of school children. The important question here is: Do schools need to actively engage in providing mental health services? A look at some statistics in mental health may help to find answers to this question.

WHO (2011) report states that over 85 countries in the world have less than one psychiatrist available per 100,000 people. Grover, Dutt and Avasthi (2010), in their review study, reported that the prevalent rate of depression was 1.61 per 1,000 school-going children in north India. Looking at some statistics across the world, the Office of National Statistics: Mental Health in Children and Young People (Children's Society 2008) reported that one in ten children between the age of one and fifteen have a mental health disorder. Further, rates of mental health problems tend to increase as children reach adolescence.

Saxena (2012) cites the SAHYOG survey (2003) that studied 1,800 Indian adolescents. 48 per cent of these adolescents reported experiencing sadness and stress. 15 per cent contemplated suicide and 8 per cent attempted suicide. The website of Vidyasagar Institute of Mental Health, Neuro and

Allied Sciences (VIMHANS) provides the following data about mental health concerns in children and adolescents:

- Attention Deficit Hyperactivity Disorder (ADHD) affects about 3 to 5 per cent children globally. 2 to 16 per cent of school aged children are diagnosed with ADHD.
- About 1.3 per cent children and adolescents in the age group of nine to seventeen years, suffer from anxiety disorders. More girls are diagnosed with the disorder than boys.
- Depression is the most common mental health concern. The diagnosis rate is 1 in every 33 children. In teenage, the chances of depression are much higher, with as many as 1 in 8 children suffering from depression.

Other common disorders include learning disabilities, eating disorders, oppositional defiant disorder and substance misuse (http://apaceinfosoft.co.in/index.php/component/content/article/38-faqs/general/215-learning-disability).

Saxena (2012) did a study of the five-year plans and pointed out the inconsistency in addressing the mental health concerns of children and adolescents at the level of planning and policy making. He highlighted that post-independence, the early emphasis on providing a supportive and caring environment to children through schools and child guidance clinics in the 1950s was not carried forward in subsequent plans. There have been only generic references to 'harmonious development' and 'general well-being of society.' The National Policy on Education (NPE) 1986, emphasised early childhood care and education and focused on the removal of disparities in society. The key focus was on child-centred education and engaging children in activity-based learning from primary stages. Other measures to promote mental health of school-going children through the provisions for remedial teaching and the practice of no detention in classes were also recommended.

The National Curriculum Framework (NCF) 2005, addresses mental health concerns through its position paper on health and physical education. Elements of coping with stress and the school's role in mental health intervention programmes have been highlighted. More recently, the RTE Act, 2009 has also emphasised the need to provide children with a school environment that is free from trauma, stress and anxiety. The provisions explicitly place a ban on corporal punishment and also stresses on the need to address psychological abuse. The RTE Act also continues with the policy for non-detention of students up to class eight. This provides space to students to learn at their own pace without feeling unduly stressed.

The statistics presented above only provide details of some aspects that are well researched and documented. Many mental health concerns and dilemmas are difficult to identify, quantify and report. Statistics, for instance, would not be able to report specific experiences of individual children.

Recession	Illness in the Family
Samira is 15 years old. She is the only child and her mother had discontinued her job as an HR executive to focus on her education during the board exam years. Her father works in a senior position in finance in an advisory capacity in an MNC. When recession hit the economy, her father suddenly lost his job. Although her parents have not discussed it with her, she can sense the tension at home. Getting another job seems to be difficult and her parents are aware that they are	Sherin is 15 years old. Her average day is spent in school with her friends. She was always ordinary in studies but lately her time in school is spent in discussing fashion styles, movies and boys with her friends. Her teachers often instruct her group to stop talking in the class. Their group is labelled as the trendiest and is very popular amongst the boys in class. At home, she spends most of her time on Facebook and on WhatsApp. She follows a fashion blog to know

eating into their savings with the heavy loans they have taken. Paying her high school fees and All India Pre Medical Test (AIPMT) coaching classes is now a burden.

Samira doesn't know how to help her parents. She is thinking of excuses to give up her coaching classes but is worried that she won't be able to clear her entrances without the guidance. On the other hand, she is wondering if her parents will be able to afford the fees of a private college. Her teachers are unaware of her dilemmas.

the latest trends and is the style icon and leader in her group.

Her mother was recently diagnosed with a serious medical condition and the doctor advised bed rest to her. Sherin's older sister studies in a college in a different city. All the household work has now fallen onto Sherin's shoulders. Although, her father helps at home, he is already busy with his own office and visiting the hospital for his wife's treatment.

Sherin doesn't want to share her troubles with her friends as she is very popular and feels that her friends will not understand her difficulties. She is trying hard to live up to her image. She has started going late to school and her interest in school activities has dipped further. Since she was never academically inclined, her teachers have not noticed any change in her behaviour. Her friends have started noticing that she is not as prim and proper as she used to be earlier. Her classmates talk behind her back and she is slowly losing her popularity.

Family Discord

Tanmay is 10 years old. He has grown-up in a joint family with his grandparents and two uncles. His house was always buzzing and he felt little need for playing outside as he had many cousins of his age in his house. All of them shared a strong bond and his house was always alive with activity. His grandfather passed away recently and though he was deeply disturbed by the incident, he recovered quickly with the help of his parents, extended family and cousins.

Lately, he can sense the tension at home as his father and his brothers are contemplating separating their business and also the household. There is a silent tension as his *Bade Papa* (father's older brother) and his father have both expressed their desire for the same shop. The women in the household also work quietly. While relations are cordial, the families know that they will not be staying together for very long. All the children study in the same school, but have started maintaining a distance from each other.

Tanmay has no other friends and doesn't know how life will be without his cousins. He spends the recess sitting alone in the class and returns home with his mother. His cousins travel with their mothers. He has become quieter. His parents are too busy sorting out family issues to think about his concerns. He has no one to talk to.

Teasing and Social Insensitivity

Amaan is a 12 years old. He is average at studies but is very popular amongst his friends. He is the class clown and children are always in peals of laughter around him. His teachers are aware of it and often join the class in laughing at the jokes he cracks. He is the favourite choice whenever there is a mono acting or extempore competition. He always leaves audiences with a smile, even when he does not win a prize.

He is often teased by his class mates for being short. He is shorter than many girls in his class and frequently hears snide remarks for it. He replies with a smile or with a witty rejoinder, sometimes exaggerating the joke to laugh at himself. In the playground, he is particularly targeted where his height acts as a disadvantage. In the last class, his friends told him to 'go and sit with the girls' instead of playing with them. His teacher noticed that his eyes suddenly welled up with tears, but he was quick to hide them and replace them with a smile. He quietly walked off from the ground and spent the rest of the period in mimicking the boys of the class in front of a group of girls. By the end of it, he was walking back to his class with all the girls. All of them were laughing heartily. The sports teacher thought he was okay now.

Specific experiences as in the cases presented above cannot be documented in terms of statistics. In fact, some other similar experiences may not be documented because they do not refer to diagnosed academic, emotional, behavioural or psychological difficulties. Many such experiences may thus be brushed aside and not attract the attention that they merit. This highlights the need to look at the recommendations and provisions of policies on mental health.

COMMON PROBLEMS IDENTIFIABLE AMONG CHILDREN AND ADOLESCENTS

School-going children and adolescents present a range of problems that vary in terms of their nature as well as intensity. Coupled with the unique psychosocial context in which each child or adolescent lives, it becomes difficult to present generalised problems and solutions that apply to all. Interactions with school counsellors, based on their experiences with students' mental health concerns, revealed that the student referrals they receive are from three sources: the students themselves, the teachers and the parents. The nature of the concerns varies according to the referral source as well as the age of the student. Counsellors report that teachers and parents are mostly concerned with the academic performance of students. When a student's academic performance is not up to the expectation, or the child shows a marked decline in scores, parents and/or teachers refer the student to the counsellor. Sometimes these initial referrals are the starting points for unearthing the underlying concerns and issues in the non-academic areas as well. When students approach counsellors themselves, it is for concerns that range from social adjustment issues, and problems with peers and parents, to feelings of loneliness, lack of confidence, lack of direction in life, concerns about puberty and heterosexual relationships.

This highlights two major aspects. First, students in school are facing a wide range of concerns that include and go beyond academics. Second, the preoccupation of parents and teachers with academic success translates into reducing all problems to academic difficulties. This means that a difficulty or concern will not be noticed till the time it affects academic performance. Further, teachers and parents sometimes feel that their responsibility ends once they have referred a child to the counsellor. On the contrary, identification is only the first step of the process towards promoting mental health of school students. Having acknowledged the need for counselling, teachers and parents need to work together with the counsellor in facilitating the students to live healthy and fulfilling lives.

Based on the discussion with counsellors, some of the common concerns that are relevant to school-going children have been discussed below. It would appear that some of these concerns are more relevant to specific age groups than others.

Academic Difficulties

As has been discussed earlier, the most frequent students' referral to counsellors is for academic difficulties. These students are most commonly identified through a dip in their academic achievement. The difficulties that students face in academics include: lack of concentration, disinterest in studies, subject-specific difficulties, fear of a subject, fear of a teacher and a poor foundation leading to diffidence in dealing with the subject. In older children, making choices about which academic stream to opt for and making career choices are also areas requiring inputs from teachers and counsellors.

In most cases, these difficulties are addressed by teachers and counsellors through focused interactions at the individual or group level. It is crucial here to not label children for academic problems that they might face. These are in fact not problems, but temporary setbacks and challenges that children can face and overcome with adult help. Further, it is important that teachers be observant over a sustained period of time and not label children on the basis of performance in one or two tests. At the same time, academic performance may at times indicate deeper ranging issues that may be rooted in specific learning disabilities or other clinical disorders. A change in academic performance may also be indicative of other personal, social or familial problems that the child may be facing.

Problems in Behaviour and Conduct

The most common occurrences of inappropriate behaviour are visible in children at the primary school level through instances of lying, stealing, cheating, temper tantrums, fighting with other children, and the like. In older children, conduct-related problems may manifest as verbal and/or physical aggression. In some cases this may also result in vandalism and violence. Very often disruptive behaviour, damaging school property, bullying others, hitting out, getting into serious physical fights with others, pornographic graffiti on the doors and walls of the school washrooms, use of abusive language and instances of substance misuse, such as smoking in a corner or inhaling chemical substances can be seen in schools.

More often than not, such behaviours are overt manifestations of more disturbing thoughts, feelings or experiences that may be affecting the child. The behaviours themselves are not the cause. The first step in such a situation would therefore be to identify causal factors that are leading the child to behave in this manner. The causes may be located in personal, familial or social settings. An inability to make friends may result in misconduct that may be attention seeking. Inability to cope with school requirements may lead to frustration and aggression. At times the child may be disturbed due to family discord. In the absence of an emotional anchor, the child may resort to aggression and violence. To sum up, the source may be located in the environment rather than in the child himself or herself.

Social Relations and Adjustment

When adults look back at their school years, the friendships and peer relationships that they had developed in school make up for some of the best memories. Yet, many children initially struggle to make friends and develop close bonds. Challenges in developing social relations and adjustment may manifest themselves through a lack of friends, inability to adjust to peers, feelings of inferiority, shyness, timidity and isolation. In adolescents, social relations may pose challenges in terms of experiencing peer pressure and developing heterosexual love relations. Although this phase may be temporary, it causes great agony and often leaves children and adolescents with feelings of isolation and worthlessness. Teachers can play a positive role to deal with this by encouraging students to engage in team work in both academic and non-academic activities. However, at times the inability to make friends may be due to other more serious emotional problems such as excessive anxiety, general anxiety disorder or even autism, among others. In such cases, it is best for the teachers to work closely with the school counsellor and parents.

Older children and adolescents increasingly face peer pressure in areas of academic competitiveness and gang identification behaviour. In the quest to find their own identity, they feel torn between making choices that they truly believe in and adhering to trends and fads. Many adolescents feel pressured to engage in substance misuse due to pressure from friends and the need to identify with the crowd. Another common concern faced by adolescents is developing appropriate heterosexual relationships. They tend to feel torn between their desires to engage with the opposite sex and conforming to social norms of what is considered acceptable. Further, this is also the time when they are most pressurised to focus on academics and make career choices. It is still not uncommon for schools to impose strict norms of behaviour and stop adolescents from interacting with the opposite sex. For instance, girls and boys are not allowed to sit with each other in the class or play together during sports periods. In some schools their play areas are demarcated, as are their entry and exit points in the school. What needs to be understood is that such practices can be more damaging than supportive. They evoke more curiosity, encourage clandestine forms of behaviour from adolescents, encourage them to be more defiant, but more importantly, prevent the development of healthy interpersonal relationships, feelings of empathy and development of understanding and respect towards the opposite gender. They fail to see the implications that this can have in the future, in terms of their relationships with the opposite gender later in life as well. It is also important to recognise that there is a natural curiosity and interest for the opposite gender at this age, so this has to be dealt with sensitively and not morally or punitively.

Adolescents need to be guided towards understanding themselves and others better during this phase. Some adolescents may also require counselling in being more responsible and mature in resisting substance misuse and sexual experimentation. Here, the attitude of parents and teachers has to be supportive and encouraging and not one of condemnation or mistrust. In recent times, schools have also reported cases of students facing domestic violence, getting involved in cases of emotionally and physically abusive love relationships and being victims of sexual abuse and harassment. Such cases require individual counselling. Group counselling sessions with the entire class, based on news articles, movies and case studies, can also help in skill building, enhancing understanding about different issues, sorting out dilemmas and learning effective coping strategies.

Clinical Disorders

Clinical disorders refer to more serious difficulties related to learning, and personal, social and emotional adjustment that require diagnosis and treatment from a trained practitioner. They show up at times in a few children in schools. For example, specific learning disabilities such as dysgraphia, dyscalculia or dyslexia are seen in a few children. All specific learning disabilities require proper diagnosis and a set of specialised strategies for which the teacher, school counsellor and special educator have to work together very closely. Here, the special educator is the key person, being the trained specialist in the area. Similarly, when social withdrawal, social isolation and emotional instability are persistent, they may be indicative of Autism Spectrum Disorder. However, this requires professional diagnosis by a clinical practitioner and also the development of an individualised education plan. Once again, the role and intervention of specialists is indispensable in such cases.

Some children show neurological disorders which surface as fits, including epilepsy. Some also show signs of depression, free floating anxiety, hyperactivity, attention deficits, mood disorders and, at times, even some obsessions and compulsions. All of these require professional diagnosis and treatment, once again, by trained practitioners. The teacher or the counsellor can help initially by identifying the child and then referring him/her to an appropriate person for treatment. Subsequently, they can sensitise the other children in the class to work cooperatively with the child and develop cordial and supportive relations and friendship with him or her as per the suggestions of the clinical practitioner. Although it is still rare, schools are moving towards the creation of inclusive spaces, where all children study together. Developing sensitivity would go a long way in helping all children to engage with those children afflicted with mental, psychological and physical challenges.

It is important to emphasise here, once again, that not all of these concerns and challenges will play out or get manifested as academic difficulties. Therefore, teachers and parents need to look at children more holistically rather than only in terms of their academic achievements. They have to pick up signs of the difficulties from varied sources of children's behaviour.

MYTHS IN IDENTIFYING AND DEALING WITH PROBLEMS

The most ignored child in class is often the one who creates the least disturbance. Consider the following case.

Sunil belongs to a middle class family and studies in class eight. His sister studies in a college. In the past few months, he has witnessed many fights at home between his parents and his sister over a boy that his sister is in a relationship with. His parents are not in favour of the relationship as the boy is from a different caste. His sister is always threatening to run away from the house and spends most of the day locked up in her room, refusing to eat. She is not allowed to go to college any more. Sunil has been advised by his parents not to talk about this to any of his friends as they fear it will bring disgrace to the family. His sister often asks him to pass on her messages to her friend. Sunil wants to support his sister but is not allowed to say anything at home. He feels scared for his sister as he has never seen his parents so angry. Yesterday, his father almost hit his sister. Nobody ate dinner. Sunil cried himself to sleep.

At school, there is little noticeable change in his behaviour. He continues to sit with a few of his close friends, although he is now quieter. He was not able to finish his homework on two occasions and his teacher asked him if everything was okay, since he always completes his work on time. He wanted to share his fears and anxieties but remembered his parents' warning. He just apologised for his mistake to the teacher. Since then, he ensures that he manages to complete his work on time so that no teacher is given a chance to complain. In fact, one of his teachers praised him for his improved behaviour since he has stopped talking during class and asking questions.

Neither his teachers nor his parents have noticed his often red eyes, constant fatigue from sleeplessness, his lack of interest in sports and loss of appetite.

In times of personal trouble, a child is more likely to be noticed if there is a significant change in his/her behaviour. Minor changes, particularly those that do not negatively influence academic performance or challenge the disciplinary norms of a home or school, often go unnoticed. The danger here lies in the presumption that 'everything is okay when the behaviour is okay.' Unexpressed emotions, feelings, thoughts, howsoever disturbing they may be for the child, are seldom noticed or given credence unless they are visibly acted out. The child may thus be left to sort out these problems by himself/herself.

Identifying a child facing trouble is not a simple task. Teachers and parents need to be particularly careful and vigilant in this regard. They have to look out for nuanced manifestations of psychological disturbance which show up in children's concentration, behaviour and participation in school activities.

The Danger of Labelling

The single biggest danger in identifying children facing challenges is the danger that labelling poses. Labelling serves the important purpose of ensuring that children get the right kind of attention. It helps in identifying the problem areas and channellising efforts towards addressing those problems. On the other hand, labelling also often leads to a sense of hopelessness about the child. The child gets labelled with being a 'problem child', 'a troublemaker', 'being poor in academics' and so on. In such cases, teachers, parents and peers tend to have lower expectations from the child. The child in turn may develop lower expectations from himself/herself. The other danger in labelling relates to the stigma attached to addressing serious cases. A student seeking counselling or clinical help for a behaviour problem, learning disability, autism or attention deficiency, for instance, may be labelled as difficult. It is not rare to hear parents and at times teachers, use the common parlance term 'mad' to refer to students with autism, cerebral palsy, mental retardation and so on. This is not just incorrect in terms of terminology, but can have a very damaging effect on the child. Students learn from teachers and parents, and end up being wary of a child with special needs. Inability to develop age-appropriate friendship bonds can further complicate the situation for the child.

Peer Relationships

Another common problem that children with difficulties encounter is in building peer relationships. This applies more to young children than to adolescents. Children are often advised by their parents to develop friendships only with 'good' children in the class. A child who hits, lies, is abusive or disruptive is often labelled as 'bad' and therefore not worthy of being friends with. So the child requiring help from peers continues to be friendless since peers tend to avoid him/her.

What complicates the situation further is that teachers and peers tend to generalise the child's problem to all spheres of his/her life. So, for instance, a child who may be facing difficulty in learning at the same pace as peers will still have the same level of emotional and social needs, but teachers tend to overlook this. Likewise, a child who has social adjustment issues will still be capable of performing academically at the same level as his peers. Yet, once again, teachers tend to overlook this. To understand this better, let us consider the following two cases:

Sushant is nine years old. He lives with his parents in an upscale locality. Both his parents work and live extremely stressful lives. He spends most of his time with the fulltime domestic help. His father comes home late every evening and Sushant is able to meet him only on weekends. His father is a strict disciplinarian and he rarely ever musters the courage to say anything in front of him.

His lack of attention and stifling environment at home has led him to develop tendencies of violence in school. He visits his school counsellor regularly. However, since the time his counselling sessions have started, teachers have started ignoring him in classes. They rarely ask him any questions and do not encourage or even expect him to participate in classes. He has no friends in class due to his aggression. He rarely completes his work but his teachers are not bothered as they don't expect him to work.

Shailly is 14 years old. Till class eight, she had managed good grades through project work. Now in class nine, in studying core subjects, she has started facing difficulties and was recently diagnosed with a learning difficulty. She has had to miss many classes because of visiting specialists to diagnose her difficulty. Eventually her specific problem was identified and communicated to the special educator in her school. However, having missed many classes, her class performance has dipped further. Her friends realised that she had been visiting doctors and there were rumours that she was mentally ill. Her teachers never addressed the issue in class. Her friends slowly stopped involving her in their conversations and games. She has started sitting alone in class. Her class teacher noticed this but feels that she should be concentrating on academics. Occasionally she asks another child to help her as she cannot 'understand as quickly as everyone else'. Her classmates look at her with a sense of pity. Shailly hates it but doesn't know who to talk to about it.

Both cases highlight how situations can become more complex when adequate attention is not given to developing healthy peer relations. Teachers at times may need to help students develop friends. Counselling may be required not just for individual students but also in helping other students to develop life skills to support their peers. It is important that they empathise and not develop feelings of sympathy.

Indifference and Abdication of Responsibility

Teachers are currently recognised as being part of the most overworked professionals. Their jobs are very demanding and as part of their role profile, they have to lead, guide, help and perform, all at the same time. For instance, while teaching in the classroom, a teacher has to attend to behavioural issues, discipline, variable learning levels shown by students, build a conducive learning environment in the class and also ensure that she covers the targeted portion of the course planned for the day. Outside the classroom, the teacher has to fulfil administrative responsibilities and be a counsellor, mentor and trouble shooter as well. Many teachers find this expansive role profile too stressful and demanding, and so focus mainly on classroom teaching. Since the culture in our society is to hold teachers as account-able for the academic performance of students, they devote all their time and energy to this. Parents and administrators too view teachers as responsible for the learning outcomes of their wards/students. Because of this too, teachers feel that they need to concentrate only on academics. The counselling role that they should be also fulfilling, takes a back seat. At times when they notice changes in a child's behaviour for instance, either they are unable to devote time to address it, or they may feel that this is not part of their job responsibility. It is only when a child starts lagging behind in academics that the teacher takes the problem seriously. As has been mentioned earlier, this often means that several problems the children face go unnoticed. The role of the teacher needs to be redefined as going beyond teaching and including caregiving. This also translates into saying that the school needs to create time and space for teachers to go beyond teaching. In fact given the paucity of counsellors and other mental health professionals in schools, teachers have to be counsellors and schools must invest time, energy and resources in preparing them for this role.

WHAT CAN AN INDIVIDUAL TEACHER DO?

Given the school and classroom context described earlier, it would appear that the individual teacher would hardly have the time or space to engage in tasks that go beyond routine teaching. However, for a driven and committed teacher, there is a lot that can be accomplished through these routine activities. What is required is a little extra thought in everyday preparation and a more expansive definition of one's work and role profile. Some suggestions are given on how this can be done in the sections that follow.

Teaching a Child Who You Know

The overarching requirement in any classroom is for the teacher to know every child. Covering the syllabus in class, lesson preparation, building resource material and managing the class are activities that are taken to be a part of her job. By simply keeping in mind the diverse abilities and capacities of her students and their interests both, while preparing for the class and engaging students in its transaction, she can factor these in and thus have a more vibrant and inclusive class than a routine, disconnected one. All that is required is that the teacher is sensitive to and aware of her students. A teacher who knows her students' social and familial contexts understands their learning styles, interests and abilities, will be able to tap these and weave then in into making her class engaging. Mrs. Alexander's class described in the box below is an example of such a classroom.

Mrs. Alexander is a science teacher. She teaches classes seven, eight and eleven. In her school, teachers are required to stay back for an hour every day, after students leave. She uses this time for her lesson preparation and evaluation. While designing her lessons, she particularly thinks about the strengths of the students in her class. Sometimes she asks one or two students to stay back and prepare for classes in the coming weeks. This gives her a buffer as she is prepared well in advance.

She distributes responsibility for lab preparation on a rotation basis among her senior class students. She works with them in organising material but entrusts them with the responsibility. They sometimes perform experiments in advance so that they can lead the demonstration in the final class. There are a group of students in her class who are interested in taking up a career in research. She often tells them the topics that are going to be taught in the coming weeks and asks them to look up for latest research advances in the field. Another student routinely brings the biographies of scientists to the classroom. Their classroom is filled with student made sketches and charts of scientists.

In her junior classes, she uses role plays and puppet shows to make her classes interesting. She asks students to volunteer for activities that she is preparing for in the coming week. She also asks them to assist her in arranging resource material for the class. They sometimes bring material that is available in their homes. She knows that one of the students sits regularly with her father to work on the Internet in the evening. She has asked her to identify and share videos in pen drives in the class. She keeps a tab on the places that children visit through casual conversations. She uses their experiences whenever she feels they would be able to relate it to the concepts being taught in class. One student has *Encyclopaedia Britannica* at home. She informs him of relevant topics in advance. He brings interesting facts about those topics to the class. Other children are also motivated to read and come.

Students look forward to her classes because each one of them feels that he/she has something to contribute to the class.

Meeting Expectations in Large Classrooms

A very challenging aspect of teaching is engaging with students in large classrooms. Teachers often feel at a loss when they have to engage with sizes that sometimes go up to seventy in a single class. Most of them end up spending all their class time in ensuring that children do not fight with each other and remain focused on the class tasks. There is little time for paying individual attention. The most common strategy that teachers use when the class size is large is to demonstrate on the blackboard, and ask students to copy the same, or solve the questions at the end of the chapter in their books. If interactive teaching is attempted, it often ends up as a one to one conversation between the teacher and a few students. The rest of the class meanwhile engage in their own personal tasks, remain passive or talk among themselves. Many teachers are uncomfortable about this but feel helpless in the face of large numbers. It is in fact larger classrooms that require teachers to go the extra mile in ensuring that no student feels ignored. Creating democratic spaces to ensure that all students get a chance to participate is an essential part of the classroom. Students will also need to be taught to take turns and develop the invaluable skill of listening to and learning from others. Preparing more hands-on activities rather than demonstrating actually provides opportunities for the teacher to engage individually with the students. She can monitor individual progress and change the complexity of the tasks, depending on individual learning levels. This allows each student the flexibility to learn at their own pace and in their own style. Engaging individually with students also helps the teacher to know students better. This also provides the important opportunity of close interaction and observation that helps in early identification of personal and/or social and emotional difficulties.

Home–School Continuity

Another significant step that the individual teacher can take is towards building strong linkages between home and school. Often the interface is restricted to parent–teacher meetings (PTMs) which have become forums for discussing the academic performance of the child and other behavioural or discipline related issues, if present. In most meetings, teachers are sometimes required to meet parents of hundreds of students whom they teach across sections and classes, so very little worthwhile communication is possible. However, it requires only some rethinking to make the PTM a forum for better home–school interface and continuity. The re-envisioning of this forum has many advantages. Parents and teachers can work together to create improved learning experiences for children. Teachers can, for instance, request parents to visit the school and engage with students by sharing their professional experiences. In senior classes, parents can also help with career guidance and counselling. It is also possible to engage individual students with parents of other children who can mentor them in their professions. Parent volunteers can also help in organising and managing field visits and picnics. A strong home–school bond helps to build consistency and continuity in the experiences and values that students grow up with. Parents and teachers are able to share expectations, aspirations, concerns and difficulties that they may be facing with each other. This in turn helps to provide better caregiving experiences at home and school and build a climate of understanding and acceptance for the students.

BUILDING A SCHOOL ENVIRONMENT

The child's engagement in school goes beyond the classroom. The school ethos and atmosphere significantly influences the experience that the child has at school. Engagement with teachers and peers goes beyond classroom spaces. The subsequent sections discuss how a school environment can be built in a manner that it promotes the development of sound mental health in its students and teachers.

Identifying Existing Spaces in the School

Every school has a set of what may be called spaces, systems and forums that provide varied opportunities to children to discover themselves, develop confidence in their abilities, learn social engagement, develop their sense of self and identity and relate to others. These include the house system, the institution of the class teacher, counselling services, sports and other cultural activities, a prefectorial system, a school assembly among others.

Class Teachership

The class teachership approach works on the model of mentorship. It operates on the basic premise of a teacher building strong personal bonds with the children in her class. Through maintaining detailed records about each child and interacting regularly with them, the teacher is able to gain insights into the world of the child which goes beyond the classroom. Background information about the student also enables the teacher to locate the child within the sociocultural world which he/she belongs to. Through class teacher periods and other occasions on which the teacher spends time with the class, personal channels of communication are opened. Parent–teacher meetings also allow the family to engage with the same teacher. All these help the child to feel a sense of warmth and connect with the teacher. The child knows that there is somebody to listen to him/her, share concerns, troubleshoot and offer advice. These bonds are even stronger when the class teacher engages with the same set of students over a period of years.

School Counselling Services

The significant role that school counselling services can play in the well-being of children is well recognised. However it is important that these services are child friendly and work towards children's development. Most schools these days employ a full time counsellor. In large schools, having one counsellor for classes from one to twelve is sometimes not enough. Irrespective of how many counsellors are employed in the school, the counselling services would not be availed of by students, if they are not at ease in meeting counsellors for sharing their thoughts, feelings, concerns and fears. In some ways, the everyday interaction between the teacher and the student also serves the important counselling function, of providing care and support. Students also tend to look up to teachers for giving them direction and helping them to take decisions. However, some situations require children to be referred to counsellors. These maybe for specific clinical problems like Autism, ADHD, Specific Learning Disabilities or more deep rooted social and emotional disorders. At times, visits to the counsellor may flow from the need for some students to be addressed separately from the rest of the class with reference to specific events or actions. Sometimes, a class teacher may also not have the time to address the difficulties of all students within the class itself and so solicits the services of the counsellor. What is important is that no stigma or label on the part of the teacher, parents or fellow students should be put on a child who visits the counsellor. These days, most counsellors plan and conduct activities across classes which address issues of psychological importance to the age group being served. For instance, these may include the themes of friendship and puberty and growing up for middle school children, academic planning and time management, effective interpersonal and communication skills, dealing with issues of love, sex and romance and preparing for board exams with senior school children. The school counsellor and teachers can together work towards building a school ethos in which students feel comfortable in approaching the counsellor. In such an environment, children would feel safe, secure and loved.

Sports and Other Cultural Activities

The school is not only meant for academic learning. It envisions education to subsume all other non-academic activities within its spectrum as being equally meaningful in the child's overall development. Activities related to sports, literature, music and performing arts, among others which schools organise and place in the curriculum, provide students a platform to discover their potential, talent and interest and also share these with their peers and family both inside and outside school. Intra and inter school competitions, school annual days and carnivals, festivals and fetes provide school students the opportunities to explore different areas and identify their interests and strengths. Through some pedagogic innovation, teachers can also easily include these activities within their teaching processes.

School Assembly

The school assembly serves multiple purposes. Gathering together every day in the morning brings order to the start of the day for students. It gives them a sense of belonging in a collective of other class-mates, schoolmates and teachers. School songs, national songs and the national anthem which are sung serve to develop a sense of pride in the school and the nation. The school assembly is also an important event for sharing information, communicating important decisions and addressing the students collectively. At the same time, it provides an opportunity to students to present their ideas, thoughts and also exhibit their skills and talents. Routine assembly activities of class-based or house-based stage performances, participating in the school choir, reading out the news or even the thought for the day, help to build confidence, public speaking abilities and leadership skills in students. Special assemblies on days of significance at the national, local or school level also help to generate awareness and build sensitivity.

On the other hand, the nature of school assembly can be such that it only serves to regiment and discipline students. Teachers often use the school assembly only for ensuring that students follow rules obediently and for identifying late comers and uniform defaulters. Such regimentation gives a flavour of militarisation to the school with little space for deviation from pre-established norms. This is detrimental to students' development of self for which free space and exploration are essential. In yet another scenario, the school assembly can be reduced to meaningless ritualised practices which students and teachers mechanically follow. Here also, there is no psychological benefit to the students. Thus every school needs to work towards building the school assembly as a constructive space.

Prefectorial System

The most important democratic system within the school is the prefectorial system. By developing a mechanism of including the class monitors, house captains, discipline monitors or prefects and head boys and head girls in decision-making, the school gives a chance to the students to develop confidence and work with a sense of responsibility. Further, it provides an opportunity to teachers and the school authorities to hear the voice of students. When students participate in decision-making, they learn important life skills of negotiation, expression and communication. They also experience participatory democracy. This helps them to be more self-disciplined, responsible and committed to school policies and ideals. The prefectorial system can also serve to mirror how free and fair elections take place by being organised as a miniature version of state and parliamentary elections.

Developing Sensitivity

An essential aspect of building a school environment that promotes the mental health of its students and teachers is through developing sensitivity.

Tolerating Alternative Behaviours

Childhood and adolescence is a time for exploration and finding one's identity. Children and adolescents explore different roles and try alternative styles of dressing, hairstyling and behaviour. Some of these are inspired by their idols that include movie stars, artists, sports stars, businesspersons, and the like. Media also puts forth certain images in this regard. Accompanied by a need to be recognised and accepted, school students feel encouraged to try out different lifestyles. Adults at school and home alike need to understand that these experiments are part of the quest for identity development. So long as they do not interfere with everyday school and home life, there is no need to overly pressurise children to align with prescribed norms.

Building an Attitude of Acceptance

An average school day lasts about six hours. It thus provides ample time and opportunities for casual conversations that include humour, jest and mild teasing. While learning to accept personal jokes is a part of growing up, it is important for both teachers and students to understand where to balance out humour. Lessons in early years form the foundation for building an attitude of sensitivity and empathy towards the 'other'. Learning to not make insensitive jokes about communities, religions, ethnic backgrounds, gender and appearances is an important lesson in this context. Since schools are secular spaces, they need to ensure this. Most importantly, children learn to not hurt one another and respect each other's feelings.

Providing Appreciation

Teachers also need to be aware of students' needs to be accepted and appreciated. Students tend to look towards their teachers for feeling a sense of worthiness about themselves. Words of appreciation over a task well done, a neatly made diagram, a poem well recited, a creative idea or a game well played, go a long way in building confidence and feeling loved. While older students turn to their peers for acceptance and appreciation, the need for acceptance from teachers never completely goes away. Teachers also need to encourage children at any age to look for positives in each other and accept all children. Appreciation may also be expressed through actions, such as in selecting children for a team, giving opportunities for monitoring the class, making charts and posters and even simple tasks such as communicating notices, collecting and distributing notebooks, and the like.

Re-visualising Relationships in School

Although in a school setup, building informal relationships with peers and teachers is inevitable, school systems often look at personal relationships with suspicion. Relationships are often seen as a hindrance to education.

Peer Relationships

It is a common practice for teachers to ensure that students do not sit with their friends in class lest they disturb classroom processes. While such practices encourage children to widen their circle of friends and learn to adjust with everyone, the underlying attitude in such practices is one of mistrust and conflicting interests. 'They just want to enjoy with their friends'; or 'Teachers don't let us sit together because we will talk in the class and not learn' are statements that point towards the belief that learning and enjoying, or having conversations are contradictory experiences that cannot go hand in hand. In contrast, peer relationships in school can be seen to support the notion of learning together. Through group work, peer tutoring, pairing and sharing, children can be encouraged to learn from and with each other. Conversations in the classroom can be directed towards building the lesson and replacing traditional views of silent classrooms.

Another problem faced in peer relationships is the unnecessary and rough competition that often comes in the way of friendships. Parents, teachers and peers, tend to pitch students against each other in terms of their performances in academics, sports or in other activities. Feelings of competition sometimes prevent students from developing supporting friendships that would have led them to excel better had they been working together.

It is important to recognise that the friendships that children build during school years often last for a lifetime. Friends from school know each other well and are often each other's biggest support systems, as they grow up. It is through friends that students learn important lessons of sharing, caring, compassion and empathy. Students learn to make sacrifices for each other and work towards common goals. Lessons in team playing, handling troubles in relationships, are all learnt in social relations in schools. It is thus important to nurture these relationships.

Teacher–Student Relationships

The relationship between teachers and students are always subjected to scrutiny and judgement. Teachers' positions are almost always characterised by authority. Even where teachers are friendly, classroom norms are often based on a model of obedience–compliance. Students are not expected to break the hierarchy of the relationship and it is the teacher who is in the position to decide the code of conduct within and outside the classroom. In such cases, students are often left with little choice but to follow teachers' instructions. Any deviation from these is seen as a manifestation of defiance that needs to be checked. Schools expect teachers to keep students under check. Transgression of authority lines is rarely accepted. However, it is important to understand that the school is a miniature society in which there can be multiple forms of relationships. For instance, students are more likely to work and cooperate whole heartedly with teachers who treat them with respect and give them space to work in their own style and pace. Being friendly and encouraging students in no way erode a teacher's authority. They only use more benevolence and democracy as stances on the part of the teacher to interact with students. As long as students do not take teachers for granted or bypass their authority, the teacher–student relationship must have space and scope for dialogue, discussion, infusion of trust and a sense of deeper bonding. This kind of relationship helps to create a healthy environment in the classroom that is free from stress and that provides an open space to learn from each other.

ON A CONCLUDING NOTE

This chapter discussed the mental health issues and challenges in a school setting. It highlighted that mental health concerns do not refer only to clinical issues and settings but occur and are of significance in the everyday lived experiences of individuals. Recognising this, there is thus a need to shift from a curative model of mental health to one that is based on prevention of problems and difficulties and promotion of psychological well-being.

Further, the chapter also brought out that mental health status is not fixed and finite, nor is it a position to be achieved. Wellness and illness are seen as two ends of the mental health continuum. Each individual has the potential to shift along the continuum towards health or illness. This fluidity and mobility have to be recognised.

The third important aspect is that parents and teachers need to look beyond the stigma attached to counselling services. The need for counselling arises in relation to everyday issues and concerns as much as it arises for clinical cases. Seeking help from a counsellor is like seeking help from a doctor, which can be as much for a common cold as it can be for serious diseases. Teachers and parents need to be particularly observant and vigilant in identifying everyday signs in their students and children that indicate the need for extra attention and special help. The same sensitivity and respect also needs to be built in students in their relationships with peers, teachers and parents.

Situating School Students

5

The chapters presented so far have focused on understanding the notion of mental health, looking at children and adolescents from their own perspective and identifying the issues and challenges in mental health school. A common thread across these chapters has been the need to understand students and teachers within the social context in which they function. The present chapter highlights this concern in attempting to situate students within the context in which they live and grow.

The process of growing up requires constant engagement and negotiation with the world around one. This includes the physical environment in which one functions. Piaget and other theorists and researchers who have built upon his theory, have highlighted how interaction with the physical world is an important process in forming new schemas and expanding knowledge construction. Vygotsky on the other hand emphasised the role of social interaction in constructing knowledge. Implications of his work point towards the importance of situated cognition. Studies suggest that the schemas that get activated in a given situation depend on the social experiences that we have (Sparrow and Wegner 2006, cited in Baron, Branscombe, Byrne and Bhardwaj 2009). One common but illustrative example of the social influence of schemas is how we learn to behave appropriately in different social settings. We all know, for instance, appropriate codes of conduct expected of us in a mall, in a restaurant, in the comfort of our own home and in a classroom. We also know that our behaviour in the classroom varies greatly depending on what we perceive our role in the classroom to be. Codes of conduct for students, for instance, are vastly different from those for teachers. The most obvious situation in which this is visible is when teachers themselves become students to pursue further studies. It is seen that the behaviours that they typically disapprove of on the part of their students, such as coming late for the class, talking in the class, disturbing the class, and the like, are the ones that they often engage in, in their changed role as students. This shows quite clearly that our behaviour is dependent on the social situation as well as on what we perceive our identity to be within that social situation.

This example highlights that not only do social situations trigger the development of certain schemas in us; they also impact how our sense of identity develops. Some of the theories that describe the development of individuals have already been discussed in Chapter 3 and will be discussed in greater detail in Section 3. Erikson's work for instance focused on the psychosocial nature of the development of identity. The works of other theorists including Jenkins (2008), Sedikides, Gaertner and O'Mara (2011) and Gergen (2011), also highlight the social nature of identity. Our uniqueness from others around us forms the basis for our development of a personal sense of identity. On the other hand, we also feel the need to identify with those around us. This forms our social identity. Our social identity is based on not just which group we belong to, associate and identify with, but also on how our group is different from other groups. Religious affiliations for instance provide clear and near binding guidelines on what is appropriate and acceptable in our everyday life. Food habits, birth and death rituals, clothing and religious symbols as accessories are some of the most obvious ways that help us to differentiate between members of different religious groups. There is no better example than religion to highlight how our social identity can serve the useful purpose of providing us with a sense of belongingness and love on the one hand, but also lead to discriminatory, sometimes violent and hatred-oriented practices on the other. The famous psychoanalyst, Sudhir Kakar in his book, *The Colors of Violence* (1995), has analysed instances of communal violence in different parts of post-independence India. The strong role that perceived threat from members of the 'other' group played in determining the actions of one group was evident in his work. Many films also depict different forms of communal tension, stemming from religious identity.

So what clearly emerges from the discussion above is that it is fruitless to understand a person as a de-contextualised being. Further, each one of us also has a social identity which influences how we perceive others. It is important for us to be aware of our own social identity when we are trying to understand the social identity of others around us.

UNDERSTANDING CHANGING PERSPECTIVES

In Indian society, it is a common sight to see several adults being collectively responsible for providing care to one child. These adults include parents, grandparents, teachers and in many cases domestic helps and nannies. The child is thus in constant interaction with adults around him/her. However, it may be wrong to assume that the growing up process for the child in this environment of protection is always very smooth. Likewise for the caregiving adults, it may not be easy to bring up the child. This is because the views and perceptions that adults and children hold about each other tend to differ. That the world views of adults and children are different on most issues has already been highlighted in Chapter 3. Let us try to understand here, how adults perceive and understand the children of today. Let us begin by examining the narratives in the boxes below.

'Our children are constantly under the influence of peers. They don't like to listen to the elders and have no respect or understanding for experience.'	'Most of their time is spent in chatting with their friends. They are either glued to their computer screens or on phone. Even if they are forced to sit in the same room, they are not bothered with what is happening in the family.'	'We used to always be polite and respectful towards our elders. But they think they know it all. They are in so much hurry to succeed and earn money that they don't care for people. The problem is that even if we try to tell them that they are wrong, they just talk back to us rudely.'

'Even young children are now so hyperactive. They don't play properly. They have no patience. They are in constant need for new games, toys, movies. It is almost like they cannot sit at one place.'	'Media has led children to grow up too soon. They want to wear the clothes that adults wear, they want the same gadgets. Their life revolves around hoarding and bragging about all that they have. They are already so focused on money, what will they do when they actually grow up?'

The narratives provide some valuable insights about the perceptions and views of adults. To begin with, they show that the adults very strongly feel that the values have changed from the time when they were children. They have also expressed feeling disrespected by the children and not being consulted, heard and accepted by them, despite all the maturity and experience that they have. Apprehensions about rising consumerism and the overpowering presence of technology in children's lives have also been expressed. These in turn have led to an accelerated pace of growing up and have also changed the nature of family relationships. As a result, children today are like mini adults in terms of their want structures, aspirations and how they relate to adults. In the yesteryears, same aged cousins were usually children's best friends as well, but now this may not be true. Often friends are closer than family. Also, the joy of spending one's vacations in one's grandparents' home is no longer true! Children now want more technology oriented forms of stimulation and enjoyment. The lack of free and natural communication between different generations within the same family, which is also reflected in the narratives, intensifies the intergenerational conflicts and creates a sense of mistrust and disrespect for each other's thoughts and feelings.

What is most pertinent to note here, however, is that in all the narratives presented above, adults have put the responsibility of the dramatic change in thoughts and behaviour on to children. This almost suggests that the adults believe that they have no role in the changing world around them. Also that they have no responsibility for the attitudes that children develop. There is resistance to the fact that these changing trends, values and mindsets of children are inevitable in a changing world and so there is a need for adults to also change their attitudes and mindsets. Most of the time however, adults make no effort to change. The result is a mismatch in the demands and expectations of children and adults. It is not uncommon to find parents, grandparents and teachers sharing the opinion that they are unable to understand the children of today. They reminisce and preach, basing on their own childhood experiences, realising little that time does not stand still. So the mismatch between the worldview of children and adults is most often a creation of the rigidities and angularities of the adults themselves and their resistance to a changing world. This creates stress, tension and conflict for all concerned. To safeguard against this, it is important that adults make space for and accept the changing values and lifestyles of growing children. In the subsequent sections, we shall discuss how social institutions both influence and are influenced by children and adolescents.

FAMILY

Family is recognised as the primary unit of socialisation. A child's first lessons in interaction and engagement with the world are learnt in the family. It is also through the family that cultures, values and social norms are passed on to the next generation. The multiple roles that families thus perform are to educate, socialise, transmit values and provide protection and guidance to children. Given this, there is no doubt that the influence of the family is highly significant in helping children to develop a sense of identity. This was also discussed in Chapter 3, where important concepts from the theory of Carl Rogers were described. Sudhir Kakar's work also highlights the significant role of family in influencing the notions of the ideal man/woman that children aspire to become. In the section that follows, the discussion will focus on how various dimensions of family life influence the mental health of children and adolescents and how family can play a very conducive role in ensuring their wellness. Many concepts that have already been discussed in Chapter 3 will be drawn upon.

Changing Family Structure

Attention has already been drawn to the fact that family patterns are changing in India. To reiterate briefly, family patterns have gone beyond the traditional categorisation of joint and nuclear family.

Many different family patterns are now visible, most of which are based on the specific needs of the family. There is also a resurgence of the joint family system where both parents are working and grand-parents are required to look after children. You may refer back to Chapter 3 for a more detailed reading of family patterns.

Each family pattern has its own unique blend of caregiving functions and responsibilities. In a joint family structure, for example, a child would grow up with many caregivers. There would be no dearth of people willing to fulfil the child's needs and desires and always someone around to protect him/her from being scolded for mischief or pranks. In a setup where the extended family lives together, children would grow up in the company of many cousins, some being of the same age group. In such a scenario, children often do not feel the need to develop friendships outside of their home. In sharp contrast to this, in a nuclear family setup, children are in contact with a limited set of people at home: their parents and one or two siblings at best. This necessitates the need to develop close friendship bonds with children of their own age group outside of the home. In yet another scenario where both parents are working, children tend to grow up and begin taking responsibility very early, but may end up feeling very neglected if their parents have no time for them. The important point to be emphasised here is that there are no clear cut implications that can be generalised for family structures. Each family is unique and would have a different set of factors and dynamics that characterise it. The mental health of children would be influenced by these.

Parenting Styles and Interpersonal Relationships

As in the case of family structure, there are as many parenting styles as there are families. Parenting styles were already discussed in Chapter 3. Most researches, which use the traditional classification of parenting styles, continue to limit it to the categories of authoritarian, authoritative, democratic and laissez faire. More recent researches have highlighted neglectful, indulgent, remote control and even helicopter parenting as more contemporary styles that exist. Depending on the specific situation of the family, it is seen that parents evolve their own styles of parenting. They are also seen to use a mix of different parenting styles to suit specific contexts. For instance, an otherwise democratic parent may become authoritarian sometimes to protect the child, or even because of lack of time. Whatever it be, frequent shifts in parenting styles tend to provide confusing signals to children. For example, it is sometimes seen that children get away with what they want to do by throwing a tantrum. Yet on other days, the parent may choose to be strict and not give in to the child. This confuses the child about what is considered as appropriate behaviour in terms of time and place. It is thus advisable for parents to set clear boundaries of acceptable and unacceptable behaviour early in life, in consultation with their children.

Children growing up with disciplinarian parents find little space to express their wants and needs. They are thus more likely to rebel when they grow up and become more verbally expressive. Like authoritarian parenting, helicopter parenting is also likely to stifle children's abilities to take decisions for themselves. They grow up feeling dependent and lack confidence in their own abilities.

Parenting styles affect the overall atmosphere of the home and also reflect the pattern of inter-personal relationships within the family. In most families, what is seen is that one parent takes the decisions regarding children, while the other parent takes a more passive position. Similarly, most homes have clear demarcating lines of responsibilities about which parent takes the responsibility at home and which one outside. Here children grow up with closer relationships with one parent, gener-ally the more indulgent one. At the same time, children tend to respect parents who are in positions of authority. A not very atypical case is that of a family characterised by domestic violence. Where young boys and girls grow up observing parents fighting with each other, or the father hitting the mother, or even themselves, the likelihood of their acceptance of violence is higher. Where mothers are not respected at home, children will not learn to respect mothers or women in general. This can be changed with adequate intervention through education and counselling. A healthy family would be one where parents participate equally in partaking household responsibilities and take collective decisions for the children through consultation and negotiation. This also goes a long way in developing gender role sensitivity.

Parental Occupation and Lifestyles

The education and occupation of parents are often seen to have a direct bearing on children's education. In most cases, parents would attempt to educate their children beyond their own education level. Besides, family atmosphere and discussions at home also steer children towards taking up the same professions as their parents. Discussions about medical cases in a family where both parents are doctors or legal cases where both parents are lawyers also familiarise children with the same terminology and encourage them to take up similar education and professions. Business families would also attune their children towards fresh ideas in expanding business and greater openness to risk taking and bearing loss. This is more likely a phenomenon visible in middle and upper middle class homes. Children of blue collared workers and business and service professionals in lower middle class and lower class household are more likely to aspire higher towards improving their lifestyles and living conditions. Parents would also encourage them to aspire higher through education.

Parental engagement in their professions also influences the amount of time they spend at home. Particularly in urban areas, the demands of corporate life and the need to succeed, require increasingly more hours being spent at work. It is common to hear of cases where one or both parents don't meet their children for days as the time schedules are not conducive to face-to-face interactions. Parents are also not willing to compromise with their careers as the late thirties and forties are also the time for them to work hard and achieve success. They also rationalise their focus towards career goals with the justification that this majorly contributes towards a better lifestyle for their children. This leaves little time for them to spend with their children at home. It is not uncommon to see urban households engage in conversation through phones, emails, social networking sites (SNS), and the like. This is as close a substitute that they can get to real time, face to face conversations. What is important in such scenarios is also the nature of engagement in the little time that parents spend with their children. Are weekends spent in staying glued to the television with no personal conversation? Parents can ensure that weekends are spent in real interactions with children, taking them out to places that they wish to visit and even helping them in their homework and studies. Personal bonds developed at this stage are significant in keeping lines of communication open between parents and children.

Parental Aspirations

The world is becoming an increasingly competitive place. Higher aspirations are a result of increasing demands, need for power and an attitude of consumerism. With technology permeating our lives, parents can be seen buying every technological product that hits the market. The same attitude is developed by children who want every toy, every game and all kinds of pencil boxes, bags and stationery. Just as consumerism transmits itself from parents to children, so does the aspiration structure. Parents want their children to achieve much more than what they have achieved. For this, they provide the best possible exposure. Even parents who are themselves not success oriented feel compelled to provide a rich exposure to their children so that they are not left behind.

This is evident in the growing urban phenomenon where there are a host of activities available for children. It is seen that every school-going child, right from primary school onwards is enrolled in a range of activity classes, like mid-brain activation, abacus, mental maths, Vedic maths, dance forms, martial arts, sports and games, craft and so on among others. The choice of classes is made by the parents. As affirmation and proof that the child is learning something, parents tend to flaunt their children in front of the extended family and their friends as a performer. The performing automaton which the child becomes is not even asked or given the space to express what he/she wishes to learn or engage in. Whether he/she is in a mood to perform is also not considered relevant by the parents. From the standpoint of the parents, these classes serve the useful purpose of keeping the child occupied, encouraging him/her to learn beyond textbooks and channellising his/her energy appropriately, particularly during summer vacations. At the same time, the number of classes that each child is enrolled in leaves no time for the child to be himself/herself. There is no space for free exploration and the concept of having personal spare time appears to be lost. Parents are often observed to share with great pride that their children learn through iPads and other technologies available at home and school. The benefits of learning in natural settings and by observation are not given due thought. Children thus grow up increasingly disconnected with the natural and social world. This furthers an attitude of insensitivity to natural phenomena in them. Constant forced engagement adds to hyperactivity and there is no enjoyment for the sake of enjoyment. The attitude that they learn is that each activity must lead to some productive result. This 'result driven attitude' increases during the middle and senior school years. Parents now begin to enrol their children in extra coaching classes for different subjects in the hope of building a strong base that will optimise performance. This begins to happen from the age of 10 or 12 years. Since children are older and more perceptive now, they begin to understand that their parents are spending a lot of money on them. This creates an internal pressure on them to excel and yield returns. All parents expect their children to be toppers and enter into the best technological, medical, management and other noteworthy educational institutions in the country and the world. However, given the large numbers and limited opportunities, many children are left feeling stressed and at times unworthy and incapable. This heightened sense of what must be achieved has increased the early onset of stress-related problems, including obesity, hypertension, diabetes and even depression. Every year around the time of the board examinations and their results, there is news of children attempting suicide. What ideally should be done is to allow each child to choose and live the life path that he/she wants. At the same time, children need to be provided guidance and reassured that parents believe in their abilities and support them in whatever best they wish to achieve.

SCHOOLING PROCESSES

The school holds much more importance in a student's life than only being a space for learning. Education extends beyond disciplinary boundaries. The school serves as another socialisation agency along with the family. In fact, experiences at school are sometimes the only exposure that children have to students of their own age. Lessons of negotiation, adjustment and communication are learnt at school.

The school also provides exposure to competition, teaching students to both win and lose. Further, it throws many new challenges towards students. Engaging and dealing with these is part of the process of growing up. Children learn to cope with stress, conflict and turmoil. Almost all the activities at school are meaningful in that the nature of engagement that the students have with them, has an effect on their mental health. In Chapter 4 we have discussed the existing spaces in school that provide opportunities for promoting the mental health of school children. In the sections that follow, we will discuss some of the direct experiences of children in school and how these are important situational factors that help us to understand them.

School Ethos

The school ethos is an all permeating dimension. It influences classroom norms, interpersonal relationships and disciplinary rules. Consider the following case:

School A

An average day in school A starts with the morning assembly. Students stand quietly in straight lines, while the principal or some other teacher addresses them. Sometimes the address gets stretched and the younger students are not able to endure standing for such long durations, particularly during summers. However, the principal looks at this as an important experience in building strength and endurance. There is no participation of the students in the assembly and they are not allowed to interact with each other. The assembly is followed by a routine check on uniforms and basic hygiene. Defaulters are made to stand apart and take rounds of the school ground or endure being severely reprimanded up by the discipline incharge. The rest of the students quietly walk back to the classes in straight lines.

CCTV cameras have been installed throughout the school building in an attempt to ensure that teachers and students reach their classes on time. Cameras within the classrooms ensure that teachers engage in teaching as per plans. Students typically quietly note down what the teacher writes on the board. There is seldom any conversation between teachers and students.

Teachers have little free time. Whatever spare time they get is spent in a common staff room where they engage in correction work. Interaction between teachers is not encouraged and they pass each other in corridors without any acknowledgment or recognition.

The school works with military like precision in terms of time. All teachers and students are always engaged in productive work with no idle time for random conversation or chatting.

The school's orientation is one of regimentation. The authorities provide a set of rules that have to be followed at all costs. This applies not just to the students but also to teachers. In such an atmosphere, there is no space for personal communication. Students and teachers are unaware of each other's contexts and concerns. Growing up in such an environment, the children feel constantly stifled. There is no space to develop and voice their opinions, reflect on social issues or question and think crucially. They only learn to follow commands.

Does this mean that the child would grow best in a school that allows complete freedom? Let's look at another example:

School B

Mornings in School B are marked by huge movement across the school grounds. The school begins at 8 O'clock when children and teachers are supposed to gather for the morning assembly. When the bell rings, students slowly walk towards the assembly ground in groups. Announcements over the mike are made for students and teachers to assemble quickly, but they take their own time. Earlier, the assembly only included a prayer and a school song. After a new teacher joined the school, a few weeks ago, she took the initiative of reworking the assembly by including students in the process. She has been able to develop a mechanism of rotational responsibility of classes in organising the assembly events. But the respective class teachers refused to cooperate with her and she was left to organise the assembly alone, on a daily basis. The students are seen to slowly organise themselves, following some order. It is not uncommon though to see students and teachers joining the assembly only towards the end. It is also seen that children are inattentive and keep on playing pranks. The class which is responsible for the assembly presentation tries hard but hardly anyone pays attention. Slowly students are seen to begin losing interest in this system.

After the assembly, the students and teachers move towards their respective classes. Teachers often first catch up with each other in the corridors or the staff room. They reach their classes, almost fifteen minutes late and their work spills over to the next period. This in turn, affects all subsequent classes throughout the day. Since classes start late, most students move out of their classrooms and can be seen in the corridors. There are frequent bursts of anger by some teacher or the other leading to noise in the corridor. Students then just move to the other corridor or the playground.

The school does not have a regular principal. One of the senior teachers officiates as the principal and so is hesitant to use administrative authority. She feels that when the new principal joins, he/she can deal with the situation.

The atmosphere in this school is exactly the opposite of the atmosphere in school A. A matter of grave concern is, what are the students learning in this shared physical space where they spend so much time? Even a teacher who is concerned and takes initiative is unable to work well as the school environment does not support such efforts. While the children have ample freedom, there is no real learning happening. There is a high chance that children will pass out-of-school without having developed adequate knowledge, communication skills, social adjustment or even learning to work within norms and standards. Unlike in school A, here, although students will be able to voice their thoughts, it would be of no consequence since the school has no organised system of addressing concerns.

The school thus has to do the balancing act of maintaining boundaries and creating space for growth. Such a case is represented by school C.

School C

In School C, the morning assembly is started with a bell indicating the start of the school day. The students are expected to report to their classes five minutes in advance by which time the teachers are already present in the rooms. Some students and teachers arrive early to catch up with friends. At the assembly time, students organise themselves in lines and move to the playground where the assembly is held. Each class knows its position in the ground and organises itself accordingly. The matter is routine requiring little intervention from teachers. Teachers use this time to observe and engage with learners about any new developments. Uniform and time defaulters are identified by the class teachers and asked to see them later for discussing the reasons and deciding future course of action.

The assembly is largely organised by the teachers. An assembly incharge is decided by rotation every year. The teacher incharge is free to decide the structure and nature of the assembly. Students are involved in every step and are encouraged to meet the assembly incharge with any suggestions for improvement or volunteering to perform at the assembly. Once a month at least, a longer assembly is organised for students of the primary, middle or secondary wing, to provide students the opportunity to present their talent or organising a special demonstration. Special arrangements are made for providing space to students to sit.

The assembly is dispersed with students and teachers moving to their respective classes. The class teacher period is utilised to discuss concerns regarding specific students, their class or the school. Suggestions or issues raised during this time are presented in monthly teacher meetings. The day proceeds according to time table. Most teachers reach in time. Slight delay is observable due to teachers moving between classes. Students take this time to relax and talk to their friends. But there is rarely any disorder. When a teacher is absent, students love to visit the open library. There is no teacher in the open library and students are free to pick up any book and read. Senior students are often seen assisting younger students in reading and comprehension. This is a model that students have evolved themselves with little intervention from teachers.

The principal oversees the entire school system and addresses students occasionally. Once a week, the principal tries to engage with students in their specific classrooms. The relationship between students, teachers and principal is open and free. This is also indicated by the door to the principal's room which is always kept open to allow access to anyone from the school.

In a school that provides the freedom to express and learn, students and teachers alike grow together. Here, relationships are not characterised by hierarchy but by mutual respect. Listening to each other for fresh ideas and opinions shows a faith in each other's abilities and trust that all are working towards a common goal of collective betterment and greater efficiency. This is in sharp contest to school A, where rules are externally imposed on students and teachers who are considered incapable of appropriate thought and behaviour if left to themselves.

In all three schools, it can be seen that the day begins with the school assembly, the time table is fixed and children and teachers are busy in their activities. What is different in the three schools is the environment that is being provided to the child. Needless to say, a child would grow to his/her fullest in an atmosphere that is characterised by love, trust and freedom.

Teacher–Student Relationship

When adults are asked to name the people who have personally influenced their lives, they often tend to name their teachers besides their family members. The role teachers play in the lives of school students, however, change as they grow up. Students are seen to associate themselves with different teachers and often aspire to be like them. This influence on behaviour, lifestyle and the meaning that the teacher holds for the student, is not usually realised till the students have passed out-of-school.

The teacher's role without doubt, is the most significant during early years in school. In pre-primary and primary classes, when the child first enters school, the teacher is often the first, and sometimes the only, friend for several days. Even the friendships developed with peers during these years are dependent on which students the teacher approves of, or who the teacher asks the child to sit with. Acceptance and appreciation from teachers at this age build confidence in facing the world. They also help a child to adjust to school life. This support in fact becomes the safety net for the child at school. Lessons in classes during these formative years, contribute towards developing moral values and learning social behaviour.

As children grow up, they continue to look for approval from their teachers. Gradually during late childhood and adolescence, friendships with peers become stronger. There is however the societal compulsion which Kohlberg called the 'Nice Boy, Nice Girl Orientation.' All children want social approval and so try hard to meet the standards and expectations of the society. As a consequence, at school, a teacher's approval continues to hold importance. At this stage, teachers also play the role of providing exposure to many different learning experiences. A teacher who does not personally connect with students, during primary classes, will not be able to provide children with a safe and secure environment in which children can learn to take initiatives, develop confidence in their abilities and learn to take on new opportunities. During middle school, with lesser personal time being spent with teachers, students focus more on peer relationships. By this time, students are searching for a space for themselves within the classroom. The significance of the teachers, for instance, for a child who is a teacher's pet will be very different from what it is for the one who is the class clown. In the senior classes, the role of the teacher is usually restricted to teaching syllabus-based content and providing occasional advice whenever required. Children in classes eight, nine and ten are often most resistant to unsolicited advice. At the same time, they are the ones in the need of maximum guidance and direction. Teachers need to be very vigilant in observing any signs of deviant behaviour at the stages of late childhood and adolescence. By identifying early signs of inappropriate behaviour, such as tendencies for violence and aggression, experimenting with substance abuse, sexual experimentation, truancy, delinquency, and the like, the teacher can work together with parents and counsellors to prevent future difficulties and escalation of problems.

During the senior secondary school years, the role of the teacher reduces further. Most students tend to look towards their peers to make decisions. The generational gap between teacher and student becomes more obvious and pronounced. Students often feel that teachers are unable to understand their thoughts and feelings. However, group counselling sessions for this age group work well for all issues related to the developmental challenges that arise, particularly career counselling, relationships, dealing with sexuality, identity concerns and so on. Some students may face more serious challenges and difficulties. They require more personalised counselling, which either the teacher or counsellor or both in tandem can address. Since students at this stage do not open up easily to all teachers, the choice of which teacher should counsel should be decided by the student's wishes.

It is also important to recognise that during the senior years, school students are in their late teens. Although still minors, they wish to be treated like adults. They feel most distanced from a teacher who is rude, insulting and disrespectful towards them. However well a teacher may teach, students feel closer to those whom they can connect with. They expect to be treated as equals and tend to talk back and rebel if they are not. Giving them opportunities to make choices and take responsibility for their actions is important in treating them with dignity. This phase is an important time in their lives for making choices and choosing between options that will, at times, affect the rest of their lives. The teacher, like parents, thus has the difficult path to tread, between being available, offering advice and not being interfering at the same time. Probably the best alternative is to provide access to information and allow students to make informed choices.

Freedom and Exploration

The three schools discussed above differ markedly in their interpretation of discipline. While on the one hand it is important for children to learn the significance of maintaining discipline, it is important to recognise that strict disciplinary boundaries act as a hindrance to one's natural tendencies. Consider the following cases:

- Tanmoy is in class nine. He is infamous amongst his teachers for always being late in submitting his assignments. Yet, every time he submits an assignment, it becomes the talk of the staff room. His assignments are the most creative in school and are a delight to read. He sometimes makes visual presentations, at other times he submits assignments through poetry and posters.
- Taruna and Sanjay are siblings and study in the same school. They are in classes eight and eleven respectively. Although they are not clear about their career goals yet, they are clear that they want to enter the fashion industry. Sanjay is contemplating being a hairstylist. They keep abreast with the latest fashion trends and are often seen in school sporting the latest makeup and hair-styles. Their parents are financially well off and are supportive of their experimentation. Their academic performance is above average. But teachers feel that students need to follow school rules and often scold the two for their wild coloured hair.
- Manisha is in class six. She is a curious child and likes to learn many new things. Although she doesn't score exceptionally well in exams, she asks a lot of questions in the classroom. Often these questions put teachers in a spot, as they also have to read more to find answers to them. Some of the teachers tend to snub her for the same. It is only a few teachers who appreciate her out of the box questions. This keeps her going and she continues to ask more questions.
- Mark's school has a feedback mechanism through a box in which students can put in anonymous letters containing suggestions. The box is opened once a month and the suggestions are read out in the school assembly. There is rarely a student who ever puts a suggestion. Mark is an exception. He is constantly questioning rules that are set up in school and coming up with alternative ideas. At times the school has accepted his suggestions and modified rules. This has encouraged him further. He also signs his letters and when asked about them, openly argues and justifies his opinions. Teachers are most miffed because he is often right.
- Garima is in class ten. She wants to grow up to be a singer. She was practicing her singing when her mother reminded her of her Chemistry exam. She decided to learn the equations through songs. When she was asked to present her equations in class, she started singing them in the rap format. Her classmates were thoroughly enjoying the class. Her teacher was also thoroughly enjoying her rendition, but was confused about whether to allow such behaviour in class!

Most schools are likely to curtail the forms of behaviour described in the examples above. In reality, acceptance of such behaviour can help such children to work towards enhancing their potential. But a common fear that teachers and other authorities have is that if they allow one child to break a rule, others will follow soon. This concern is not far from reality. What is important is that teachers and school authorities ask themselves which rules are non-negotiable. Does dying one's hair red actually come in the way of learning mathematics? If not, then should there be an objection to behaviour that does not disturb others and does not transcend personal space? Can pedagogy be modified to include alternative viewpoints and modes of expression? Is it possible to allow students to participate in collective decision-making at the class level and through representatives at the school level? Would this allow for greater freedom with responsibility?

School Values

School values are reflected in many different ways. The most basic aspect is that of the kind of infrastructure and facilities that the school provides its students. Elite schools often translate good infrastructural facilities to mean providing students individual technological access and air-conditioned classrooms and transportation. While this does help to create a conducive learning environment, the danger is that children from a very early age move away from nature and become technology dependent. Such early technology dependence reduces their adaptability and adjustment to varied physical environments. Some schools also offer meditation classes to develop self-awareness. This helps in a better understanding of oneself, provide a sense of peace and promote psychological well-being.

Another common value that schools tend to promote is excellence. Most schools value meritocracy and the same is communicated to students through parents and teachers. School authorities often put pressure on teachers to ensure that their students secure the highest marks, gain interschool and state positions and their results show higher pass percentages. Here, success is valued in terms of the marks the students score. Little appreciation is given to alternative viewpoints, unless they help in winning accolades and prizes in interschool competitions and bring more prestige to the reputation of the school. One common example in this regard is giving greater importance to the science and commerce streams over humanities. This is because jobs in the fields of science and management pay higher and are better reputed in society. Furthermore, the subjects that fall within the humanities stream are considered easier. Most schools have a tendency to send low achieving students in the humanities stream. This lowers the prestige of the stream and at times, students who by choice would like to take humanities end up not taking it, for the fear of being labelled as less bright. A humanities student is usually only respected if he/she eventually becomes a civil servant! In the longer run, this influences what values students grow up with. They start to value success in terms of money earned and power positions in society. Students invariably grow up wanting to take up professions that are likely to get them better paying jobs and will allow them to live a more lavish lifestyle. It is much later in life that they realise that the path they are treading is not what they truly wanted to be on. They get stuck in a circle of greed with little awareness of their true interests and potentials. This is evident in the many examples of graduates from the top medical and engineering colleges shifting gears to engage in entrepreneurial endeavours. Cases of management graduates taking to farming, bee keeping or managing farms, dairies and stables and living a laid back life in the countryside are also increasing.

In many co-educational schools, it is common to see teachers asking students, particularly in senior classes, to refrain from interacting with the opposite gender. In sports periods, too, students are expected to play only with the student of the same gender. In classrooms, they are asked to sit on separate benches.

Sometimes, during the middle school years, being asked to sit with classmates of the other gender is used as a punishment. Irrespective of whether it is a single gender or co-educational school, many children grow up without learning to appreciate the concerns and challenges of the other gender. What they learn are the lines of demarcation and at times discrimination between the two genders. Where contact is limited, they do not learn to value each other, understand each other's problems and to participate in each other's growing up journey. This often prevents them from developing healthy relationships with each other in later life. It is important to recognise that the school is a gendered space. Teachers at times unconsciously discriminate between genders on the basis of preconceived biases. For instance, during school functions, boys are often asked to rearrange furniture and girls are asked to decorate different school spaces. School uniforms can also be hindrances to girls playing in the playground. In senior classes, girls are often encouraged to take home science with hardly a handful of schools offering the same subject to boys. Similarly, girls are encouraged to take up medical science as medicine is a profession involving compassion in comparison to mechanical engineering and even management. Schools need to provide adequate exposure through workshops, interaction sessions and create opportunities to learn from each other.

PEER RELATIONSHIPS

The common thread that is visible across all age groups in the above two sections is the relationships between peers. Developing healthy friendships requires learning adjustment, negotiation and social skills with people of one's own age. Children learn to share with each other and develop empathy through peer relationships. School is a space where children learn to engage with others of their own age. At home, parents, grandparents and other members of the extended family provide adult engagement and are often indulgent towards children and more tolerant of their behaviour. Siblings are often older and younger, creating a hierarchy in relationships. It is thus only at school that children are likely to engage with same age friends.

Peer Pressure

Peer pressure can be both healthy and unhealthy. Healthy forms of peer pressure are commonly seen in children through casual teasing and healthy competition. Casual teasing allows a child to cope with external pressures and laugh at himself/herself. The child also learns to look beyond limitations and shortcomings. In terms of competition, children often tend to attempt outdoing other students through academic achievements, excellence in sports or other activities. This creates a form of healthy stress on children to stretch their abilities and perform better than they were performing earlier. Both of these can quickly turn into unhealthy practices. Parents and teachers sometimes pitch students against each other. This stops them from learning with and from each other. This also causes undue rifts and at time prevents the development of friendships and what could have been better learning opportunities. While occasional teasing is often a part of learning to grow up, it can become detrimental if children engage in teasing that is insulting and discriminatory. Where children are judged constantly on the basis of how they look or the habits that they have developed, they start to feel unworthy and unwanted. This can be damaging to their self-esteem. Teachers and parents need to be careful in ensuring that unhealthy teasing, particularly one that discriminates on the basis of gender, region or religion among others, is checked and stopped immediately.

Besides teasing, unhealthy forms of peer pressure include bullying and coercion. This is particularly common amongst older children and adolescents. Peers encourage each other to engage in risk-taking behaviour including bunking classes, substance abuse, sexual experimentation and illegal activities including vandalism and stealing. It is often believed that in such cases the offender and the victim can be clearly identified. In other words, there are one or two bullies who encourage or pressurise peers in their group to rebel or comply with their demands. Recent researches have shown that the lines of demarcation between the victim and the perpetrator are not so clear. The perpetrator is often someone who was a victim himself/herself earlier. At other times, the perpetrator is victimised in feeling compelled to bully others lest he/she is bullied.

Embracing Diversity

We have discussed in an earlier section how the school is often a regimented space providing little freedom to children to find space for themselves and develop identities. In such settings, informal relations with peers are an important outlet for children to engage in conversations about what they truly like and dislike, share their talents and hone their abilities. Appreciation and acceptance from peers for their hidden talents, often unrecognised at home or school, provides the much needed recognition that contributes towards building a sense of identity. Peer subcultures are also visible among school students. Here, students form groups on the basis of shared likes and dislikes. Some of these groups are based on a shared interest in a common sport or game. For example, students form a group on the basis of common interest in chess, or Rubik's cube, or crossword puzzles. Groups may be formed on the basis of common aspirations, such as a study group to prepare for a common entrance exam. Members of the football team or debate club can have yet another group. In other instances, groups may be formed on the basis of the social class to which one belongs. The elite students in class can have a group for discussing the latest fashion trends. Peer subcultures are not restricted to occasional meetings but are marked by clear memberships and loyalties. Some groups may also have behavioural norms and codes of conduct. This would make their group distinct from others. What adds to the complexity of the nature of peer subcultures is the tensions it creates between groups and sometimes for individual students. For instance, a student may want to participate in several groups but may not be allowed due to strong in-group codes. For groups that base on social class backgrounds, memberships are discriminatory and often create feelings of jealousy, longing and disrespect.

Sense of Belongingness

Peer subcultures as discussed above in relation to a particular grade, house or school provide a great sense of belongingness. Peers provide love and support in situations where adult support may not be either welcome or forthcoming. Shared moments with partners in crime are often the basis for strong friendship ties. An absence of strong interpersonal friendships, not belonging to a group can leave a child feeling lonely and even lose interest in activities in school. The past two decades have witnessed a phenomenal rise in social networking and microblogging websites. These lend a new dimension to the nature of friendship. Presence on an SNS is a mark of being 'in' with the times. These sites have become substitutes for real time conversations and all communication takes place through written texts. It is not uncommon to see a group of teenagers sitting together, all of them busy on their smart phones, tablets or laptops. Digital communication is almost an obsession with children and adolescents. They are seen to be online all the time. The need to be constantly connected is also related to the felt need for image building. Everything that an adolescent engages in is uploaded either as a description, or through photographs or both. The need to communicate and be heard is evident in the number of posts and status updates, as also in receiving appreciation through 'comments' and 'likes.' Further, adolescents also engage in image building through posting photographs frequently. Some of these photographs are not a reflection of their real self and context, but are posted to build popularity. When these image building attempts fail to make a mark on peers, adolescents tend to feel depressed and lonely.

Parents need to keep a careful watch on children befriending and sharing personal details with strangers in an attempt to increase their number of friends. This engagement with technology may be seen as an adolescent fad that is likely to go away with time. It becomes a matter of concern where interaction over these sites poses a danger to healthy familial and social relationships. We have already discussed earlier how some parents feel the need to connect with children through websites and chat rooms.

COMMUNITY AND SOCIAL LIVING

Many aspects of society at large influence children directly. We have already discussed that home and school act as socialisation agents. They tend to reinforce social norms and beliefs, and encourage children to abide by the same. Children learn to live according to social norms and adjust to the culture and community. On the other hand, this very adjustment to social norms often tends to prevent children from growing to their fullest. A healthy, well-adjusted individual lives largely by the rules of the society. Yet, it is our culture that poses unhealthy restrictions and provides us with a predetermined set of rules to abide by. Some of these rules are enforced on individuals by virtue of being born in a particular socio-economic background, religion or gender. In this section, we will see how caste, class, gender, religion and sexual orientation are strong influences through childhood and adolescence.

Negotiating with the World

Often biases and discriminatory practices start right at the time of birth. Kakar (2005) describes how the birth of a male child is celebrated, while the birth of a girl is not marked by similar festivities. While the child may not be aware of the celebrations at the time, older children in the family observe these events and understand the development of a gender identity. These gendered attitudes continue later in life and mark all experiences of the child. Earlier in the chapter, attention was drawn to how school can be a gendered space. In many communities, girls may not be allowed to enrol in educational institutions. Discrimination on the basis of gender can still be seen on the basis of availability of food, clothing patterns and access to public spaces. Clear restrictions are visible on girls' participation in spaces beyond the boundaries of their homes. Travelling outside of their hometown is often not allowed. This is a great restriction on pursuing secondary and higher education. At home as well, preferential treatment towards boys gives a clear indication to relationship between siblings. Even where the boys in the family are younger to the girls, they are asked to accompany girls outside of home for providing security. This is particularly true in lower socio-economic class (Saraswathi 1999).

Social class is a strong influence that shapes the lives of children and adolescents. In fact, the socio-economic class to which one belongs determines access to facilities and the cultural capital of the child. These in turn influence the opportunity structures and aspirations of children. Through policy provisions, the government is attempting to increase access to educational opportunity across social class groups. Compulsory admission of students from the Economically Weaker Section (EWS) in private schools, as part of RTE 2009 is a step in this direction. The idea is to provide similar exposure to all children. Teachers and parents often complain that the presence of children from the EWS background tends to lower overall performance and lead other children to learn inappropriate behaviour. The resistance that this provision met from parents, teachers and many school principals is indicative of the discriminatory practices still visible in society.

Similar discrimination is also seen on grounds of caste. Children are often referred to by their castes instead of their names. This is despite article 15 of the Constitution of India which expressly places a prohibition on discrimination on grounds of religion, race, caste, sex or place of birth. Teachers carry many prejudgements about students of a particular caste or tribe as being incapable of studying. So they make very perfunctory efforts to teach them. In some schools, children do not eat together in school on the grounds of caste. Children are not allowed to drink water from the same public water facility or even play together if they belong to particular caste backgrounds. All this creates an attitude of discrimination in children. Further, those being discriminated against grow up with a sense of inferiority. Coming out of this false sense of inferiority adds to the challenges of facing a discriminatory world. Some children also drop out-of-school due to such unfair treatment.

Caste, class and gender are not the only grounds of discrimination. Post the 9/11 attacks in the USA, many children reported being discriminated against in schools on grounds of being Muslim. Sikh boys have long been laughed at for wearing turbans. Similarly, there have been reported incidents of discriminatory behaviour against people from the north eastern states of India. School children are also insensitive towards people with alternative gender identities and sexual orientations. Insensitive attitudes by students, teachers and parents are also visible in how they engage with children with physical, visual and mental challenges. What this highlights is that children face challenges on an everyday basis at home, school and society which flow from the social and personal context to which they belong.

Self-awareness

The discussion above highlights a number of challenges that children tend to face on an everyday basis on account of their personal and social backgrounds. Often, children look at these as hindrances in their progress. So they resign to their fates. When they are repeatedly told that they are incapable of achieving anything, they actually start believing it. With respect to gender identity, boys and girls are socialised to fit into gender stereotypes. An alternative gender identity usually is not accepted.

The first step is often to accept one's identity. In attempting to fit into social roles, adolescents particularly attempt to disengage with their true selves and assume an identity that will be accepted. An example of this would be an adolescent who has homosexual tendencies, attempting to form heterosexual relationships to be accepted by his peers and family. Similar attempts are also visible in cases of cross dressers and transgenders.

In other cases, children and adolescents tend to disassociate themselves with their peer group and only develop friendships with 'their own kind.' Here, boundaries between self and others are clearly defined. Examples of this include peer groups formed on the basis of religion, caste or physical abilities.

Teachers need to develop sensitivity themselves and go out of their way to ensure that children are able to accept themselves and each other for who they are. In dealing with social issues it helps to encourage children to learn personal and social histories to understand their position in society. This also helps build a sense of pride in their own identity. Acknowledging one's emotions also contributes in building a sense of identity. In fact, children need to be provided opportunities to share their thoughts, feelings and experiences with each other. This helps to build empathy and support towards each other.

Challenging Societal and Family Norms

While we recognise that class, caste, religion, gender and sexuality are significant factors affecting one's identity, it is equally important to acknowledge that childhood and adolescence are important life stages during which families and school can help develop the right attitude towards each of the concerns identified above. Social change can be brought about only if we encourage all children to be sensitive towards and accepting others. The attitudes, biases and discrimination that exist, need to change towards ensuring a more just and free society.

Besides acceptance of oneself, children also need to be encouraged to break away from social norms that are discriminatory, biased and unjust. Not every child or family will be in a position to rebel against the world. However, change can begin at the personal level. Changing attitudes can lead to a better society in the future. The school space can be used to provide exposure to many ideas and thoughts from across the world. Through biopics and biographies children can be presented with possibilities and role models. Workshops with parents and awareness camps in the community are other ways through which sensitivity can be built at the societal level.

ON A CONCLUDING NOTE

This chapter has highlighted that the child is embedded in the social context in which he/she lives. Family, school, peers and the larger world, all influence the lives of students. Each of them interplays to form a complex network, with the child in the centre attempting to negotiate complexities presented by the various dimensions. It would be meaningless to attempt to understand and facilitate growth of the child without due consideration to the social factors in his/her life.

6

Taking a Proactive Stance

In the overview section of the book at the very beginning, different perspectives to understanding children and adolescents in schools were discussed. It was also highlighted that children in schools face several mental health concerns and challenges, based on personal factors and age-related developmental concerns. The contexts in which children and adolescents live and experience the world are extremely important, be it family, school or society at large, in understanding how children deal with the challenges and concerns that come their way. This aspect found elaborate discussion in the previous chapter where the need to understand children in their situatedness was emphasised.

Keeping this backdrop in mind, the present chapter focuses on the need for teachers and schools to take a proactive stance to promote children's well-being. There are usually four stances to children's well-being: to prevent stress, conflict and tension from tinting the child, to promote his/her sense of wellness by building resilience and suitable skills, to conserve the child's happiness and to provide curative intervention to help those children who face problems. In the curative approach, the school, the teachers and parents become alert only when the child manifests behaviour that is inappropriate, shows decline in academic performance or exhibits a lifestyle change that is markedly different from what he/she usually follows. In contrast, a preventive stance works towards addressing issues before they become a cause for concern. A conservation stance focuses on maintaining mental health and a promotive stance helps the child to move towards wellness. Here the focus would be on enhancing life skills, coping abilities and personal and social adjustment. Table 6.1 provides a brief suggestive list of school activities and processes that have the potential to work towards preventive, promotive and curative aspects of mental health.

You would notice that many of these activities and facilities provide benefits that overlap in the preventive, promotive and curative dimensions. Further, this list is by no means exhaustive. You can draw up a similar list for your school to see what the existing services are and what needs to be worked upon, depending on the specific context of your school and the needs of the children studying there.

TAKING THE FIRST STEP

The first step to be taken by teachers, counsellors and school authorities is acknowledging the need to address mental health concerns and recognise that the school has the potential to do the same.

Acknowledge the Need for Addressing Mental Health

Very often the school, in its endeavour to complete the syllabus and meet academic goals, ends up ignoring the mental health concerns of students. The past two decades have seen an increase in the

Table 6.1	Preventive, Promotive, and Curative Aspects of Mental Health: Some Suggestions for Schools

Preventive	Promotive	Curative
– Teacher–student relationships	– Exposure to many activities	– School Counselling Services
– Space to students to voice their concerns	– Opportunities for participation and expression	– Parent–teacher meetings
– Encouraging friendships	– Prefectorial system and space for democratic participation	

Source: Authors.

number of schools that promote holistic development. The same has also been recommended by several policies in education in independent India. In practical terms, this translates into introducing a number of activities in the school such as music, art, dance, swimming, horse riding, martial arts and so on. This, albeit beneficial, is only successful in creating an illusion that these activities should be enough to fulfil all the needs of children and adolescents. However, the truth is that these are seldom enough, especially given the uniqueness of every child. Providing a set of common experiences while important in itself is not enough to cater to the needs of all students. Usually, children have very specific needs, concerns and problems and thus require individual attention. It is only through a personalised approach of reaching out to each one of them that the school can hope to address the mental health needs of children and adolescents in schools. The school space has to be understood as more than merely an amalgamation of infrastructural facilities and a series of organised activities. After all, it is also a space for developing bonds, interpersonal ties, mutual sharing, social living, enhancing life skills and personal grooming.

Remove Taboos and Stigmas

Sumira, a practicing psychologist, recounts her experience as a student of psychology in University of Delhi. As part of her undergraduate programme of study, she was required to visit a mental health institution in the city. The institute, earlier known as Shahdara Mental Hospital, had been rechristened Institute of Human Behaviour and Allied Sciences (IHBAS). New to the area, Sumira asked another passenger in the bus for the appropriate bus stop to reach IHBAS. The passenger answered her query, stared at her for a few seconds and then quickly got up to sit somewhere else in the bus. The incident highlights the stigma attached to psychological problems, people undergoing treatment and even mental health institutions.

Although the past decade has seen an increase in importance accorded to psychology as a disciplinary area, society at large is far from accepting the need to see psychological well-being as important domain in everyday life. People seeking professional help are still seen with suspicion mixed with awe and curiosity. This sense of awe is somewhat natural as there is a lack of awareness about psychological disorders. People can acknowledge that you can visit a medical doctor for cold as well as for heart ailments. But they may not acknowledge that psychological concerns are just as widespread and diverse. Any person is thus identified as 'mad', 'disturbed' or 'crazy'. Similarly, any child with learning disability, or on the autism spectrum, or having an ADHD is labelled in a single category of 'special' and thus incapable of studying with 'normal' children. This is further compounded by the fact that many people are apprehensive around people undergoing psychological treatment. They tend to be cagey and try to avoid interaction and contact once they know someone is seeing a psychologist.

The stigma attached to seeking professional help places a taboo on discussing matters of concern. People end up avoiding discussion, which only results in complicating and aggravating the problem further. A conscious effort by the school in generating awareness and developing sensitivity can help in removing taboos and stigmas. Sessions with parents and the community at large can help to spread acceptance of seeking help from a professional, when the need arises. This will help to further openness and sharing of experiences, voicing thoughts and seeking help on the part of students. The first step in this direction is for schools to have at least one full time counsellor whom students and teachers can approach.

Avoid Passing Judgements

The discussion above highlighted that people tend to be judgemental about those seeking professional help for psychological problems. However, passing judgement on others is not restricted to only those who are taking treatment. The previous chapter had briefly presented the case of siblings who wished to enter the fashion industry. The following is an excerpt from the daily diary that eight-years-old Taruna maintains.

Once again today my class teacher scolded me for not scoring well in the test for mathematics. This is when I have scored 18 on 20. Many students scored less than me but Ma'am didn't say anything to them. She insulted me in front of the whole class. *Fashion mein dhyaan hai bas tumhara. Itna dhyan padhai mein lagao to pure number aayenge* (You only pay attention to fashion. If you concentrated this much on studies, you would have scored full marks). I was so upset. What is wrong in being interested in fashion? This is what I want to do. At least I know what I want to do. Most of my friends don't know this for themselves. I had learnt a new way of making a plait from the Internet. My hair was neatly tied but this new style is not okay with the teachers. I overheard some teachers comment when I was returning to my class from the assembly. *Ye aur ladkiyon ko bhi bigad degi* (She is going to spoil the other girls as well). The teachers have asked parents to keep their children away from me. I am into fashion and all those in fashion are not of 'good character'. Some of my classmates have actually stopped sitting with me. They told me that all who are successful in the fashion industry are on the basis of how much they can party and drink. They believe that everyone in the fashion industry changes boyfriends every other day. I don't know where they come up with these notions from. I feel terrible in school.

The diary entry highlights the inner dilemma that Taruna experiences every day. Her interactions with teachers and her classmates are clouded by the perceptions of society. Stereotypes perpetuated by media usually also contribute towards building opinions and views. What is of utmost concern in Taruna's case is that people of all age groups have formed opinions about her, even before interacting with her. Many of these biases and preconceived notions about her or those who aspire to be in the fashion industry act as a deterrent to any effort to know the person. This is how myths and stereotypes get perpetuated and are then used to judge and typecast others.

Taruna's case is only an illustrative example of what an individual student undergoes or can undergo on an everyday basis. Students are often judged on a variety of aspects such as submitting late assignments, not adhering to norms of the school uniform, inadequate expression skills and so on. Some of these judgements are formed on the basis of isolated incidents. At other times, students are judged on the basis of isolated aspects of their personality that may or may not be reflective of the person as a whole. Needless to say, such judgements tend to curb potential and force children into conformity.

Be Tolerant of Experimentation

Children and adolescents tend to experiment with different lifestyles in their quest to find meaning and identity. It is through experimentation that they are able to choose their life positions and make commitments. It may be recalled that this was discussed as part of Erikson's theory of psychosocial development in Chapter 3.

In general, it is seen that schools and homes show little tolerance for children's experiments. Consider the case of Riddhi.

> Riddhi is 10 years old. She studies in an international school and is recognised as an above average child on the account of unusual questions she asks in the class. Her parents are encouraging and are cognizant of her multifarious abilities. She had initially joined abacus classes but did not like them much. She was also admitted to classes for Kathak and Sitar. When she didn't like these, she tried to learn synthesizer. She also occasionally attends theatre workshops. Although she has performed reasonably well in almost all the things she has tried, she has never wanted to continue the classes. Every few months, Riddhi's parents start looking for classes that she can join. She has recently joined a ballet class. Her mother feels that she may have finally found her area of interest. She is very committed and never misses a class. Although there are long hours of practice, she is happy in the time spent in this class.

If Riddhi's parents had not been supportive, it would have been near impossible for Riddhi to find her interest. In most cases, parents encourage children to choose their interests before joining the class or to stick to the classes that they have taken up. If the child is lucky, she/he may find her/his areas of interest. Otherwise, she/he just has to commit to whatever choices are available. In most cases, money is a constraint and parents are in a hurry for children to choose what they want to pursue further in life. At a young age, it is unreasonable to expect children to commit to one activity. They are often interested in everything and it is only with time that they narrow down their focus and make specific choices. During this period of exploration and making choices parents need to be patient.

In older children, this exploration extends itself to all domains. Pre-teens and adolescents may try on different hairstyles and dressing styles. They may be fascinated by rock stars, scientists or ideologies. Often these are temporary fads that keep changing or get toned down on their own with time. Since most of these fads are temporary and harmless, home and school can provide an environment in which these can be tolerated and sometimes even channellised positively.

> Nakul, for instance, had the habit of collecting face masks of ghosts, zombies, and the like. His parents thought that it was a waste of money but he continued to use a substantial part of his pocket money to buy these. His teacher was aware of how disturbed he was because of the lack of support at home. The perfect opportunity came when the school decided to have a dance drama

in the school's annual day function with a Good versus Evil theme. All the masks that he had collected came in handy for the various characters. His knowledge of specific colours and styles of costumes was very useful in the entire conceptualisation. He even helped with the background score and song composition. His name was announced at the function. He received appreciation and recognition from both home and school. His parents don't question him on his passion any longer. He is able to concentrate better on his studies and is generally more cheerful.

What the cases of Riddhi and Nakul highlight is that children and adolescents need the time, space and opportunities to discover and make the best of their passions. However, not all passions and experiments are completely harmless. Adolescence and preadolescent years are also marked by experimentation with cigarettes, alcohol and drugs. Parents and teachers should try to detect early signs of substance misuse and keep a check on the same. Similarly, sexual experimentation, in the quest to find one's sexual identity, can lead to heart break and engagement in abusive relationships. At times activities undertaken such as video recordings, sex chatting or sexting and so on can lead to serious consequences. Adolescents and the elders around them need to be careful about any kind of addiction including gaming, chatting and Internet addiction.

ENCOURAGING SOCIAL ADJUSTMENT

Healthy relationships are a key to living a fulfilling life. In a society that emphasises relationships with family and society, it is important that children learn to live in social settings. Schools are probably the most important spaces that require children to learn social adjustment. We have discussed earlier how the home environment is often characterised by relationships that are marked by inherent restraint in interactions between members of different age groups. In school, however, there is little consideration between peers. They are of the same age group and are under no obligation to give undue consideration to each other. This necessitates that children learn important lessons in social adjustment, of sharing, mutual compromise and cooperation. Teachers need to ensure that children learn social adjustment, by providing many opportunities to them to interact with each other. During adolescence, social relations and adjustment once again become difficult as adolescents work towards finding their individual identity within collective settings. Teachers can take several small steps to encourage better social adjustment.

Observe Behaviour

One of the first steps that teachers need to take is observing the behaviour of the students in their class. When young children come to school, they bring with them the baggage of their contexts and backgrounds. Lifestyles and food habits depend on a variety of factors including family settings, class, religion and regional background. What is considered appropriate behaviour by one family may be considered inappropriate by others. The classroom is a heterogeneous space, so there will always be students in class who would have different habits, or ways of behaving from the rest. Sarabjit, a student of class two, had to eat lunch alone every day because he brought eggs and salami sandwiches regularly. Most students in his class were vegetarians and refused to eat with him. Slowly they started distancing themselves from him saying that he smelled of eggs. In the case of Sarabjit or similar cases, teachers would need to be observant and keep a check on the class to ensure that no child feels left out or victimised on account of behaviour-based discrimination.

Acknowledge Peer Subcultures

In slightly older children, it is important to first acknowledge the existence of peer subcultures in the classroom setting. Teachers often tend to treat students of the same age group as a homogeneous cohort that comes to schools with the aim of studying and scoring high marks. However, what is important for teachers to note is that children will differ on many aspects such as interests, aims, motivation, abilities and attitudes. Often, children form friendships in the class on the basis of one or more of these commonalities. Peer subcultures are considered a hindrance to studying well in schools. Teachers often try to separate friends in the classroom, arguing that they concentrate and study better when seated separately. This may be far from true. Allowing children who get along well and have common interests may actually allow better collaborative learning.

At the same time, teachers have to be careful in telling children that although they may be close to a particular set of friends, they should learn to get along with others in their class as well. Peer subcultures can create artificial hierarchies and structures that children find difficult to transcend. This creates a sense of elitism and seclusion in groups. These form an important part of building one's identity, based on belonging to a particular group. At the same time, it may create feelings of jealousy and envy among children which are often unhealthy.

Build Sensitivity as Part of Life Skills

Recent years have seen an increase in emphasis on life skills in schools. WHO has recommended that apart from academic studies, the school needs to focus on developing a set of life skills in students. These include problem solving, critical thinking, self-awareness, interpersonal skills, decision-making, negotiation, empathy, cooperation and emotional and stress management. These skills focus on encouraging the development of positive and adaptive behaviour. It may be seen that most of the life skills emphasise better personal and social adjustment. Adolescence Education Programmes across the country focus on promoting life skills. These skills provide an important first step in moving towards building a more sensitive classroom and school environment. By strengthening interpersonal skills, children also learn to develop awareness and empathetic understanding towards others. Through interactions with others who are unlike themselves, children learn to appreciate varying cultures, lifestyle patterns, attitudes and learn to form opinions on the basis of outward appearances.

Look Beyond Stereotypes

Our life experiences teach us to form opinions about people which later guide our actions. This is an important although automatic mechanism that protects us from repeating mistakes and getting hurt in interpersonal interactions and relationships. Sometimes our opinions are not based on our own experiences but on the basis of what others around us have said, or what is represented in popular media. People forming opinions on the basis of these at times, end up judging others not for who they are, but for which gender, region, religion or caste they represent. Stereotypes can be perpetuated on the basis of skin colour, body structure and other physical features as well as family background or personal habits, such as being left-handed or the level of personal hygiene. Almost everyone falls in one or the other category of stereotyping. This results in limited interactions as people view each other with suspicion and mistrust. Among school children, these stereotypes are perpetuated through parents. Children form opinions on the basis of what they hear at home. At an impressionable age, they sometimes form opinions about others in their class even without interacting with them.

If teachers encourage them to look beyond stereotypes at school, students may be encouraged to find common interests with others and form strong friendship ties that they may not initiate otherwise. A slightly more proactive teacher would be one who would take the initiative to organise workshops for building sensitivity in parents and in the community.

NEED FOR COMMUNICATION

A common complaint that many adolescents have is that they are unable to communicate with their parents and teachers. Any parent or teacher would tell you that this feeling of being unheard is mutual. This gap in communication can arise for a number of reasons. What it results in are feelings of being misunderstood, unwanted and unappreciated. To bridge this gap between two generations, there is a need to build lines of communication that are strong and effective. As elders, parents and teachers may be required to take the first step in this direction.

Active Listening

A key ability that needs to be developed for strengthening interpersonal communication is that of active listening. Sometimes even when teachers and parents engage with children regularly, they get accused of not listening or being unavailable. At other times, the belief that elders would not listen to them is so strong that children and adolescents refuse to share their thoughts and feelings with them. Let's see a case to see why this could be so.

Mira is in class ten. She wanted to go out for a movie with some of her friends but her parents refused to allow her. She and her friends bunked school one day and watched the movie. Her teacher happened to learn about it and the next day confronted her in the school. Mira wanted to put her point of view across. But the teacher told her that she had already called her parents. They told her that she was irresponsible and that she would score less marks if she continued like this. Mira was wondering if she had ever left her work incomplete. She had done well in all her class exams and was an above average student. This was the first time that she had broken a rule. But she didn't say anything as she knew that her teacher and parents and had already made up their minds.

When students feel that teachers or parents are merely pretending to listen and are genuinely not concerned about their viewpoints, they may bottle up their feelings, which burst some day and cause unpleasantness to all concerned. Teachers make no effort to reach out to those who don't speak or voice their views in the class. They assume that the student had nothing to say. Sometimes, children don't speak in class or at home because they know that their views will be sidelined or countered. It is difficult but extremely important to keep discussions from becoming arguments and confrontations and adults have a great responsibility towards this.

The way to break this impasse is to ensure that children feel that they are being heard. Providing a listening ear and building trust through communication can build the bridge between elders and children. What is important is that the process of listening should be authentic. In other words, it is not merely physical presence that can build trust; elders have to actively participate when listening to children. They should express their openness in listening to the children and pay attention to their words through non-verbal gestures as well.

Opportunities to Participate in Decision-making

School-going children are full of fresh ideas. However, in most situations, decisions are taken for them. This implies that they have little control over what is happening in their lives. While for young children this may be justified in most circumstances, as they grow older, their involvement in decision-making needs to increase. Older children and adolescents feel very frustrated when they feel that the locus of control is external to them. The urge to take control over their lives is an indication of their attempt to find their identity. They wish to define themselves in their own ways, learn from their mistakes and chart their own life course. Over interference by elders in their lives can stifle their capabilities and lead to feelings of suffocation and unhappiness. This also is sometimes the cause of rebelling against home and school rules. It further creates strained relationships and a lack of mutual trust and understanding.

Another very important reason for elders to give space to children in decision-making is to help them to develop faith in their abilities. Children feel more confident of their own abilities when the decisions that they take are accepted and sometimes even followed by others. Involvement of children in decision-making can be in simple tasks such as allowing them to choose the clothes that they will wear or helping you to choose what you can wear. Even asking them to choose from a limited range of options is an important exposure to decision-making. Asking them to share why they are making a particular choice also helps them to lend voice to their own decision-making process.

Involving children and adolescents in decision-making at home and in school can develop a sense of ownership and responsibility.

Teachers at a senior secondary private school were very distributed by the excessive use of cell phones by their students in the school. The school had clear rules against the use of cell phones in the school premises. Phones were confiscated from any student who was found using it in the school. Parents were asked to come and retrieve the phone. Despite all this, students continued to use phones openly. This often disturbed the teachers. The school principal and senior teachers together decided to hold a meeting with the school prefects and class monitors of the concerned classes. They were given time to discuss with their classmates. In the meeting, the students shared that many students from senior classes went for coaching classes from the school itself. They were required to carry cell phones with them to stay in touch with their parents. The teachers accepted their argument. The whole committee then together drafted rules for the use of cell phones in school. Student representatives then communicated the same to their respective classes. Since the rules were drafted by the students and teachers together, there were hardly any violations. The classes ran much more smoothly.

What is important here is that decision-making was not a one-way process. The school authorities sat together with the students to present their viewpoints and develop a set of rules that were acceptable to both. In other words, decision-making should, as far as possible, be a participatory process.

Space to Voice Their Thoughts

If we for a moment try to recall when children initiated a conversation with adults, the instances would be few. Most of the times, conversations between children and adults are initiated by adults. Parents, for instance, may ask children how they spent their day at school. Teachers may ask content-related questions in the class. Conversations may be initiated when children engage in behaviour that teachers or parents may not approve of. A commonality across these situations is that the time and topics of conversations are decided by elders. Children have to adjust themselves according to the schedules of classes. As children grow older, this adjustment can lead to distancing them from their parents and teachers.

Instead, elders should try to create a relationship where children find them approachable and available. Children should feel that it is not only when they have to give an explanation that they are asked to speak. Their presence at home and school needs to be acknowledged. They should not feel left out or ignored. Further, recognising their place at home and school helps to involve them in the everyday life of the home and school. Besides developing a sense of self-worth, they develop feelings of belongingness and a sense of ownership. It opens up channels of communication and fosters involvement in relationships and family and school matters.

Space for voicing their thoughts can be created in several ways. Children can be encouraged to share their thoughts and views on specific topics in the school assembly. Class teachers can spare some time in their daily or weekly schedule to discuss aspects that are relevant to, or of concern to, the children. Students can themselves be asked to choose what they wish to discuss. It is significant here to remember that this will only be possible if elders engage in authentic listening, as has been discussed earlier.

Listen Without Judgement

Another key aspect to developing strong channels of communication is to listen without judgement. When children are asked to give an explanation for their actions, they feel threatened. They feel that parents or teachers are trying to find fault in their explanations. This perception of being judged prevents them from sharing their thoughts and views honestly. In pedagogic processes as well, teachers often focus on fault finding. When asked to explain a concept in class, students are often probed and asked to find out the missing points in each other's answers. Similarly, in evaluation processes, the focus is often not on what a child can do but on what a child has faulted in doing.

Students carry forward this feeling of being judged in the academic sphere to other aspects as well. Thus, when a student is called to the staff room or the principal's room, it automatically generates feelings of anxiety, suspicion and fear. Where students do not feel judged, they are able to share their ideas more freely. The support required by children in translating some of their dreams into reality can only be gathered if they are able to express their thoughts. School-going children, for instance, may have ideas for developing computer programmes, starting community awareness drives or have some suggestions for improvement in the school. If they feel judged, these ideas will be stifled. More importantly, restrictions of these kinds place boundaries on thoughts. Divergent thinking and out of the box ideas are slowly replaced with run of the mill notions. Children become followers instead of leaders. The consequence of stifling expression is lower level of creativity.

During adolescence, the intergenerational communication gap tends to increase. The relationship between adolescents and elders is often marked by feelings of mistrust owing to a lack of understanding. Adolescents often feel that parents and teachers oppose everything that they propose. There it is only through building strong relationships that are based on trust that open lines of communication can be maintained. Adolescents need to believe that they are being heard and not judged. It was earlier discussed as to how at this stage the role of elders is often restricted to facilitating informed decision-making. Instead, parents or teachers end up preaching in their attempt at stopping adolescents from taking the wrong decisions. This is a further deterrent for adolescents to share their concerns.

Anshika is in class eleven. She recently joined a social networking site. Her friends have been on the site for many years. In her quest to match them in the number of friends she has on the site, she has added many people she doesn't know. Her friends told her that it was normal to befriend strangers on the site. She recently befriended a very good looking boy and has been exchanging personal messages with him. He expressed a desire to meet her and she agreed to meet him one day after-school, when her parents were away at work. It soon became a routine. He soon professed love for her. She had never been happier. Although she was doubtful, he was older and he said that it was alright for people to express their love physically. She acceded to his requests but was not happy as she felt her parents would disapprove of her relationship. She told him so the next time that they met but he had secretly clicked their photographs. He blackmailed her into agreeing to his wants. She didn't know who to share it with as she felt her parents and teachers will never accept her and blame her for everything that she had done. She was in a trap. He had now started bringing his friends and asked her to be physically close to them as well.

The case above highlights how students can get trapped in difficult circumstances. They may need help from adults but may not be able to approach them or share their difficulties, if they feel that the adults will judge them.

ROLE OF TEACHERS AS COUNSELLORS

In recognising the need for mental health in schools, teachers also need to take the first step towards acknowledging their own role as counsellors. Besides home, students feel most comfortable with teachers. School-going children spend a considerable time in engaging with teachers. Sometimes the same teachers teach them across many classes. Years of familiarity have the potential to breed trust and confidence in sharing thoughts. For this, however, the teacher must define her role as going beyond academic inputs. She must subsume counselling as an integral part of her engagement with students.

Understanding Counselling Processes

For teachers to act as counsellors, they need to develop an understanding of counselling processes. To some extent, pre-service and in-service teacher education courses orient them towards the process of counselling. Here, a brief description of the types of counselling has been presented to familiarise teachers and parents with counselling approaches and techniques for school-going children.

In its simplest explanation, counselling is the process of providing help to someone who is disturbed, facing problems or emotionally distressed. Counselling may extend to personal, academic, emotional and/or familial domains. It may be undertaken at a personal level or with an entire group on a common theme. In both cases, interaction between the counsellor and students has to be based on trust and aimed at gathering insights into the issue at hand. There has to be an acceptance of working together towards a common goal.

Counselling may be directive or non-directive. In directive counselling, the counsellor understands the problem and takes on a dominant role in showing direction or the future course of action to the one seeking help. The counsellor works on the presumption that the person is unable to take a decision due to lack of information or inability to think clearly. An advantage of directive counselling is that the counsellor takes on the dominant role and the counselee only has to follow directions. It is fast and benefits from the maturity and experience of the counsellor. However, a major disadvantage is that the counselee would never be able to work independently of the counsellor. The counselee is presumed to be incapable of taking decisions for himself/herself.

As against the counsellor-centred process of directive counselling, non-directive counselling is counselee-centred. Propounded by Carl Rogers, non-directive counselling focuses on creating an atmosphere in which the counselee feels comfortable and is able to solve his/her problem. The counsellor's role is restricted to creating a level of comfort and allowing the counselee space for free expression of feelings. Through paraphrasing and analysis, the counsellor and counselee together develop new insights about the situation, thereby helping the counselee to arrive at a decision or solution. Here the counselee is able to function independently of the counsellor and is able to take his/her own decisions. However, it is a time consuming process that may not be suitable for younger children.

In general, it is seen that most schools follow an eclectic mix of the two approaches. As has been mentioned in earlier sections, it is advisable to allow students to arrive at their own decisions and the focus should be on providing them appropriate information that would help them to arrive at solutions.

Knowing the Child

In earlier chapters, we have already discussed the importance of understanding the child from his/her world view. We have also addressed the significance of locating the child in the specific social and familial context in which he/she lives and the important role played by the school in building a conducive school environment. Earlier in this chapter the need to be observant for signs that indicate the need for counselling have also been highlighted. Many concerns of children can be solved if the child feels loved and cared for. Where teachers show genuine concern and interest in the well-being of the child, the child also feels comfortable in sharing difficulties with the teacher.

During early childhood, children may face difficulties in social adjustment and adapting to the routine of the school. Differences based on socio-economic class among students also create difficulties in adjusting to peers. At times, some students may require extra help in coping with studies but may be hesitant in expressing the same to teachers where relationships are formal and distant. With young children, teachers have to pay extra attention as this is often the first time that they are away from the care and comfort of their home.

During late childhood, children focus on finding their potential and developing healthy peer relationships. Areas that require counselling include time management, lack of concentration on studies, interpersonal problems with peers and family members, among others. Some children may also be facing serious problems including domestic violence, substance abuse and so on.

Adolescence is first and foremost marked by changes associated with puberty. Adolescents need to be helped in coming to terms with physical and hormonal changes they are experiencing. This stage is also marked by the trials and tribulations in dealing with heterosexual love relationships. There is increasing peer pressure on the children to engage in love relationships and to use the Internet and technological services. Each of these issues has the potential to cause distress and may require support from teachers. This is also a crucial time for adolescents to build their career and make choices. Increasing conflict at home and academic stress are also important aspects that may require personal counselling.

What is important in a student–teacher relationship, throughout the school years, is that teachers should be supportive of students. Students must know that teachers are with them unconditionally and while they disapprove of some of their actions and decisions, they will never disapprove of the students themselves.

Bridging the Home–School Gap

Another significant role of the teacher as a counsellor is in bridging the home–school gap. In the discussion above, we have already discussed that students may need personal counselling in cases of domestic violence and increasing conflict with parents. Practicing teachers also share that young children at times get sandwiched between parents and are often asked to take sides. Increasingly, cases of dysfunctional families are coming to the forefront. These may not only be limited to families undergoing divorce. Children are often witness to everyday fights between parents and grow up in an atmosphere marked by strife and conflict. There is little academic or emotional support provided to children. Where parents are undergoing divorce, children may have to experience custody battles. It is not uncommon for parents to visit children in schools to encourage them to support them in court cases. All of this places a lot of stress on the children. They may turn to teachers for emotional anchoring. It would be unfair to attribute this experience of stress through family strife only to young children. Children of any age group would need support, love and care to deal with the stress associated with family discord.

Families also need to be counselled about issues of relevance to school-going children. Regular counselling sessions and workshops help in filling the gap between home and school. For this, parent–teacher meetings need to be redefined. Besides sharing the academic progress of the child, the meetings need to encourage open discussion between parents and teachers about common concerns related to the child and the school. These are also opportunities for teachers to counsel parents about their engagement with children at home. It ensures that families and schools are working together towards a common purpose and with a common vision.

Seeking Professional Help

The discussion above has highlighted the very important role that teachers have to play as counsellors. It is equally important for teachers to recognise that they will not be able to address each and every problem. At times teachers are too busy to address serious problems that require more than routine discussion. This may be due to paucity of time. At other times, teachers who are genuinely concerned feel helpless as they are unable to help students beyond a point. In such cases, if the students are not referred to professional counsellors, the severity of their problems may increase. It is therefore necessary to ensure that proper help is available at the right time. A fundamental requirement for this is to have counselling services available in school. Availability of a permanent school counsellor provides ease of access. Teachers are able to refer cases of students to the school counsellor as they deem fit. The flip side is that teachers often feel that their work is over once they have referred specific cases to the counsellor. In fact, the school teacher and counsellor need to work in tandem if they wish to make a difference for students. At times they may have to involve the family in the process.

Besides recognising the limitations of teacher training in dealing with specific learning and psychological difficulties, teachers also need to work towards removing the stigma from personal counselling. This has already been discussed earlier. To reiterate, teachers teaching at all levels of school education should make an effort to build a classroom environment where the students feel it is okay to visit the school counsellor when the need arises. Further, parent–teacher meetings should be used as a forum for building a similar mindset in parents through workshops and discussion sessions.

Teachers have to recognise what they should consider as beyond normal. It is okay for any child to be angry, score low or be defiant once in a while. It is only when the behaviour persists over a period of time that the child actually needs to be taken for professional counselling. Similarly, early signs of ADHD, learning difficulties, autism and so on need to be identified. But every child who is seeking the teacher's attention in the class need not be an ADHD case. Incorrect labelling can cause more damage than provide help. Thus, teachers need to be careful before labelling children. Low achievement in terms of marks can be due to multiple reasons, learning difficulties being only one of them. Similarly, it is normal for adolescents and even adults to have suicidal tendencies once in a while. But a person who shows perpetual low moods for several weeks or months needs to seek help. Having said this, it is important that teachers do not hesitate to work with counsellors in dealing with academic, behavioural and psychological problems.

ON A CONCLUDING NOTE

School counselling services extend beyond the school counsellor and also include the teacher as a counsellor. In an average senior secondary school, where hundreds, sometimes over a thousand children study, it is near impossible for the school counsellor to meet the needs of every child. The teacher thus must recognise her role as going beyond teaching and to be inclusive of meeting the emotional and psychological needs of children. Teachers must also be extra careful in identifying signs of any emotional, psychological or academic difficulty that children may be facing and which requires professional support. All of this of course, will only be fruitful if the school recognises its significance in promoting the mental health of children.

Addressing Mental Health Concerns

The first section in the book raised several important concerns about the mental health of school children. The discussion in Chapters 1 to 6 revolved around understanding the psychosocial world of the child. It also highlighted the role of the school in addressing these concerns. The assumption was that the development of self and identity takes place in the matrix of sociocultural factors that are present in the child's world. In this context, there is no denying that family and school act as primary agents of socialisation. The time spent at home and school and the wide range of experiences that children get in these spaces, contribute significantly towards shaping their thoughts, beliefs and values. They also teach children valuable lessons of coping, adjustment and resilience. Peer relations, academics and competition are important aspects that children get exposed to. School and family also help children to identify, develop and further their talents, abilities and interests. This in turn helps to affirm one's sense of self and identity.

It is important here to point out that this argument is not mere rhetoric. A genuine attempt at addressing the mental health needs of children requires taking concrete steps to translate all the ideas that have been discussed in the foregoing chapters into reality.

In the second section, this book aims at presenting practical suggestions to build the school space as a mentally healthy and enriching space for children. Although the focus in this section is on providing indicators towards many different kinds of activities that can be organised in school settings, these suggestions are only indicative, and are meant to lead teachers to think towards building similar activities that suit the specific needs of children in their class and school.

Six of the seven chapters, in this section, address one issue that is of relevance to students in school. These are behavioural problems, addictions and abuse, communication and expression, interpersonal relationships, sexuality and associated concerns, self and identity, and stress and anxiety. While some of these may be more relevant to specific age groups and developmental stages, you would notice that these concerns are relevant to students across different ages in varying forms. Thus, each chapter is relevant for students of all age groups. The final chapter is focused on developing counselling skills in teachers and parents that would help in implementing the suggestions made in the earlier chapters.

Identifying and Managing Behavioural Problems

7

The present chapter addresses the different behavioural problems that are commonly seen in school-going children. Some of these problems are age-related and they tend to go away on their own as the child grows older. However, many of them require focused attention, so that they are managed and prevented from becoming more complex. The chapter begins by discussing some of the common behavioural problems observable in school-going children. Some of these problems are related to specific developmental stages and need to be dealt with accordingly.

UNDERSTANDING BEHAVIOURAL PROBLEMS

Any behaviour of a child that is substantially different from other children of his/her age group, continues for a significant period of time, and has the potential for causing harm to oneself or others, can be termed as a behaviour problem. Here, 'harming self and others' includes but is not restricted to only physical harm. Stress, isolation, emotional abuse and difficulty in social adjustment are also ways in which a child's behaviour can be problematic. Examples of such behaviours are lying, cheating, stealing, hitting, abusing and so on. If left unchecked, these can develop into disorders which require professional treatment. The role of the school and family in identifying and recognising these problems is important but they may not be able to deal with them left to their own devices. Often it is seen that during early childhood parents and teachers are very indulgent and therefore fail to take cognizance of early symptoms of behaviour problems. It is only when children start showing the problem more severely in their behaviour that professional help is sought. An attempt has been made in the subsequent sections to present the typical behaviour problems that children show and ways of dealing with them.

HABIT FORMATION

Developing behavioural habits is a common phenomenon in children. Habits help them to develop social skills and adjust to the world around them. Positive habits such as greeting people, washing hands before and after meals, maintaining personal hygiene, contribute towards living a healthy life. Young children can also be seen engaging in repeated actions that appear to be meaningless to others. Circling an object or a spot, rotating one's head in a circular motion, flapping of arms, chewing pencils and so on are other habits that develop in children. Initially, these habits are ignored as childish play by parents and teachers alike. In most children, these problems tend to disappear on their own as they grow up, and thus may not be a cause for concern. However, in some cases they may be the indicators and signs of larger problems and concerns. Arm flapping, for instance, is commonly seen in children with autism. However, this does not imply that all children with the habit of arm flapping will be autistic. Repeated

Table 7.1   Identifying Behavioural Problems

1	Does your child have a behaviour habit, such as arm flapping, rocking, repeating words and sounds, head banging, which are not observable in other children of his age?
2	Is the behavioural habit persistent and observed frequently? (If yes, keep a record of the frequency of the habit.)
3	Is the behaviour repeated at particular times or at fixed time intervals?
4	Is your child's behaviour disturbing others around him/her?
5	Is the child's behaviour a cause of reduced concentration for the child?
6	Does the child repeat the behaviour under specific conditions?
7	Does the behaviour provide comfort to the child in times of stress or anxiety?
8	Does the child show this behaviour only in some situations or in all situations? If only in some, which are those situations?
9	Does the behaviour come up when the child is with a particular person? If so, who is the person?
10	Is it easy to deal with the child's behaviour when it emerges?

Source: Authors.

behaviour, such as running inside the house aimlessly, chewing pencils and so on may be signs of anxiety and stress. If unchecked, these can result in further psychological complexities. What is important therefore is to carefully observe the child and his/her environment. Table 7.1 contains a list of questions that can help parents and teachers to identify behavioural problems.

The checklist given in Table 7.1 serves the important purpose of identifying and acknowledging the problem. Once identified, it is important to take the child to a counsellor or psychologist to address the issue. A word of caution is required here. Undue visits to the psychologist may create feelings of self-doubt in the child and loss of self-esteem and may lead to social withdrawal, complicating the situation instead of helping to resolve it. New age parenting and increasing access to the Internet has added to the list of parents who tend to see problems in their children where none exist. In other words, caregivers should use available information on popular psychology-based websites or SNS with caution. To reiterate, any of the habits formed at a young age tend to dissipate on their own. A very significant question to ask is if the child's habit is harmful for the child or others around him. An example of such a habit would be of throwing tantrums or hitting people or throwing objects when their wishes are not fulfilled. Children need to learn impulse control and better social adjustment. This can be dome through simple everyday activities.

Teaching Impulse Control

An important aspect of growing up is to learn the norms and codes of conduct of the society in which we live. Both school and home play a vital role in the process of socialisation. A key learning in this context is to control impulses. Infantile desires are often fulfilled by primary caregivers in the best and fastest way possible. As children grow older, they learn that all their demands will not be met immediately. This delay in gratification of needs sometimes results in temper tantrums, crying, screaming and so on during early childhood. At this stage, it is important to provide children with many opportunities to learn impulse control. Impulse control teaches patience and develops an understanding that all needs will not be met immediately and some will not be met at all. These are important lessons in social adjustment and building healthy relationships outside of the home. Parents and teachers thus need to take measures to ensure that this transition from being pampered and cared for, to learning independence is smooth. Some simple suggestions for how impulse control can be developed have been presented in the subsequent paragraphs.

Turn Taking

A lack of impulse control often results in children dominating in games and group activities. This may be because children in the early years are yet to develop abilities of perspective taking and understanding the needs and points of view of others. Further, till the time children are at home, that is, during infancy and early childhood, they spend most of their time in the company of adults. Adults tend to indulge children into making the first choices, setting rules in games and so on. This experience is not repeated when children go out to play with other children of their own age. Several simple steps can be taken to teach children to adjust to their peers.

- *Encouraging children to participate in group games outside of their homes*. This would provide more group experiences and opportunities to adjust to social settings through observation and interaction with children. Care should be taken to restrict adult supervision and interference as far as possible.
- *Organising group activities within the classroom*. Teachers can supervise classroom activities and observe the behaviour of various students. Students who tend to dominate or be submissive can then be checked. Those who dominate can be encouraged to allow everyone to participate. In contrast, submissive students can be encouraged to take greater initiative towards participating in activities.
- *Using indoor board games at home and school*. Popular board games such as carrom, ludo or chess for older children can provide opportunities to children to learn turn taking as these inherently require children to wait for the other/s to finish their turn.
- *Assigning Authorities by Turn*. Children love to be in positions of authority that allow them to make rules that others are required to follow. This adult like behaviour gives them the position of control and can lead to a tendency to dominate over others. Parents can ensure that siblings take turns to set up rules in the games that they play. Similarly, teachers can create situations in the classroom or the playground where each child gets an opportunity to make choices, set rules, take decisions and learn to work with others.

Teaching to Win and Lose Graciously

In a society that values success and achievement, children are bound to learn to focus on winning rather than on the joy of being a part of something. Almost all activities that children engage in have become competitive. Thus the focus is on which painting competition, poetry competition and sports activity has the child won, rather than on the joy of discovering, learning and engaging in new activities. Because of this overemphasis on winning, children tend to feel exceptionally disheartened when they lose at an event. Sibling rivalry and jealousy between peers can come in the way of healthy relationships. Some simple steps provide ways for addressing this concern:

- Parents and teachers must appreciate the efforts of each child who has participated in a competitive activity. Besides announcing the winner, the teachers or the judges should ensure that adequate feedback is provided to every child.
- As many different kinds of activities should be organised at the class, school and/or interschool level, as is possible. The focus should be on providing every child the opportunity to acknowledge and share his/her strengths.
- Efforts should be made to organise at least some non-competitive activities. Children need to be encouraged to not focus on winning but on participating.
- A listening ear and a caring hand go a long way in developing confidence and faith in ones abilities. Children must be repeatedly told through verbal and non-verbal gestures that they are not being judged for their performance. They must feel loved and accepted irrespective of their having won or lost in a competition.

Behaviour Control Strategies

Besides attitudinal adjustments that have been discussed above, children need to learn simple strategies that help them to control their impulses. Counting slowly till twenty before they react strongly to a situation is one such strategy. Moving away from a situation that agitates them and taking a short walk is another simple technique. The basic idea is to divert their attention from what annoys or frustrates them. Likewise, when angry, children can be asked to sit in another room and write their thoughts or record them, in order to vent out their feelings.

Dealing with Anxiety

As has been discussed above, children tend to develop certain behavioural habits as a way of dealing with stress and anxiety. In such cases, it is not just the behavioural habit but the underlying anxiety that needs to be addressed.

Talking It Out

Parents and teachers can set out special time every week, or if required every day, when children can vent out their thoughts and feelings. In school, the class teacher, along with the school counsellor, can build trust in students. The students should feel that teachers are available to discuss their problems and share their feelings. At home, parents need to ensure that they regularly follow the routine of spending exclusive time with children and conversations do not take place only over housework. This will be particularly required in families where both parents are working and have little time for conversation on an everyday basis. When families face conflict or distress, parents will have to put in an extra effort to make children feel comfortable and secure. An important aspect of this exercise is that adults need to restrict themselves only to listen to their children to understand their feelings or point of view. They should not intervene while the child is sharing something or expressing himself/herself. Children should be allowed to speak freely without being told to feel or think differently.

Identifying Patterns

While everyone experiences anxiety, some people are more prone to it than others. Children as well as adults can have a greater than average tendency to experiencing anxiety. This may be due to heredity factors or may be learnt from overanxious parents around them. It would be helpful for teachers and parents to identify situations in which children feel anxious such as public speaking, unexpected changes in routine, meeting new people, changed settings or visiting new places. To help children to deal with their anxieties, located in specific experiences, adults can:

- Talk to children before going out to a new place; apprise them with the routine.
- Explain a backup plan and make children aware of what possibilities have been prepared for.
- Arrange for rehearsals before they are asked to speak on stage.
- Provide many opportunities including both guided as well as independent experiences.

Building Confidence

An important way to deal with anxiety for children is to build confidence in them. This requires the school to provide exposure to a range of different situations and activities. Wider exposure allows children to deal with different situations and feel more confident of their capabilities. Opportunities at school need to be distributed among all the students equally. Teachers experience a lot of pressure to ensure that the school wins in interschool events and that students bring accolades to the school in the public eye. This results in the same children being selected for representing the school in many different activities, denying others a chance. Teachers will have to attempt to know the potential of every student and create opportunities for them. This has already been discussed in the first section of the book.

LYING, STEALING AND CHEATING

Almost all children engage in lying, stealing and cheating at some point or the other. This shows that these are a normal part of growing up. Some part of them may also be learnt through the socialisation process at home and school.

Lying

Children learn to lie both from their parents as well as their peers in school. Isolated incidents of lying can be ignored and need not be seen as cause for concern. Repeated lying, however, must be addressed, particularly with a focus on understanding why children are lying.

Fantasy Cognition

Children engage in fantasy cognition and are fascinated by the imaginary world of fairies and prince and princesses. Being a part of the magical fantasy world is a wondrous experience and children like to engage in role play and converse with imaginary characters. You would see toddlers engage in conversation with people who only they can see. This in itself is not unhealthy, and children tend to outgrow this fantasy world. However, in some cases, the fantasy world tends to overlap with the real world, particularly where the world of make-believe provides more security to children than the real world.

Parents should understand that this imaginative world is a part of growing up experiences. Where the fantasy world starts to interfere with everyday relationships and routines, parents would have to talk to children and help them to make a distinction between the real and the imaginary. An example of this would be a young child who has eaten a whole cake and explains it as being eaten by an imaginary friend, or a young child who spills milk but blames it on a person who nobody else has seen. For this, parents must be open to first listen to children's stories and beliefs, however silly they may sound. As has already been mentioned, if children find greater security in the fantasy world, parents should try to find out the source of their child's anxiety and deal with it.

Nice Boy, Nice Girl Orientation

A major reason why children lie is because of the emphasis that we place on being the ideal child. A child is considered to be 'good' and worthy of being loved when she/he meets the standards that have been set by adults. When they transgress from the norms and rules that they are expected to follow, they tend to lie to save themselves from impending negative consequences. These consequences may not be rooted in reality or past experience. Consider the case of nine year old Manisha.

> Manisha studies in class four. She spends the afternoon playing by herself when her mother takes a short afternoon nap. One day when Manisha was playing, she accidently dropped a box full of biscuits that was on the dining table. She was scared that she would be scolded for having dropped the whole packet and wasting food. She quickly picked up all the biscuits and threw them in the dustbin. Her mother later asked her if she had eaten the whole packet and she swore she hadn't. Her mother didn't believe her but Manisha kept repeating that she hadn't touched the packet and didn't know who ate the biscuits.

In the case above, Manisha feared that she will be scolded or even punished, although she had actually made a genuine mistake. Her lying was only motivated by her intention to be in the good books of her mother. Many children tend to focus on maintaining their Nice Boy or Nice Girl image and resort to lying to save their face. Adults need to reassure them that they are not being judged for their actions and will not be loved less if they deviate from social norms or break rules. This would give them the confidence to honestly share their thoughts and acknowledge their mistakes.

Rewarding Honesty

An important way of preventing lying is by encouraging children to be honest. This can be done by rewarding them for honest behaviour. Simple acts, such as treating them to an ice-cream or allowing them half an hour extra to play, are important means through which children can be encouraged to remain truthful. In the case presented above, Manisha was scared that she would be scolded by her mother. This may or may not have been rooted in a previous experience. Here, her mother can use this opportunity to encourage honesty. She would be required to communicate to Manisha that she would not scold her if she shared that she had committed a mistake. Rather, she would appreciate her honesty.

Removing Fear

Besides rewarding honesty, parents would also need to develop feelings of trust in their children. Relationships need to be based on mutual trust, where parents and children know that they can accept each other even with all the mistakes that either of them makes. Children should not feel afraid of parents. A parent who is verbally and/or physically abusive will not be able to build this trust. A relationship which is based on fear would leave no room for mistakes and scare children into lying.

Stealing

Somewhat less common and more serious than lying is the habit of stealing. During infancy, children are encouraged to share their possessions with others to develop good personal relations and develop friendship bonds. However, as they enter school, they are asked to be careful of their possessions and share them only with those whom they trust will return them. This creates a conflicting situation for children and they occasionally give in to their impulses which may result in stealing something.

Understanding Needs

Children are impulsive and are fascinated by new things. As they move out of their houses and interact with others in school, they try to assimilate everything that they see. Friends indulge in playful comparisons of their possessions and children who do not have as many or as colourful possessions as others around them do often feel inadequate and sometimes even inferior. Adults must understand their needs and feelings. The intention with which they pick up each other's things is not one of stealing but of fulfilling wants. However, this does not justify stealing and so this needs to be communicated to children firmly.

Giving Choices

Parents play an important role in preventing children from indulging in stealing. Middle and upper middle class parents would often notice that children tend to want everything that they see with their friends and try to grab many different things in malls. Parents need to be firm in addressing the needs of children and can ask children to make choices. For instance, when buying a product for children, they can ask children to choose from between the various choices available in terms of styles and colours. They can also develop an attitude of valuing money by giving children a fixed budget in which children can be allowed to choose as many different products as they desire. Using the concept of a fixed pocket money enables decision-making in children and creates a sense of ownership in the material possessions that they take. This allows them to limit their needs and focus on what they have rather than stealing.

Consequences

The above discussion focuses on stealing that is occasional and not intentionally harmful. However, children can sometimes develop the habit of stealing and, if unchecked, can develop kleptomania. This can create serious problems in the long run. To prevent stealing from becoming a regular feature, teachers and parents need to make children aware of the consequences of stealing. For young children, the Nice Boy, Nice Girl orientation discussed earlier is helpful in taking moral decisions. In other words, children can be told that 'good children do not indulge in stealing'. Other consequences in terms of loss of respect, losing friends and legal implications can also be discussed with children. All of this has to be done in a manner that children do not feel accused. A simple way to address this in the classroom is for the teacher to share stories with children. An example of such a story, appropriate for students in primary classes, has been presented below.

Jhumpa, the cat, had recently joined the animal school. She had a beautiful black body and a shiny fur that made her popular with the other students immediately. She was very happy to have adjusted so well to the new school. Lina, the pigeon, and Mili, the ant, were her best friends. The three spent all their time together.

In the past week or so, many students in the class reported having misplaced many of their things. Everyday someone or the other lost an eraser, a pencil, a book or even a ribbon. Thrice in the past week, Mahesh, the elephant, returned to his class to an empty lunch box after the assembly. Everyone in the class was very upset. But they were all good friends and no one wanted to blame anyone. They took permission from their teacher and started taking turns to guard their bags during assembly and lunch time. For a few days, everything was in order. However, one day, their teacher found a crayon box missing from the class supplies. She was very angry. She asked the students to return the box to her privately. But none of the students came forward. The next day, the teacher asked them in class whose duty it was on the day that the box went missing.

It was Jhumpa. The teacher asked her to stand up. Jhumpa started crying and confessed to have taken the box as well as all the other things from her friends. The teacher took her outside the class and asked her why she had done it. She said that her friends had such lovely objects with them, while she only used ordinary objects. She was popular in class and needed to maintain that image. She could not stop herself from stealing. She used to eat Mahesh's lunch since she never carried lunch from home and used to feel hungry.

When they returned to the class, all the students had realised that she was the one who had been stealing from them. Nobody spoke to her and she sat alone in a corner for the rest of the day.

Based on the above story, students can be asked to discuss the following questions:

* Do you think Jhumpa's behaviour was justified? Why do you think she was stealing?
* Could there be any other reason which can justify stealing?
* Do you think she will continue to be popular in class after the students have realised that she steals? What will Lina and Mili do next?
* What should the teacher do next?
* How can Jhumpa be helped to give up her habit of stealing?

Cheating

The number of news reports of cases of cheating in examinations, false admission processes and of forging documents are steadily increasing. While this emphasises the desperation of people to achieve success and the value that is attached to achievement, it also shows that honesty and self-worth are not valued as much as success is. It would be incorrect to presume that the tendency to cheat only develops after children grow up. Young children can be seen to indulge in cheating during group games in order to win. The same gets slowly generalised to tests and examinations.

Valuing Honesty

Quite obviously, the first thing to focus on in children is to build the value of honesty in them. Sessions on life skills development that focus on encouraging honest behaviour can be used to supplement everyday classroom interaction. The following is a conversation between a teacher and student that can be used to discuss the value of honesty.

> Sushant studies in class nine. In his Geography test, he was asked to do map work. The maps were distributed in the class by the teacher and all students were busy doing their work. After a while, Sushant went to the teacher and told her that she had not signed as an invigilator on the map that she had given to him. He had already completed his map work and only wanted her signature before he could submit. She quietly signed the map and kept it along with other submissions. Two days later, the checked maps were returned to the students and Sushant had scored full marks in the same. Sushant could not make eye contact with the teacher. The teacher regularly discussed all students' assignments individually with them and she did so with Sushant as well.
>
> Teacher: *Sushant, you have done very well in your map work. I hope you are happy.*
>
> Sushant only nodded. He kept his eyes on the ground.
>
> Teacher: *I hope you will work hard for your final examinations and perform equally well there as well.*
>
> Sushant: *Ma'am, I will try.*
>
> Teacher: *Do you think map work is difficult?*
>
> Sushant: *It requires regular practice.*
>
> Teacher: *Do you think you could have done this on your own, instead of bringing a map from home and replacing it with the one given to you?*
>
> Sushant was too surprised to react and merely looked at his teacher.

Teacher: *Yes, I saw you exchange the maps but if you wish to give examinations like this, I do not want to impose on you. I am not reporting to the head teacher, nor sharing it in class with your friends. You are free to learn the way you want to. I would have appreciated if you were more honest and had scored less rather than score full marks but through cheating. This means that you have learnt nothing in Geography. Could you not have marked any answer honestly?*

Sushant: *Ma'am, I knew most of the answers but I wanted to get full marks like my other friends do.*

Teacher: *But these full marks don't mean anything. I am giving you the option of giving the test again during lunch break today. You can revise till then and give the test today. If you do not come to the staff room, I will just give you full marks like you have scored. You can return to your seat.*

Sushant quietly returned to his seat.

The discussion questions can be as follows:

- Do you think Sushant's actions were justified? Why did he want to score full marks?
- Have you ever felt tempted to cheat?
- Do you think the teacher's response was appropriate? What should she have done?
- What should Sushant do next?

Presenting Role Models

Another simple way of encouraging children to refrain from cheating is to help them to value honesty, by providing adequate role models. Parents and teachers need to themselves present model behaviour. Children look up to adults to shape their own behaviour. Parents who lie and cheat are likely to observe their children doing the same. Simple acts such as ensuring that the right amount is being paid to the shopkeeper, or not lying to neighbours and bosses, are important in building a foundation in children to learn not to cheat. In addition, stories of people who were honest and successful also need to be shared with children. Further, it needs to be reiterated that it is much more important to be honest than to cheat and be successful.

Behavioural Contracts

If children are found engaging in cheating on a regular basis, it may be because they have developed a habit that is now out of their own control. This can be checked using behavioural contracts. A behavioural contract is a set of terms of behaviour which the person who is signing the contract is expected to follow. It mentions clearly the terms to be met, the rewards that would follow and the consequences that would emerge, if they are not met.

Kapil Singh studies in class ten. He is an intelligent student and usually scores well in his tests. However, lately he has developed the habit of cheating in examinations. He does well in his tests anyway but compulsively cheats, sometimes to countercheck his answers, and at other times to just try and increase his score by half a mark or more. Most of the times, he gets no help from his peers who score less than him anyway. Yet, he cannot stop himself from cheating. His teachers have been complaining and he is scared that his parents will be called to school soon. He has consulted his school counsellor for the same. The following is a behavioural contract drawn up by his school counsellor to help him overcome his habit.

Young Achievers School

New Delhi *09 August 2015*

I, Kapil Singh, promise to not cheat in the next class test of Mathematics. I understand that I will be given two marks extra if I do the paper honestly. However, if I am found cheating in the examination, I will not be allowed to play with my friends in the sports period for the next two weeks.

Signature *Signature*

Kapil Singh *Sushant Kumar*

X B *Counsellor*

A behavioural contract is particularly helpful since it makes children responsible for their own actions as well as their consequences.

TRUANCY

Truancy refers to missing school or classes without appropriate reasons. Often, students may be missing classes without the knowledge of their parents. Truancy is generally noticed in older children. It often starts as a quest to experience the thrill of breaking rules and getting away from the discipline of school life. Stepping away from adult supervision provides freedom that cannot be experienced at home or school. This freedom soon becomes addictive and an easy outlet to the restrictive environment of home and school. Besides academic concerns arising out of missing school, truancy can lead to safety concerns. Usually, truancy provides a sense of independence and makes children more confident in their abilities to face the world. However, at the same ce shutdown time it also leads to undermining the value of schooling and opens up the possibility of defying adults.

Causes of truancy can range from the need to rebel, to disinterest in studies, peer pressure and avoiding punishment at school. Along with the causes, the frequency of truant behaviour and the peer group also needs to be identified. In contemporary times, schools use technology to keep a check on students. Parents are informed through SMS if the child is not present in school. Nevertheless, these efforts are not infallible and truancy is common in middle and secondary school classes.

Creating Free Spaces

One of the major causes of truant behaviour is the imposed restriction that is experienced by children. Curbing freedom can result in children feeling the need to rebel against their parents and school. Although children spend time with their friends at school, most of this time is spent under adult supervision. There is a constant check on students and the kinds of activities that they engage in. Although the nature of the activities that they engage in may not be any different from what they do in school, children would still like to experience the independence of unsupervised time. If free space through post-school engagement with friends is provided on a regular basis, the probability of engaging in truancy may reduce greatly. Parents can take the initiative of driving their children and their friends to a mall, to the movies or to a restaurant and leaving them alone to interact with each other. This ensures that children are safe within the physical space defined by the parents and yet are free from their interference and prying eyes.

Negotiating Spaces and Rules

Another significant reason for truancy is that students have no involvement in the rules that define schooling. This makes them feel disengaged with the schooling process. Further, they feel that school rules have been imposed upon them. The school can create a democratic environment where students are involved in the process of deciding rules and the codes of conduct. Schools that involve student representatives in decision-making have fewer cases of deviation and indiscipline. A writing activity can be organised in senior classes on the following themes:

- Which school rules do you find restrictive and would like to change?
- Do you think students should participate in decision-making in school? In which aspects and why?
- Suggest suitable ways of involving students in school decision-making.
- Would you like the school to be a more free space? How do you think free spaces for student engagement can be created in school?

ON A CONCLUDING NOTE

The chapter discussed the different behavioural problems that are manifested during childhood and adolescence. Most of these problems can easily be managed if identified in time. However, it is important that parents and teachers remain aware about how to identify and manage the problems. It is also significant to recognise that many of these problems are related to specific developmental stages and require a deeper understanding of the life context of students before they can be dealt with.

Dealing with Addiction and Abuse

8

The previous chapter discussed different behavioural habits that develop across developmental stages. Some of these habits develop as early as infancy and early childhood. Some of them are rooted in emotional causes and are best resolved through addressing the identified root causes. In older children, behavioural problems *may* also manifest themselves through addiction and abuse. This will be more evident during late childhood, pre-teens and adolescent years. The present chapter will address these concerns.

UNDERSTANDING ADDICTION AND ABUSE

Addiction and abuse are often taken to be adult afflictions. Contrary to popular belief, addiction and abuse may start during childhood itself. The form and intensity, however, would be different from what it would be in adults. Addictions may manifest themselves through behaviour but can have both physical and psychological causes. Stress, for instance, can result in developing addictions.

Besides personal experiences, the social environment also plays an important role in children developing addictions and abusive tendencies. For instance, children who grow up witnessing domestic violence are likely to believe that abusing is okay. Violence in the neighbourhood, mistreatment of family members, use of profane language, road rage and so on are all social influences that push children towards similar behaviour. Media also contributes significantly to the development of addiction and abuse. For instance, until a few years ago, cigarettes and alcohol were openly advertised and attracted a lot of attention from children, adolescents and young adults.

Likewise, the chief protagonist of many movies and TV serials is often seen indulging in substance abuse. This contributes to the image of what is considered 'cool'. The good man in movies, who presents himself as the social role model, is also seen as being violent and resorting to consuming alcohol, both in times of distress and celebration. Both overt and covert messages are given through this. These are some examples of how media acts as a significant stimulus in drawing children towards addiction and abuse.

In the present chapter, addiction and abuse have been presented as interrelated concepts. Although, in behavioural terms, these are completely different categories, they are both closely intertwined. The tendency to abuse for someone who is an alcoholic is much higher than for someone who is not. In the context of abusive relationships or even self-abuse, being abusive can itself be an addiction. It is in this context that no clear demarcation has been made between abuse and addiction. Each of the sections below focuses on some form of abuse and/or addiction. However, you will see overlaps in the discussions across all the sections. As a beginning point, it is important to identify abuse and addiction. Like it was discussed in the previous chapter, it would be unwise to label any person on the basis of isolated incidents. In other words, experimentation may lead to but need not be an indication of addiction. It may help to ask the following questions in order to identify an addiction:

* Does he/she spend excessive amount of time in engaging in the activity?
* Is this activity distancing him/her from family and/or friends?
* Does keeping him/her away from the activity, even for short durations, make him/her excessively irritated?
* Is his/her activity harmful to him/her or to others around him/her?
* Has the engagement in the activity led to change in his/her behaviour and/or relations with others around him/her?
* Has the activity led to a substantial change in his/her everyday routine?

In secondary and senior secondary classes, students can themselves be asked to think of the various forms of addiction and abuse. A movie screening of a popular Bollywood movie can be organised to facilitate the discussion. Many movies that address adolescents and young adult issues address the issue of addiction and abuse. *Dil, Dosti*, etc. (2007), *Udaan* (2010) and *Dev D* (2009) are some of these movies. Students can, for instance, be asked to watch *Dev D* at home so that they can come prepared for the discussion. Alternatively, the movie screening can be organised in the school premises. The teacher may choose to show excerpts of the movie to save time. A summary of the movie and follow up discussion questions have been presented here.

Dev D, **2009** (Director: Anurag Kashyap, Actors: Abhay Deol, Kalki Koechlin, Mahi Gill)

Summary

The story is an adaptation of the Bengali novel, *Devdas* in contemporary times. The movie begins with Dev having been sent abroad and in a long distance love affair with his childhood friend, Paro. Even on his return to India, the love story never blossoms, because of mutual insecurities and misunderstandings. Paro gets married to someone else. Lost in love, Dev lives the life of a maverick till he meets Leni/Chandramukhi/Chanda. Leni's involvement in an MMS scandal when in school, and her father's subsequent suicide, leads to her social rejection and her entry into the world of prostitution.

Dev's and Chanda's lives eventually intertwine. He also attempts to reunite with Paro, but ends up with a bitter experience. He later struggles to accept Chanda's profession and continues to lead an aimless life. It is after several months of aimlessness, his father's death, a near-death experience and an accident, the realisation dawns on him that he needs to mend his ways. He then decides to go back to Chanda and starts his life afresh.

Themes that can be addressed:

Forms of Abuse depicted:
* Sexual: Involvement with an adolescent and MMS scandal, prostitution
* Physical: Car accident, Suicide
* Emotional: Involvement with a married person
* Substance abuse: Alcohol, Drugs

Discussion questions:

- Was Leni's involvement with an older man incorrect? Would you call it sexual abuse? What does the law state?
- Who was responsible for the MMS scandal? What was the role of peers, parents and school in the case? Who was the victim and who was the perpetrator?
- What would have been the parents' thoughts and emotions during the MMS scandal? Could the father's suicide have been prevented?
- Who is responsible for Leni's eventual acceptance of sex work? What could have been the alternatives for her?
- What were the reasons for Dev's indulgence in substance abuse?
- Was his hit-and-run incident connected to substance abuse? Can you see other ways in which different forms of abuse connect to each other?
- Which of the lead characters in the movie were not involved in any form of abuse?
- Can you think of forms of abuse that you may have seen your friends indulge/engage in?

INTERNET AND SOCIAL NETWORKING

One of the most common forms of addiction in contemporary times is addiction to the Internet. Out of the average time a person spends on the Internet, a substantial time is spent on SNS. While this is true across all age groups, it is particularly true for school-going children and adolescents. Even younger children are now seen spending their time on the Internet. Part of this is because of the nature of home assignments by the school which require them to do Internet searches on different issues. However, more and more children feel the need to be connected to their friends all the time. This can also be addictive. It may also be on account of peer pressure and keeping up with the group.

Monitoring Habits

Foremost in the ways of preventing Internet addiction is to monitor the habits of children. This is most important and equally tricky for adolescents. The web opens up the opportunity for a wide ranging exposure. This need not always have a positive impact on them, however. The basic level of keeping a tab is to regularly check the history settings of the browser and keep privacy settings that restrict content that is inappropriate for children. It may also help for parents to keep the home computers and laptops only in common living spaces. Similar restrictions can be placed on computer servers used by students in school.

With younger children having access to smart phones and laptops, the complexity of keeping tabs on their activities increases. At the same time, adolescents would rightfully want their personal space that will be curtailed by helicopter parents. It is natural for adolescents to want to keep their activities private, even when they are not engaging in inappropriate behaviour. It may be better for parents to engage in frequent discussion with children and adolescents about the various forms of information available on the Internet and how some of it may not be appropriate for their age.

Nevertheless, parents would notice that children are increasingly engaged on the Internet, spending excessive time away from the family. Addiction can be noticed when children start to stay connected all the time and infrequent breaks in access to connectivity cause distress. Online activities can also seem to take precedence over what is happening in the world around them. An example of this is the popular news of a girl who had burglars in her house and chose to write about it on a microblogging website, rather than calling the police.

Acknowledging the Problem

It is firstly important to acknowledge that addiction to the Internet is a problem. Until recently, Internet addiction was unheard of and it is thus increasingly difficult to acknowledge. Working parents encourage their children to play games on laptops and computers so that they remain engaged and do not create disturbance for the elders. This soon converts into an addiction and parents do not realise that it was they who had initiated their children into this state. It is important, thus, for parents to themselves acknowledge and also help their children to recognise the unhealthy habit of Internet addiction. Once the problem has been identified, parents and/or teachers can conduct a simple exercise that would help students to move towards a healthier life.

The exercise can begin by asking children to list the reasons why they find the Internet useful and enjoyable. They can be asked to share the same in the class and listen to what they have learnt from the Internet and how the Internet has made their lives better.

How Internet Has Made My Life Better
I am more aware.
I am in touch with my friends.

Following this, students can be asked to share some of the things that have changed in their lives because of being online.

How Internet Has Changed My Life
I haven't actually met my friends for months.
I spend lesser time with family.
I don't read books anymore.

It is important that the parents or teachers do not pass judgements or force children to write. They should be allowed to comfortably share their experiences. The effort has to be made towards helping children understand the effects that Internet has on their lives rather than dictating what they should or should not be doing.

Setting Time Away from the Internet

In the previous section we had discussed how children need to be urged to accept that they are addicted to the Internet. It is equally important for parents to accept that they themselves may be addicted to the Internet. Many parents have resorted to using emails and SNS as a way of communicating with their children. This builds bonds at one level, but also increases the chances of lessening real time, face to face interaction. Parents are themselves online all the time and are in touch with most of their friends through smart phones and other gadgets. This helps overcome problems of time but also implies lesser offline engagement with the world around them. Being addicted themselves, they are less likely to recognise and acknowledge the same signs in their children. Parents must act as role models and set time aside for themselves and their families. It may be advisable for the family to decide a fixed time every day or every week, when the whole family is disconnected from the Internet and engaged with each other. Family members can also help each other to decide on a set of offline activities that they enjoy and motivate each other to regularly engage in them.

Inform about Harmful Effects

In some cases, teachers and parents may feel the need to inform children about the harmful effects of Internet addiction. Besides its being a distraction from studies, children may be told how this can affect relationships with family and friends. For instance, children can be asked to think of their own experiences on SNS and think of how honest or dishonest they have been in interacting with people. The notion of projecting an image that may not be close to reality also needs to be discussed. A simple activity may involve sharing a copy of a profile on a social networking site, discussing the perceptions that are formed on the basis of the profile and then showing how these can be far from reality. Some of the questions that can be asked are:

- Would you befriend this person on SNS?
- How do you decide who you wish to befriend on the site?
- Would you like to meet the person in reality?
- What perceptions have you formed about the person behind the profile?
- How will you check if the person is being honest?
- Do you see any distinction between online communication and face to face communication? Where are you more expressive? Where do you think your expression is better understood and you understand others' expressions better?

Meeting strangers through SNS seems fascinating as it opens up a world of possibilities of meeting new people and developing friendships from across the world. However, it comes with its own set of dangers. The number of cases reported for being duped by people who teenagers met online for establishing illicit sexual relationships, blackmailing or extorting money is increasing. In addition, the importance of engaging in a variety of different activities also needs to be emphasised.

SUBSTANCE ABUSE/MISUSE

Substance abuse, or substance misuse as it is now popularly called, is a common occurrence among school-going children. The past decade has witnessed an increase in the number of school students engaging in substance misuse as also the lowering of the age at which children start to smoke and use drugs. The phenomenon cuts across class boundaries. Although there are variations in the forms of substance misuse that children engage in, it is not restricted to any particular social class. Another common myth is that addiction to drugs and other forms of substance misuse is restricted to boys. Girls are equally likely to experiment with and become addicted.

Substance misuse is also commonly associated only with drugs such as marijuana, heroin, cocaine, and the like. It, in fact, includes all forms of drug addiction including tobacco and alcohol. School-going children also engage in cheaper forms of substance misuse such as inhaling glue, drinking whiteners or using over-the-counter medicines such as pain relieving balms.

The school and the home have to work together towards recognising the problem and spreading awareness. It is common to hear schools and parents refer to substance misuse as a problem of 'others'. The first step is always to accept that this can be a problem that our children face. Each child is equally capable of indulging in cigarettes, alcohol and drugs, and equally capable of getting over the habit, if he/she gets addicted.

Getting Started

Children and adolescent are likely to engage in substance misuse under peer pressure or even out of curiosity. Particularly where children see their parents or other family members smoking or drinking, they are more likely to engage in the same. This is because, first, they have more access to cigarettes and alcohol at home and can use them in the absence of their parents. Second, they are also likely to think of these as habits that are permissible for adults and therefore cannot be harmful. Having separate standards of judgement for adults and adolescents also acts as a challenge for adolescents. This can in fact become a source of encouragement for some adolescents to try smoking and drinking in their attempt to imitate adultlike behaviour.

The two activities that are discussed below aim at highlighting that substance misuse often starts as an experiment and becomes a habit soon.

The first activity targets children in secondary and senior secondary school. Students can be asked to write a short story or a paragraph on how adolescents start smoking cigarettes. The following format may be used.

Up in a Puff of Smoke*

It was a regular day and I was walking back home with my friends. There was nobody at home today and I could take my time in going back. _____
_____
_____
_____
_____
_____
_____
_____
_____
_____
_____
_____
_____
_____
_____ *I had never thought that I would be an addict!*

*Title taken from a 1970s song by Polly Brown

Students can be asked not to write their names on the story and, if they wish to, they can share their real life experiences through this task. At the end of it, select anonymous stories that can be read out in class or displayed on a notice board for everyone to read. This can serve as a means of sharing the different ways in which cigarette smoking starts and becomes an addiction before they realise it.

The second activity focuses on upper primary and middle school children. The activity is particularly useful for children who may not have encountered substance misuse in their personal lives yet. The purpose is to forewarn them of what situations they may experience and thus prepare them to prevent addiction. The activity may also be conducted with senior classes. The following story can be shared in class.

School was just over and I was walking back home with my friends. One of my friends mentioned that he had learnt how to make smoke rings. I knew he had started smoking a few months back. As we crossed a kiosk, my friends urged him to show them how to do it. We stopped and bought a few cigarettes. We passed them around to each other. I didn't want to smoke. My friends were making fun of me for being a child. It's not that I didn't want to, it's just that I had never smoked earlier and I didn't want to make a fool of myself. I just left for home. I could hear them making fun of me as I walked away.

Once I was out of their sight, I went to a shop and purchased a cigarette. The shop keeper knew me and asked me if I have started smoking at this young age. I didn't reply and just took it home. I waited till my parents had left for their evening walk. Once they had left, I quietly lit the cigarette. I coughed terribly after the first puff. I was wondering why people liked it so much. But I was determined to show my friends that I was not a child. I smoked the entire cigarette but I was tired of coughing in the end. I quickly sprayed some room freshener in case my parents could later on smell the smoke. This soon became a routine for me. I continued with one cigarette a day till I had mastered making smoke rings. I had started liking the taste of it as well. I felt powerful with the cigarette in my hand. Like a hero from the movies. I often stared at myself in the mirror, holding the cigarette in my hand.

A few months later, it was I who was leading a group of friends on our way back from school, teaching them how to make smoke rings. Board examinations were around the corner and I wanted to excel in my studies. I had heard that smoking relieves stress. I started smoking late nights when I used to study for all the entrances. It helped. Initially, I tried to hide it from my parents. But the number of cigarettes that I smoked through the night increased, and my parents soon found out. I didn't care. I had to clear the entrance, and I couldn't do it without cigarettes.

Post activity discussion should also highlight that once substance misuse becomes an addiction, it will be much more difficult to get rid of it. Effects of substance abuse on everyday life also need to be highlighted.

Addiction to Drugs

Drug addiction is less common than tobacco and alcohol consumption. Yet, it is important to address it in school to prevent children from engaging in it. After the activities mentioned above are carried out, the teacher can lead the discussion forward by highlighting how drug addiction is even more danger-ous than smoking and drinking. Depression, academic stress, a troubled family life and socio-economic difficulties, often lead children to develop a sense of meaninglessness. They may turn to drugs to help them cope with this stress, physically as well as emotionally.

Drug addiction is particularly dangerous since addiction to drugs is much faster than to other forms of substance misuse. De-addiction in contrast is much more difficult and slow. While there have been cases of smokers and alcoholics who have given up on the habit with some help from family and friends, drug addiction requires professional help, sometimes requiring addicts to live at de-addiction centres.

Besides affecting the health of the addict severely, it leads to problems in his/her behaviour as well as in social adjustment. With a weak immune system, addicts are more prone to diseases. Using needles to inject drugs also increases the risk of HIV. The strength of drug misuse lies in the sense of calmness it provides through changing one's state of mind. With an altered sense of consciousness, people find an escape from the real world. If one is happy in one's real life, this escape may not be desirable. Schools and homes must actively work towards providing a happy and caring environment that is supportive of the child and adolescent.

Another downside of drug addiction is that it is expensive and thus leads people to steal for gener-ating funds for drugs. It may begin by taking small amounts of cash from parents' wallets. Once the addiction grows stronger and the need for drugs is more frequent, it overpowers one's sense of right or wrong and compels one to steal. There have been many reported cases of students stealing bags and random objects that can be sold for small amounts. The purpose is not to steal but to fulfil their craving for drugs and anything that can yield cash would be appealing. Others resort to drug peddling them-selves so that they can earn enough to fulfil their own needs.

Finally, children must be told about the legal consequences of drug misuse, as well as drug peddling.

PHYSICAL ABUSE

Besides substance misuse, physical abuse is also a major problem encountered during the school years. While school is generally perceived to be a safe space, children often witness accounts of physical violence during their school years. The school may not always be the site of violence and aggression. Home and the neighbourhood at large can also serve as spaces for violent activities.

Violence and aggression can be directed towards both people as well as objects. Children will be influenced not only by witnessing people who hit each other, but also by people who damage property or throw things in a fit of anger. Family and society give subtle messages to children stating that a little bit of violence and aggression is acceptable. For instance, a child can witness a parent scratching the car, or breaking the windshield of a car that has blocked his parking space. Children also witness violence and aggression meted out by family members against each other. Parents and teachers hitting children for instance are an indirect way of telling children that it is okay to be violent when you are in a position of power. Children also learn gender roles when they witness domestic violence.

One of the worst forms of physical abuse is that of sexual abuse. Sexual abuse of children is routinely reported in the newspapers. The real number of incidents of sexual abuse of children may in fact be much higher than those that are reported. Sexual abuse of children can influence their lives several years after they have grown-up. The school must thus make an effort to address it as well.

Anger Management

Besides being told that engaging in violent and aggressive behaviour is incorrect, children also need to be taught anger management. In comparison to adults, young children are less in control of their emotions and thus tend to experience extreme emotions that are detrimental to them as well as others around them. During early childhood, parents tend to give in to their children's temper tantrums which then leads to lesser control for the child over his/her temper. With time, parents need to teach control to children by telling them that their every wish cannot be fulfilled. A young child may, for instance, believe that if he throws things in the supermarket, his parents would buy him what he wants, just to stop him from causing damage to the property and bringing embarrassment to the family.

To teach anger management, a few simple techniques may be taught. Counting till their emotion subsides, drinking a glass of water and so on have already been discussed in Chapter 7. Other techniques that can be used are:

*   Taking a walk away from the source or cause of anger.
*   Engaging in some other activity, such as painting or hitting a punching bag
*   Finding other ways of expressing emotions such as writing or making video journals.
*   Children and parents can take time to review their thoughts and set a time to negotiate and discuss the issue.
*   Schools need to involve children in decision-making and teach children to negotiate with each other, instead of fighting.

Taking the Glamour Out of Movies

Parents and teachers must encourage children to understand that the reel world is not the same as the real world. Children need to understand that heroes on television and cinema encounter different situations that are not rooted in reality and their actions are meant to present larger than life characters and situations. By doing this, children can be encouraged to understand that everything they see, though fascinating and impressive, should not be copied.

Classroom exercises on discussing recent Bollywood movies need to be organised regularly so that children can develop an opinion on what is acceptable and what is not. Schools and parents also together need to develop the culture of ensuring that children watch movies meant for their age group.

Sensitising Parents

An important initiative that schools and neighbourhoods need to take is to sensitise parents towards the dangers of violence. Parents often encourage and provide facilities to their children that lead them to engage in aggressive behaviour. The most common example of this is providing motorised vehicles—two wheelers and four wheelers—to underage children to drive to school and tuitions. While this encourages independence in children, parents need to understand that it is against the law and also a traffic hazard. Schools have also now started creating a separate space where students are allowed to park their two wheelers when they come to school. Often this initiative is taken as part of traffic management outside schools. However, this is both illegal and dangerous for children and for society at large. It is not uncommon to see school-going boys and girls driving two wheelers rashly and often without helmets. The thrill attached to speeding can be dangerous for them. While children themselves need to be sensitised, it is equally important for parents to act responsibly.

The school can initiate a community sensitisation programme in which school children can themselves be motivated to prepare a skit that can be performed during parent–teacher meetings or in the local parks and markets.

Even more dangerous is for parents to give access to children to weapons at home. Incidents of bringing and using knives/guns to school have also been reported in the recent past. Parents, if they need to own weapons, must be extremely careful in ensuring that children do not have access to them.

SEXUAL ABUSE

Another form of abuse is sexual abuse. While many schools focus on talking about sexuality, they seldom talk about sexual abuse. Further, these sessions are restricted to classes with adolescent students. Discussions in class need to be organised around how to prevent sexual abuse. Here, the focus has to be both on understanding the perspective of the perpetrators as well as that of the victims. This is keeping in line with the recent trend of school-going children engaging in abusive behaviour. Discussions should also include dealing with emotions after facing abuse. This would include dealing with guilt, restoring self-confidence and building trustworthy relationships.

School Rules for Prevention

The school must set specific rules for prevention of sexual abuse within the school premises. Some of the practices that schools follow are:

- Have separate washrooms and changing rooms for boys and girls.
- Segregate private spaces for older and younger children. There should be no room for engaging in unsupervised interaction between students from secondary and primary school. This also helps teachers to keep an eye on any suspicious activity.
- Not allow one to one interaction between teachers and students in a closed room.
- Have clear rules for interaction between teachers and students outside of school. Many schools place restriction on interaction between teachers and students over SNS.
- Set up a disciplinary committee and sexual harassment committee for addressing any forms of sexual abuse identified or reported in school.
- Have regular sessions for addressing sexuality-related concerns of school students.

The specific strategies to operationalise each of these will be covered in greater detail in Chapter 10.

SELF-ABUSE

A form of abuse that does not harm others and does not overtly present itself in behaviour is self-abuse. Since it is not harmful to others, it often goes unnoticed and thus unaddressed. Self-abuse can take many forms. These include physically harming oneself to endure pain, indulging in crash diets or taking steroids for body building. Psychological troubles often motivate people to take drastic steps such as cutting their hands. The pain provides them a kind of solace that distracts them from everyday life. This form of abuse is not very common and is rarely seen in school children. Dietary abuse would much more commonly seen. Anorexia and Bulimia are two forms of eating disorders that many children and adolescents fall prey to. Inspired by thin bodies projected by media, children may desire the same kind of bodies and resort to extreme dieting that is unhealthy for them. This can often go unnoticed particularly in school, where teachers can only monitor recess time eating. This is more prevalent among girls. In contrast, boys wish to build muscles in keeping with the Bollywood and Hollywood actors and heroes from different sports. Body building requires a lot of patience and effort. Adolescents may find it simpler to take steroids for temporary gains. A lack of guidance and awareness of the detrimental effects of steroids can lead many of them to focus more on immediate rewards.

Developing Faith in Themselves

A key aspect of helping adolescents to prevent and/or overcome the tendency to be self-abusive, is to help them build faith in themselves. This can be done through a variety of ways that help to provide them with opportunities to find their abilities and strengths. One of the simplest and most effective ways of doing this is to ask them to do a SWOT (Strengths, Weakness, Opportunities and Threats) analysis of themselves. This can be done by asking them to fill out the grid given below. An example has already been filled out in each section.

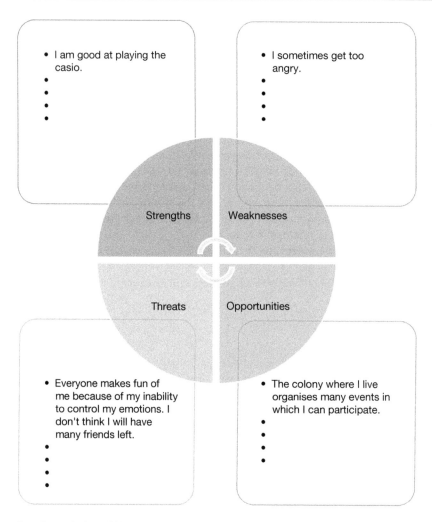

- I am good at playing the casio.
-
-
-
-

- I sometimes get too angry.
-
-
-
-

Strengths   Weaknesses

Threats   Opportunities

- Everyone makes fun of me because of my inability to control my emotions. I don't think I will have many friends left.
-
-
-

- The colony where I live organises many events in which I can participate.
-
-
-

The exercise above helps children to identify their own strengths. Every student would be able to look past their weaknesses and focus on the strengths that they have. A class discussion can also help in discovering new talents and potential in every student. This can help each of them to build confidence in themselves.

Building a Supportive Peer Group

A supportive peer group goes a long way in helping children building confidence. Peers help in reaffirming faith in our abilities even when we have lost faith in ourselves. Developing sensitivity in children helps them to learn to help each other. Children must learn not to bully, tease or make fun of each other when it starts to hurt the other person. They should also learn to appreciate the good qualities of each other. To help them to build this attitude, a list of students can be circulated in class in which each student is required to mention at least two good qualities about each of their peers. In this way, they would be forced to think of positive attributes of each other. Each student can then be given a list of all the attributes that others have mentioned about them. When students get to know of the positive things that others think about them, they will develop better faith in their own abilities.

ON A CONCLUDING NOTE

We have discussed five major forms of abuse and addiction in the present chapter: Internet Addiction, Substance Misuse, Physical Abuse, Sexual Abuse and Self-abuse. Sexuality and related behaviours also present themselves in the form of addictions to sexting and adult literature. This, along with sexual abuse, will be discussed in greater detail in Chapter 10.

It is important to conclude the chapter with a word of caution. Abuses and addictions are more common than they are recognised in the social sphere. Children and adults alike engage in abusive behaviour without acknowledging even to themselves that they are facing difficulties. In such a scenario, it is of utmost importance for the school to provide a listening ear to the children so that they may share the difficulties they are facing in their personal, familial and/or social life.

9 Fostering Expression and Building Healthy Interpersonal Relations

In the beginning of this book, it was highlighted that the mental health of an individual is influenced by both personal as well as social factors. In other words, to promote and conserve mental health, it is important to build strong and healthy social relations. Strong social bonds help to prevent mental ill health. Friendship bonds results in mutual sharing and caring, and serve a cathartic role. A friend listening to your problems may not be able to solve them, but will provide empathy, support and comfort in times of distress. This support goes a long way in helping individuals to cope with stress and deal with conflicts in personal, familial and social spheres. Thus, social bonds perform preventive, promotive, conservative and curative functions.

As a social being, every individual feels the need to interact with others around them. There is a felt need to communicate one's thoughts and feelings and a need to be heard. This is in line with the third stage of social needs mentioned in Maslow's Need Hierarchy theory, already discussed in detail, in the third chapter of this book.

It is through sharing, expressing and communicating that one also develops empathy and the ability to understand the other person's perspective. Empathetic understanding is an important aspect of integrative personal and social adjustment. Being able to voice one's emotions and thoughts requires self-confidence. If one is not accepted for the thoughts he/she has expressed, it can lead to low self-esteem. This in turn can hamper social relations.

The present chapter aims to address both these aspects: need for expression and building social relations. While these are interrelated concepts, the need for expression goes beyond just building interpersonal relations. Recognising this, the two concepts have been discussed separately.

FOSTERING EXPRESSION

This section presents a discussion on fostering the ability to express oneself. Expressing oneself behoves being able to lend voice to one's thoughts and feelings. Expression is important at both the interpersonal as well as intrapersonal levels. At the interpersonal level, fostering expression involves being able to share one's thoughts and feelings with others. Schools most often provide very little time to children to engage with each other in casual conversation and non-academic discussions. Classroom discussions are also often restricted to teacher led, subject-based questioning. Students thus get very little space and opportunities to share what they really think.

At the intrapersonal level, it is important that one's thoughts and feelings are accepted by oneself before they are shared with others. A school and home atmosphere that gives credence to only adult talk and undermines the nature of children's conversations, dismissing them as immature and childish, reinforces the same in children themselves. Children thus start believing that what they 'think' is not important enough to be voiced. This repression of thoughts extends to feelings as well. From a young age, children are taught to exercise impulse control and restrain the expression of their emotions, particularly in social settings. Over a period of time, they learn to keep their feelings in check and try not to express them. From these experiences, the child infers that being emotional is not a good habit. Thus, it is not just expression but also the experience of emotions that is checked. This in turn prevents them from recognizing and accepting their own emotions.

In other words, children learn not only to stop expressing their emotions but also to stop feeling them. This is particularly true in contemporary urban settings, which place excessive emphasis on competition, success and high achievement. The subsections that follow focus on fostering expression at both the interpersonal and intrapersonal levels.

Building Confidence

The first step towards fostering expression is through helping children to build confidence in them. Self-confidence helps children to voice their thoughts, however trivial they may seem. One reason why children feel uncomfortable in expressing themselves is because they do not possess the vocabulary and language skills to express what they feel and/or think. A key focal area would therefore be language abilities.

Opportunities to Perform on Stage

Homes and schools need to look beyond language classes to provide children the opportunities to improve language skills. Some of the ways in which this can be undertaken have been suggested below:

Classroom Presentations

Assignments requiring additional reading and students' presenting them in their own words are some ways of helping them to improve language skills. They can also be asked to present their work in the class, so that they overcome the fear of public speaking. Encouragement needs to be provided for the positive aspects of the presentation. For instance, a child may have good ideas but may lack the language skills to express them. Another student may have the language skills, but not the ideas. It may help to pair both the students and ask them to present the same on stage.

School Assembly

The school assembly serves as an important opportunity. Before venturing into participating in school and interschool competitions, children can be encouraged to present their ideas in the school assembly. The benefit of the school assembly is in the opportunity to address a large crowd without being judged for the performance. Initially, students may be asked to present items that do not require creative work, such as reading out a quote or the news headlines. Once students develop confidence in their speaking skills, they can be encouraged to present their own creative work on stage. Here the school assembly would have to be envisioned beyond the stereotypical ritual of a morning prayer, announcements and the national anthem.

Community Programmes

Home and community can also play an important role in helping children to build confidence in their abilities. Organising functions in the neighbourhood to celebrate festivals or special days such as Children's Day are important ways in which children can be provided the opportunity to showcase their talents. By creating a system of rewarding each child, the society can ensure that every child feels loved, appreciated and encouraged.

The motivation that schools and homes provide by sharing children's creative work is the first step towards encouraging them to have confidence in their abilities to think out-of-the-box and come up with innovative ideas.

Developing Sensitivity

Another important aspect in helping children to build self-confidence is to develop sensitivity. Each child has positive qualities and strengths. How to identify these strengths has been discussed in detail in the previous chapter. However, where peers and/or caregivers are insensitive, some of these strengths go unnoticed. A child, who stutters, for example, may never be encouraged to engage in public speaking. This has two clearly detrimental effects. First, the child would learn to value only fluency of speech and not the thoughts behind the speech difficulties. Second, the child would never develop the confidence to face the public and overcome his/her stutter. In fact, by systematic planning of opportunities much can be achieved. The following steps may be observed:

- Asking the child to communicate his/her work through written tasks, to the teacher.
- Reading out the work to the teacher.
- Reading out the work to a peer or bench partners.
- Reading out the work to the whole class from his/her own seat.
- Reading out in front of the class.
- Presenting creative work in the school assembly.
- Participating in competitions at the interschool level.

This whole exercise would, however, be fruitful only if the other children in the class are supportive. Often in class, children make fun of each other when one child starts to stutter or stammer. Teachers would have to encourage healthy interpersonal relations, so that peers help each other to overcome challenges and difficulties.

Another reason why children who stutter or face other learning difficulties feel uncomfortable in class is because of the teacher's own reactions. Teachers are often in a hurry to finish their course and complete the lesson planned for the class. This leaves them with little time and patience to listen to children who are slow in expression. Even when opportunities are given to speak in class, the time taken by a child who stutters is often too much and so most teachers quickly move on to the next child who is likely to know the answer and will be able to present it faster. This lack of patience is also then transmitted to the students in class.

To build sensitivity, therefore, it is necessary that teachers themselves develop sensitivity and keep a check on any bullying in class. There may be challenges or difficulties that children face that cannot be overcome or solved. Children need to be encouraged to develop acceptance towards these challenges in themselves and others, so that they can together work towards helping each other learn better.

Expressing Oneself through Writing and Art

Not all children will be comfortable with oral expression. Many children prefer the written medium to express their thoughts. Others may prefer to express themselves through art. It would be counterproductive to force children to express themselves in a medium that they are not comfortable with. Thus, equal opportunities for both oral and written expression would have to be created. Similar opportunities would have to be created for art work. Some forums that provide or have the potential to provide such opportunities are discussed below.

Display Boards

One of the simplest avenues is provided by display boards in schools. Wall magazines can easily be created where children's written work can be displayed for all to read. This helps children to build confidence in their writing abilities. It also serves to motivate them to write. Teachers can provide encouragement and directions for the future.

At home, parents can use small display board to put up the work of their children. Seeing their own work on the board, gives children an immense sense of pride and happiness.

Magazines

Another forum through which children's work can be shared is the school magazine. The annual school magazine can be an important platform for children to showcase their work. Students also get opportunities to act as editors for the magazine. However, teacher mentorship is essential for scaffolding the process.

A similar initiative can be taken by the neighbourhood. Parents and/or Residents' Welfare Associations can take the initiative to provide periodic opportunities to submit works for the magazines of the colony. In school or residential spaces where funds are not available, e-magazines may provide a solution. E-magazines require little funding if the designing and editing is undertaken by the school or neighbourhood.

Parents and teachers should also encourage children to submit their works to websites and newspapers that publish children's work.

School Websites and Blogs

Another alternative is provided by the Internet. Schools can set up their own websites and create a students' corner that is periodically updated with latest works of the students.

A simpler alternative may be to create a blog where each students is allowed to create a page and share his/her thoughts or other creative work including stories, poems, articles, paintings and so on, the blogs can be created at the school or even at the class level. The class teacher, for instance, can create a blog to encourage students of his/her class to share their written work.

Improving Public Speaking

As has been discussed earlier, some children may face difficulty not in language but in oral expression. This may be due to poor speaking skills or due to a lack of confidence. Some specific strategies can be suggested to children to help improve public speaking skills.

Peer Pairing

Peer pairing is an effective strategy that has been discussed earlier as well. Through peer pairing, children can also be asked to share their work with each other, give feedback to each other and practice together. This may be done during or after-school hours. Pairs maybe made based on the comfort level of students or on the basis of their residence to ease after-school engagement.

Audio Recording

Students can be encouraged to use simple recorders or even phones, to make audio or video recordings of their presentations. By replaying these recordings, children will be able to identify the portion which they wish to work on, in terms of pronunciation, voice modulation, expression, body language and so on. This exercise can be undertaken by children alone or along with teachers, parents and/or peers.

Facing the Mirror

Children can also be asked to practice speaking in front of the mirror. Repeated practice helps improve eye contact, body language and confidence. Initially, children may face difficulty in speaking without any written reference. Facing the mirror can be distracting. Hence, it would be helpful if children begin by reading exercises and slowly move to spontaneous speech.

Encouraging Emotional Expression

Being expressive is not restricted to sharing thoughts with others. It is equally important to be able to express one's emotions and share feelings with other. Although it is not often acknowledged, identifying and expressing one's feelings is one of the most difficult exercises.

Valuing Friendship

Young children need to be taught to appreciate the valuable role that friends play in their lives. Friends are not merely play mates but also secret keepers and confidantes. Further, it is with friends that one shares joys and sorrows throughout the school years. Children thus need to be encouraged to develop close friendship bonds that are lasting. Parents will have to take the initiative in encouraging play dates and provide children the time to build bonds. A similar relationship can also be developed between siblings.

Self-talk

Children and adolescents can also be encouraged to engage in self-talk. There may be times when they do not feel comfortable in sharing their emotions or thoughts with anyone. Further, in heightened emotional states, it may be difficult for children to express what they are feeling. In such situations, they may feel better in engaging in self-talk.

Self-talk can also be encouraged in children when engaging in SWOT analysis as discussed in the previous chapter. This would enable them to reinstate faith in their own strengths and also help in developing a positive attitude.

Diary Writing

For children who express better through written words, diary writing provides a very good option. The introduction to diary writing can be given by teachers and/or parents. However, they must assure children that their diaries will not be read. When children are asked to share their diary entries, they often end up screening their thoughts and feelings. This defeats the whole purpose of diary writing. Diary writing should in fact be a voluntary exercise that children engage in to write their deepest thoughts. This manner of writing can be cathartic if children know that it is not being judged by anyone. Children can also be told that they are free to share the diary entries that they wish their parents and/or teachers to read.

Teaching Listening

Children also need to be encouraged to listen to each other. The best way to do this is through role modelling. This has already been addressed at the beginning of the chapter. A simple exercise can help children to build listening skills. Children can be asked to sit in pairs. They will first be given a few minutes to think or write about anything new, exciting or novel that they did or felt in the past week. They would then be asked to share it with their pair. The children can be asked to make presentations in pairs to talk about what they have learnt about each other through this exercise. The exercise emphasises the need to listen to the other person. Class teachers can make this exercise a part of zero or class teacher periods on a weekly basis.

INTERPERSONAL RELATIONS

The discussion in the section above focused on encouraging communication and expression with self and others. The focus was on providing opportunities to children to express themselves and improve on their sense of self. In this section, the focus will be on interpersonal communication. Good expression is essential in building strong interpersonal bonds. It is in this context that this section will discuss some of the concerns with reference to interpersonal relations.

Relationships are delicate and experience many ups and downs. Maintaining strong bonds requires actively working towards understanding each other. Communication is the key to developing understanding. Communication is not merely the ability to express oneself; it is also the ability to listen actively. This has already been discussed in Chapter 6. To reiterate briefly, listening actively involves showing empathy towards the speaker and giving him/her one's full attention. The speaker should feel that the listener is paying attention. This can be conveyed through body language and maintaining eye contact. One of the best ways to teach active listening is by role modelling. When teachers and parents take out the time to listen actively to the children, they are teaching them the importance of valuing the other person's perspective and giving credence to their thoughts. This is one of the keys to building strong interpersonal relations with people across age groups. In the subsequent sections, the discussion centres on the possibilities of developing strong peer relations and fostering intergenerational communication.

Strengthening Peer Relations

Strong peer relations are often seen as a threat to their own authority by teachers and parents. Adolescents, in particular, are constantly told to spend less time with their peers and more on their studies. In such a situation, the message that gets conveyed is that friends are distractors and not a suitable influence, since they eat into study time. The reality is very different. Peers are actually the biggest support system. It is easiest to share one's problems with someone who is going through the same life stage, and is therefore likely to be facing similar problems. Even in studies, peers help in concept clarification, discussion, debate and perspective building. They must be perceived in terms of their potential as a collaborative group.

Encouraging Bonds

Keeping the above discussion in mind, teachers and parents should encourage children to build strong interpersonal bonds with their friends. Friends made during the school years can actually be the strongest support throughout life. Having grown-up together, they know each other well and the sheer length of knowing each other presents a strong opportunity for many shared experiences in and out-of-school.

However, teachers and parents will have to be vigilant in identifying the close friends of their children and students. In times of peer conflict and difficulties, parents, teachers or siblings can help children to patch up and make peace with their peers.

As has been mentioned earlier, friends are often seen as being oppositional to parents and teachers. This is a preconceived notion and must be contested. In reality, when parents and teachers approve of their child's/student's friends, there is a visible sense of pride and reassurance that the child feels. Through this, parents also remain in the know of what their child is doing and whom he/she is engaging with.

Ensuring that No Child is Left Alone

Teachers play a very important role in helping children adjust to school. They are the ones who can encourage children to develop friendship bonds and a sense of comradery with every child in the class.

It is important for them to see that no child gets left alone. Biases about dressing sense, personal habits and sometimes even academic performance often lead specific students to be isolated. It is not uncommon to hear a school child remark that he/she will not sit with another because that child doesn't study, talks all the time, copies from others or is untidy in his/her dress. The notion of a 'bad student', often learnt from parents and teachers, leads children to form these ideas and ignore particular students. In turn, the ignored child has a higher likelihood of falling behind in studies. Similar treatment is often meted out to children facing physical challenges and/or learning difficulties. If the teacher develops a spirit of caring and gives support to all the children in her class, the same would percolate to students. They would learn to care for and interact with each other. The fact that adults play a very important role in influencing students' interaction with each other needs to be recognised. Often, teachers build and perpetuate stereotypes and biases by the statements, comments and at times labels and titles that they use for denoting certain children. Other children are quick in picking these up. This may have an adverse impact on how they behave with those children. Teachers thus need to be very vigilant and cautious about this.

Encouraging Out-of-School Interaction

In the section on fostering expression, we have discussed how the school provides little space for informal interaction between friends. Allowing children to return home together, spending extra time after-school in engaging in conversation and ensuring that they engage in activities together are helpful in providing time for informal interaction. For younger children, this may simply translate into parents taking them to the birthday parties of their friends and playing together in the neighbourhood. For adolescents, parents will have to lend greater space at home and outside where they can interact with each other. Joining activity camps and classes together during vacations is another way in which children can be given the space to develop bonds. This allows children to know each other's social contexts, appreciate different lifestyles, family spaces and accept varying cultural settings.

Building Intergenerational Ties

As children grow up, relationships at home are marked by conflict and strife. Parents and children never seem to agree with each other. The two always feel and appear to be at cross purposes with each other, resulting in frequent arguments and little real conversation. The culture and habits that people have been socialised into tend to change with time. The resultant gap in perspectives is even more strongly felt in families where grandparents and adolescents live together. In this section, a series of activities have been suggested that can be conducted in school to help bridge this intergenerational gap. The school would have to play a proactive role in fostering family ties and thereby, maintaining home–school continuity.

Understanding the Other

The first step towards building strong ties is to understand the other person. Most conflicts are a result of children failing to understand the parents' perspective and vice versa. Parents in turn continue to treat adolescents as children and take decisions for them. Children feel the need to participate in decision-making, particularly in areas that concern themselves. Parents, however, tend to ignore them and do not listen to their perspective. Accepting the autonomy strivings of children by parents and teachers is important.

Orienting Parents

One of the ways in which this intergenerational gap can be addressed by the school is through organising and conducting orientation programmes with parents. These can be organised over weekends or during parent–teacher meetings. Parents need to be oriented towards engaging in active listening. This is only possible when they take out time from their everyday schedule to listen to children. Although parents may know more about decision-making owing to their own experience, children need to be given opportunities to express themselves. They would also need to be told the rationale for not taking their suggestions. This is an important lesson for them in learning weighing options and decision-making.

To build communication between families, parents may be encouraged to use technology to stay in touch with children. However, parents would have to be told to interact with children and decide what forms of communication they can have with their children.

Role Play with Role Reversal

An activity that can be organised with parents and children can be 'Role Play with Role Reversal'. This activity can be organised together for parents and children. A topic can be given on which parents and children would have to enact each other's roles. The purpose of this activity is to help them to understand the way in which the other perceives them. This can be followed by a discussion on the possibilities of negotiation and developing guidelines for future interactions. A theme on which this activity can be organised is 'the amount of time spent in interacting on phone'.

If it is felt that parents and children would not be able to work together on the activity, separate sessions of role plays can be organised. A theme can be given on which children will be asked to write and enact a role play. This can be conducted in the class itself. Some of the areas on which role plays can be organised are:

- Surbhi is in class nine. She has been invited to spend the night at her friend's place when her parents are away. All her friends are going but her parents have refused.
- Sunita has just turned 16. She has learnt driving on her brother's car and now wants to take the car to school every day instead of taking the school bus.
- Rajiv is in class twelve. He has joined coaching classes for engineering entrance preparation. After the class, he likes to spend a little time with his friends outside the centre before returning home. His parents think that he is wasting his time and is not studying at all.

Appreciating Others

The next two activities focus on appreciating the lives of others. Parents often feel that children spend their day doing nothing. Children in turn, often lack the appreciation for the efforts put in by their parents. In this context, the first activity involves listing out the tasks that the other does for them. The following formats can be used. Some examples have been filled already.

FOR PARENTS	FOR CHILDREN
What do children do for you?	**What do parents do for you?**
My son makes tea for me in the evening.	My mother cooks for me every day.
My daughter gives me a head massage when I return from work.	My father drives me to my classes and to my friends' place.
My daughter goes to the market to buy things from the grocery store.	My mother helps me in my homework and projects.

Through this activity parents and children learn to appreciate each other and care for each other.

Similarly, in the second activity, parents and children can be asked to describe a day in the lives of the other.

Name: _____

Son/Daughter's Name: _____

Complete the following paragraph writing on behalf of your son or daughter.

DESCRIBE YOUR DAY

I am _____. I study in class _____. I am _____ years old.
I wake up in the morning at 6:00 am on a school day. _____

_____
_____
_____
_____
_____
_____
_____
_____
_____
_____
_____

A similar format can be given to the students for parents.

Name: _____

Father/Mother's Name: _____

Complete the following paragraph writing on behalf of your mother or father.

DESCRIBE YOUR DAY

I am _____ . *I live in* _____ . *I start my day*
at _____
_____
_____
_____
_____
_____
_____
_____
_____
_____
_____
_____
_____

This activity aims at developing a sense of appreciation for the busy lives that each one lives and how it influences family life and interpersonal relations at home.

Celebrating Special Days in School

The school can also take the initiative of celebrating special days. These can be the conventionally popular ones such as Mothers' Day, Fathers' Day or Grandparents' Day. Other specific days can also be specially created and celebrated, like Bonds with the Family Day, Appreciate Senior Citizens Day and so on. Traditionally, celebrating special days involves exchanging cards and gifts or flowers. However, this does little to develop sensitivity towards each other. Further, these are celebrations organised at the individual level rather than as collectives. Some suggestions for alternative ways in which special days can be celebrated in school are presented in the subsequent subsections.

Bulletin Boards

One of the ways to express thoughts and emotions is through bulletin boards. This was also discussed in the section above. To celebrate special day, bulletin boards or a wall of the school can be used for a graffiti competition or for writing slogans. Some other ideas for organising bulletin boards are:

- Making a collage of photographs of parents showcasing their achievements.
- Writing the special moments enjoyed with their parents/grandparents and presenting it on the bulletin board.
- Making a wish list of things they would like to do with their parents.
- Making a list of things that they would like to do in the future that would bring joy to their parents.

Invite Your Parent to School Day

The school teachers can take the initiative to organise a celebration in school in which parents are invited to school and students are asked to introduce their parents to the class. This can be done over several days or one day every week for the whole year. This helps students to develop a sense of pride in their parents while introducing them to class. The teacher can help them to write appreciative introductions. Alternatively, in middle and secondary school, teachers can invite parents to take sessions on specific professions so that they can guide the students of the school. Care should be taken to invite parents from a wide spectrum of professions and across social classes. This can also be organised in groups. For instance, all medicine professionals, across specialisations can be invited together. Similarly, all entrepreneurs, small and large, can be invited together.

Community Sensitisation

Another important aspect is that of community sensitisation. Rather than only celebrating Grandparents' day by making cards and giving to grandparents, students can be asked to organise various activities for their grandparents. Walkathon, *antakshari* and quiz competitions are simple activities that children can organise. Handmade gifts can be distributed to all participating grandparents. Health check-up camps are another initiative that can be undertaken with the support of the school and local hospital.

Going beyond grandparents of student studying in the school, children can be encouraged to prepare street plays that can be performed in the local community centre, markets or residential areas. Posters, placards, pamphlets can be used to develop sensitivity about the needs of senior citizens. These can be used in community awareness walks.

Visits to Centres

Besides celebrating special days, schools and parents can take the initiative of encouraging children to visit old age homes in their local area. Care should be taken that these visits are not restricted to only specific festivals and days. While these are important activities as students undertake the task of decorating old age homes and helping senior citizens to celebrate festivals, they often become token gestures and fail to convert into habits. More routine visits during or after-school hours help children to develop a sense of empathy towards the senior citizens. This encourages closer interaction through everyday exercises of helping them in reading, playing board games with them, accompanying them on walks and so on. Children gain from the wealth of wisdom that senior citizens can provide.

ON A CONCLUDING NOTE

The present chapter focused on fostering expression and building strong interpersonal relationships. Communication and expression help to build self-confidence and support better personal and social adjustment. Reducing intergenerational conflict is also important for helping familial relationships and opening lines of communication between children, parents and grandparents.

10 Sexuality and Related Issues and Concerns

Sexuality has been a very controversial issue over the past two decades. For a long time, policy makers, school authorities and parents have continued to believe that sexuality should not be talked about in schools. This is particularly true in smaller towns and rural parts of India.

Indian society tends to attach morality to all sexuality-related issues. Sex-related crimes are therefore seen in relation to the family honour. In the recent past, many 'honour killings' against inter-caste love and/or marriages in some parts of India have been witnessed. Till date, the term 'sex' and all other ideas, notions, feelings and queries associated with it, are considered taboo subjects in many parts of India. Very few homes and communities permit discussion of issues related to sex. Likewise, homes provide very little or no support to children to deal with puberty and related bodily and psychological changes. So children are left to their own devices to deal with the changes in their life. Girls may be told something about menstruation by their mothers, sisters or aunts, but this too is limited. The hesitation about openly discussing sex-related issues can be seen in media projections as well. For instance, until recently, advertisements for sanitary pads barely mentioned what they were used for!

Not surprisingly, therefore, a society that places restrictions on talking about pubertal changes and sex also opposes sexuality education in schools. Sexuality education was, and still is, by some, understood in the narrow sense of sex education. In fact, sexuality refers to a wider domain that includes an understanding of sex and gender, constructing a gendered identity, understanding our bodies, sexuality-related adolescent issues and alternative sexuality, among other things.

In the present chapter, an attempt has been made to address sexuality and related concerns and suggest possible ways in which these can be addressed in schools. The first section focuses on the key debates that are relevant to sexuality education in schools.

KEY DEBATES IN SEXUALITY EDUCATION

Should Sexuality be Addressed in Schools?

Concerns about sexuality are relevant to every individual. In the paragraphs above, we have discussed how society places a lot of restrictions on discussing sexuality-related concerns. To address these concerns is therefore even more relevant in schools, since children are less likely to receive any guidance from homes. Lack of proper guidance encourages children to look for information elsewhere. Most of them end up with half-baked knowledge that is gathered from the Internet, magazines and from their peers. Some of this information may not be reliable and accurate. This leads to the creation and propagation of myths and misconceptions. If there is no sexuality education programme in schools, children and adolescents will have no place or forum to clarify their misconceptions.

What is the Right Age to Discuss Sexuality?

As has been discussed above, sexuality includes a host of areas that go beyond sexual activity. Children of different age groups would have different sets of issues that need to be addressed. Hence, sexuality education needs to begin early. This is particularly true in light of the rising cases of child sexual abuse being reported. Young children need to be taught the difference between 'good touch' and 'bad touch' to prevent sexual abuse. Older children would need to be spoken to about sexual experimentation and dealing with pubertal changes. Thus, there is no right age to discuss sexuality. In fact, sexuality education can begin during primary school. The issues to be addressed, however, need to change over a period of years. The developmental needs and vulnerabilities of a particular age would be the best indicators of what needs to be discussed.

Does it Address or Generate Curiosity?

Another key question that dominates the debate on whether schools should provide sexuality education is whether it really addresses or generates and incites curiosity. Parents have often objected to sexuality education in schools, since they feel that it will lead to children becoming more curious and excited. However, parents and schools need to acknowledge that curiosity about sexuality is natural and needs to be addressed. So, even if schools don't take it up, curiosity in children will not cease. The danger is that unreliable sources will be tapped, leading to misguided, partial information and several myths and misconceptions.

It is thus advisable that sexuality and related concerns be seen as natural processes that need to be talked about. Children and adolescents require a lot of support and help in dealing with these issues. So, instead of being treated as taboos, these issues need to be addressed with a positive approach and sensitivity. The first step towards this would probably be to convince parents and teachers that these issues need to be addressed.

The subsequent sections will discuss the key issues that need to be addressed as part of sexuality education.

CHILD SEXUAL ABUSE

One of the key issues that need to be addressed as part of sexuality education is child sexual abuse. Statistics by the Ministry of Women and Child Development show that 53 per cent of children face sexual abuse in India (cited by Kumar, Pathak, Kumar, Rastogi and Rastogi 2012). This translates into every second child having faced sexual abuse. Given these statistics, protection of children must be our foremost priority. Child sexual abuse can be categorised into two main categories: where the perpetrator is an adult and where the perpetrator is a minor himself/herself. Children and parents need to be guarded against both these forms of abuse.

Prevention

The school must take a preventive stance towards child sexual abuse. An issue as sensitive as this needs to be addressed by synergetic efforts of the home, school and community. Measures would have to be taken to prevent sexual abuse in schools, as also to generate awareness about the same in parents as well as children.

Parental Awareness

Simple measures can be taken to spread awareness among parents. Some of these have been suggested below:

Organise a Documentary Screening

Documentary screenings can be organised exclusively for parent groups. Popular documentaries that can be used include *Chuppi Todo* (Break the Silence) by Sanjay Singh. Screenings of Aamir Khan's popular show *Satyamev Jayate* can also be organised. It should be noted that mere screening of the documentary is not enough. This must be followed by a discussion between parents and teachers about the issue and finding concrete ways of preventing it.

Seminars and Workshops

NGOs that work in the area of child sexual abuse can be contacted to take special sessions with parents about the issue. These can be in the form of discussion-based seminars or specific workshops that help parents learn the techniques of talking about the issue with their children.

A seminar can also be organised by the school counsellor. If the school does not have a full time counsellor, a few teachers can take the initiative to organise a session for parents. Some of the themes that can be covered are:

- Ensure that your child feels comfortable in talking to you about everything. This prevents the child being threatened or being blackmailed into doing things that he/she does not wish to do, lest he is complained against to the parent.
- Teach your child to differentiate between good and bad touch. This must be done in a sensitive manner. Two- to three-year-old children should be taught to wash their private parts themselves and told not to allow anyone else to touch them.
- Be clear about who the child can trust. Teach the child to not talk to strangers and to never accompany strangers. Ensure that the same person(s) pick up the child from school or other places so that he/she can notice a change in pattern immediately.
- Never force a child to spend time with an older person who he/she is not comfortable with. This should be followed irrespective of how close a relative it may be. Instead, try to talk to the child and find out why he/she does not like the person. In contrast, you may also wish to find out when your child becomes too friendly with an adult, what the reasons for this are.
- Keep a check on the kind of play that children engage in. If you are not supervising their play, talk to them afterwards to know the games that they played and encourage them to share the incidents of their play time. This should be done irrespective of the age of their play mates.
- Observe your child regularly for any change in behaviours. If a cheerful child suddenly becomes withdrawn, try to find out what has led to this change. Ask a lot of questions without being threatening.
- Carefully screen any written material or media that is available at home. Screen the television channels, programmes and songs that children are allowed to watch or listen to.

- Use child locks on televisions and computers to restrict access to content that is inappropriate for their age. Share the same with your relatives or friends who your child is likely to visit.
- Stand up for your child if she/he complains to you about inappropriate touch. The child should know that you are there to defend her/him.

Awareness of School Rules

Parents must be informed about who to contact in case their child complains about sexual abuse in schools. The school's policy and the ways in which the school's committee on sexual abuse can be contacted must be informed to parents. This communicates to parents that the school does not take the issue of protecting children casually and is making every effort to keep their children safe. Further, parents can then share this information with children so that they know whom to contact if they feel threatened.

Documentary screenings and seminars should pave the way for future discussions. Parents and teachers must understand that sexual abuse of children cuts across social classes and gender. The notion 'because I have a boy, I don't need to worry about sexual abuse' needs to be changed. Further, parents also need to be encouraged to teach their children to neither be victims nor perpetrators of abuse.

Precautions at School

Besides making the parents aware of what they can do, the school must take precautions to prevent sexual abuse in school premises.

Sensitising Teachers and Non-teaching Staff

The first step is to sensitise teaching and non-teaching staff. The school must communicate a zero tolerance policy towards sexual abuse to all its employees. They must understand that any such incident should be reported. Teachers must also be sensitised to bring any reported incident to the authorities so that appropriate action can be taken against the perpetrator. Teachers attempting to protect their colleagues and friends should also be warned of disciplinary action.

Building an Environment of Trust

The school should build an environment in which children feel comfortable in sharing any incident of abuse. Teachers should not be authority figures who appear to be distant and unapproachable. Students must be able to contact teachers within the class in a group or individually.

Prefectorial System

If the school has a prefectorial system, the students must be sensitised to keep an eye on the activities of other children in school. Any suspicious behaviour by adults or children seen in school must be reported.

Entrance and Exit to School

The entrance and exit gates of the school must be watched. Any unauthorised entry must be prevented. This can be done by keeping a register at the gate with the watchman and ensuring that every visitor signs it. Timings for visits by parents and opening and closing of gates can be fixed.

The school guards must also be encouraged to keep an eye on who the child leaves the school with. Any suspicious person must be stopped and reported to the teachers or school authorities. The class teachers of students in junior classes should keep a tab on who comes to pick up children from school. This is particularly true for schools in urban areas where parents have to depend on private vans for transportation. If possible, the school should issue i-cards to van drivers who are allowed to enter the school premises.

If the school provides school buses, there must be a teacher or a woman employee accompanying children at all points, till the last child is dropped home. The bus routes and timings must be clearly communicated to the parents. A verification check of all bus drivers and attendants who are school employees must be carried out.

Setting Up Rules

Some rules can be made that would prevent child sexual abuse within the school premises. For instance, clear demarcation between spaces that are utilised by older and younger children can be made to prevent any unsupervised interaction. Washrooms and changing rooms for girls and boys and older and younger children should be built separately to prevent inappropriate interaction.

Teachers should not be allowed to engage with children individually in isolation. Class rooms and staff rooms should suffice for spaces for interaction. When children wish to have personal conversations with teachers or the school counsellors, attempts should be made to have these conversations in open spaces rather than closed rooms.

Students and teachers must be clearly told that assessment does not depend on personal equations between students and teachers but on the basis of the students' academic performance. Teachers should be accountable for the assessment they submit to the school.

Helping Children to Cope

Prevention is of course the first step to addressing sexual abuse. However, helping children to cope with the trauma of having been abused is also an important aspect of dealing with abuse. In the first section of this book, we had shared the story of Sohaila Abdulala. The story highlights how social and familial support goes a long way in helping people deal with trauma and anxiety and move on in life. The subsequent sections discuss some aspects that help build a supportive environment for victims of abuse.

Protecting Privacy

When children report or share incidents of sexual abuse within or outside the school premises, care must be taken to protect the privacy of the child from all. Only the teachers who need to address the child directly should be told about the incident, so that the child can be dealt with sensitively. As far as possible, other children should not be told about the identity of the child so that further harassment, insensitive conversation or unfair treatment can be prevented.

Dealing with Guilt

The child must be assured that it is not his/her fault that the incident took place. As far as possible, comfort should be provided to the child. The child must be assured that he/she would not have to face the perpetrator again. The school counsellor and teachers who the child is close to should be available to the child whenever he/she needs to talk. Every effort should be made to ensure that the child continues with the school regularly. If required, a few of the child's friends can be taken into confidence to help the child cope. For a few days, the child should not be left alone. Parents, teachers and any other person close to the child should be warned to not repeat conversations or questions about the incident unnecessarily, as this can be traumatic for the child. No question should ever make the child feel that he/she did something that brought the incident on to the child.

Removing Stigma

Another key aspect in helping children cope with sexual abuse is through removing stigma. This needs to be undertaken at home, school and community level. School-going children have the power to change the society and its attitude towards sexual crimes. The notion that honour and respect of the person is lost when he/she is sexually abused must be challenged. Children should be taught that the victim is deeply wounded and needs comfort. He/she should not be ostracised or treated with a sense of curiosity and wonder. They deserve to be treated fairly and with sensitivity. Children should be encouraged to help the victims of sexual abuse to recover quickly.

Children do not learn discrimination till the time they are taught the same by their families or society at large. If the school takes the initiative, children can be encouraged to develop sensitivity in others around them. Community awareness programmes through street plays, putting up posters and so on can be initiated. Students of the senior secondary school can also be encouraged to take a stand when they see someone being abused or being treated unfairly by society for having faced abuse earlier.

SEXUAL EXPERIMENTATION

The above section discussed how sexual abuse can be prevented in school-going children. We highlighted that sexual abuse can be perpetrated by adults or underage children themselves. In this section, we will specifically focus on sexual activity in school-going children. While intentional sexual abuse among underage children cannot be ruled out, much of sexual abuse between underage children can be because of sexual experimentation by school-going children.

Sexual experimentation involves engaging in any form of sexual activity that may be undertaken to fulfil curiosity, mostly seen in pubertal and post-pubertal children. Many children engage in sexual behaviour that may not be appropriate for their age. This may be a result of having experienced child sexual abuse themselves or age inappropriate exposure to media. The need to imitate what they have seen is also a reason that explains why children might engage in experimentation.

Sexual experimentation can be engaged in by children with others of their own age or younger children. Incidents of older children engaging in the sexual abuse of younger children are no longer uncommon. The complexity of situations where children are engaging in sexual abuse increases manifold because underage children lack the maturity to understand the consequences of their actions. This is even more so in the case of consenting minors of the same or opposite gender, where, sometimes, the responsibility of the event cannot be ascribed to any of the two. Further, sometimes children are ignorant of the sexual nature of the activities that they are engaging in. They often report complex feelings related to incidents of sexual abuse and sexual experimentation. In the case of sexual experimentation, they may feel pleasure sensations but may end up with an unpleasant experience. This leaves them with confused feelings. This complexity cannot be dealt with by the children alone. Through adult support, they can be helped to deal with the complexity by learning what is appropriate or inappropriate and the underlying rationale for the same. This would help them in their future behaviour and choices.

Besides conducting sexuality education sessions in general, some specific aspects that must be discussed with children on matters of sexuality are presented in the text that follows.

Learning to Say No

Children must be given assertive training to teach them to express displeasure when they wish to. Saying 'No' goes a long way in preventing sexual abuse. At the same time, saying no is also important to resist involvement in sexual experimentation. All children and adolescents must have the confidence to stand up for themselves. Particularly in the face of peer pressure to engage in sexual experimentation, they should be able to say 'no'. Peers, for instance, may decide to watch pornographic videos together. Sexual experimentation includes asking each other to remove clothes or engage in inappropriate touching. Often these incidents may not be termed as sexual abuse. For instance, teenagers may generally greet each other by hugging each other. This casual gesture can take sexual connotations when done with sexual intentions. A child who feels uncomfortable in such a hug may not be able to say so for fear of being rejected or rebuked by his/her peers. It is thus important that children be taught how to deal with such scenarios. The idea that friendship is more meaningful when there is mutual respect for each other, and acceptance of each individual's values and space, must be discussed. The problems that result from blind conformity to the peer group should also be discussed.

Learning to Accept 'No'

Equally important as saying 'no' is accepting 'no' as an answer given by others. The idea that one should not force someone else to do things just because one thinks that it is fun has to be taught early. Many young boys in our country and around the world are socialised into believing that saying no to them is a way of insulting them. Having their way with everyone is seen as a mark of authority. When others say no to them, they feel a loss of power and control over others and get agitated about this. Many sex-related crimes, even beyond childhood and adolescence, are because of the lack of acceptance of the other person's right to say no.

Peer subcultures demand compliance by all members to what may be called the peer group norms and standards. Any deviation from them is seen as breaking the code of friendship and is frowned upon. Generally children's closest friends are drawn from their peer group. They thus need to learn that friendship does not mean that a person cannot have his/her own views, ideas and beliefs, while being a member of a peer group. In fact, the closest form of friendship is when friends accept each other unconditionally. They can be part of a group without blindly participating in all the group's activities. The freedom and space to differ are very much part of true friendship.

A simple class discussion may suffice to build this sensitivity and understanding in children. They can also be asked to share instances when they were compelled to do something that they did not wish to do, but were forced to do it by their friends. The following story may be used in middle and senior school.

Shumayla is in class nine. She is part of a close knit group of six friends, others being Deepak, Rachel, Monica, Jasbir and Sohail. The six are almost always together in the school. They live close to each other and spend many afternoons in one or the other's home.

One day, during summer vacations, they had all gathered at Deepak's place. A recent Bollywood movie had just released and he had downloaded it on his computer. He always downloaded movies and the six of them would often watch them on his laptop. Everyone kept asking him which movie he had downloaded this time, and he refused to share its name. He played it on his laptop and the jokes soon died down. Everyone waited for the name to be displayed. As soon as it happened, Shumayla quickly got up and turned the movie off. She said that it is an adult movie and their parents did not want them to watch it. Deepak had a different opinion. He said they were all grown-up enough and it didn't hurt to watch a movie. He told her to sit down and watch the movie. A huge argument followed. Monica supported Shumayla. Deepak and Jasbir by then had lost their cool. They told Monica and Shumayla to leave if they wanted to. As the two got up to leave, Deepak told them that they cannot leave and should just sit and watch the movie instead of behaving like babies. But they decided to leave anyway. Rachel joined them. She said that she was not comfortable in watching an adult movie when there was no other girl. This made Sohail very angry. He said that the six of them are so comfortable with each other, gender had never been a problem and they shared everything about their lives with each other. He asked why had that become a girls versus boys issue? The three girls left anyway. The boys were all upset and ended up not watching the movie.

Next day they all met in school but nobody was talking to each other properly.

This story can be followed by a set of questions to aid discussion:

- Whose opinion do you agree with and why?
- Should Deepak have forced Shumayla to watch the movie? What should the group have done?
- Why was Deepak so upset when the girls wanted to leave?
- Is Sohail justified in his anger?
- How would this incident have changed their friendship?
- Should they have seen the movie together? Is it common for students of their age group to watch adult movies together?

The discussion in class should focus on healthy friendships between boys and girls and how friendship means respecting the other person's perspective. The teacher should first allow students to share their views and arrive at a consensus themselves. Her approach should not be didactic or moralistic.

Accepting Heterogeneity

Another aspect that is commonly discussed among students and is a taboo in social settings is alternative sexuality. Effeminate boys and masculine girls are often joked about. Children continually ridicule boys who are feminine in their mannerisms. Stereotypical images of what men and women should be like have contributed to this black and white notion of gender. Academics have long since woken up to a more fluid construction of gender identity. Yet, this has not become part of the popular culture or belief system. Effeminate men are still shown as homosexuals in popular media projections. Taking cue from the same, students continue to tease some boys in their class or school, often calling them derogatory names. Research shows that these boys are also more prone to sex abuse. Schools also promote these stereotypes by not giving certain options such as home science, psychology and so on, in higher classes to boys. Although this trend is slowly changing, the number of boys in these streams is far less than those in other streams. A reverse trend is visible in non-medical sciences and commerce, where boys tend to dominate.

Some teachers may reprimand students when they tease a boy in class. However, merely reprimanding students does not contribute to changing their attitudes and perceptions. Individual children with different sexual preferences and behaviours than others from their own gender tend to face difficulties in accepting their own identity. They have feelings of bewilderment and awkwardness about themselves. They may require counselling and support in accepting themselves and firming up their sense of identity. Likewise, others around them, particularly their peers, have to be sensitised to their alternative sense of identity. For this, class sessions that discuss the LGBTQ (Lesbian, Gay, Bisexual, Transgender and Queer) Movement can be held. Newspaper articles and biographies of people who are otherwise successful but marginalised by society for their sexual identity can be shared in the class and discussed. All discussions on this issue should be free of moral judgements. In fact, they should be held in a relaxed manner that permits free expression, so that children do not shy away from voicing what they truly believe in. Myths and misconceptions such as homosexuality being unnatural, transgenders being peculiar human beings and so on should be openly discussed and clarified.

Sexting and Pornography

Sexting, and watching and reading pornography have also become fairly common. This is particularly true for adolescents and young adults. Chatting over the Internet and phone are slowly being replaced by sharing sexually explicit messages and photographs or selfies, through the telephone and the Internet. Most youngsters find it as normal as chatting. While this phenomenon has been documented more in the western world, it is equally widespread in India as well.

Pornography and addiction to watching it are commonly believed to be problems that are faced by adults. However, it is fairly widespread among school students as well, particularly during their adolescence. In a culture where discussion on sexuality is generally avoided, adolescents resort to vicarious knowledge and draw from pornographic literature and films to satiate their sense of curiosity and wonder. Watching pornography has become more common since it is easily accessible through the Internet. In almost all urban homes, adolescents have access to the Internet through phones, laptops and/or cyber cafes. This ease of access may also be a contributory factor to increasing addiction to pornography. With little restriction, the urge to control what will be a pleasurable experience would be difficult to resist. The following is an excerpt from an article on adolescents' engagement with pornography.

ADOLESCENT ADDICTION: WHEN PORNOGRAPHY STRIKES EARLY

Sarah Israelsen-Hartley (Jan 1, 2014)

WALES, Utah—Justin was 11 when he first saw pornography. He'd been looking for remote-controlled cars and found a cool YouTube video showing one making a huge jump.

He watched it repeatedly on his home computer, trying to ignore the sketchy video suggestions popping up on the side. But when his friend showed him the pornographic website those sketchy videos brought up, he was instantly hooked.

'At that moment, I wanted more', said the 18-year-old Justin, which is not his real name. 'I looked up more. It was a constant need. I had no idea what it was. I was never happy with what I found. Even if it met my sexual preference, it didn't make me happy. I (just started) clicking and clicking and clicking and never stopped'.

He's been struggling for years. He is just hoping he can stay in his latest inpatient facility in central Utah long enough to make some real changes.

'The urge to stop has been there for two to three years in treatment', he says. 'It just hasn't reached the point where it's strong enough to overcome the temptation'.

Justin is just one in a growing body of teenagers who find themselves unable to function because of an increasing appetite for pornography—which was often first found during an innocent Web search on a home computer. Experts say the age of first exposure is continuing to fall and is currently around 11 or 12 years old.

Not every adolescent who struggles with pornography will need something as drastic as a stay in an inpatient treatment center, and even if they did, the huge price tag is prohibitive for many.

For other teens, the struggle is still so private and hidden that the thought of opening up and asking for help is an impossible obstacle.

The complete article can be accessed at : http://national.deseretnews.com/article/802/
Adolescent-addiction-When-pornography-strikes-early.html

Although the article is not drawn from the Indian context, we must accept that a large number of adolescents in India are also engaging with pornographic websites. Rehabilitation facilities may not be available in India and like the article mentions, may not be required by most adolescents. However, many adolescents would have a number of questions, queries and experiences which they would like to discuss. This article can in fact be used as a starting point to initiate discussion with adolescents on the issue of viewing pornography. If a class discussion does not seem feasible, the teacher can encourage students to discuss the article in groups or pairs. A full class discussion would benefit all the students. Students can be asked if they know of anyone who has had similar experiences so that they may share their own experiences anonymously. The harmful effects of viewing pornography and sexting can also be discussed in class.

Violence and Media

Primarily, the purpose of pornography is recreational. However, it is common knowledge that many of the actors who work in the pornography industry do so out of coercion rather than out of their own will.

While some actors in the international scene have openly accepted that this was their career choice, this is more an exception than the norm in the Indian context. The sociocultural values and morality with which we are socialised give no space for sexual entertainment. Yet the industry continues to thrive. This, despite the fact that production, distribution and possession of pornographic material is a punishable offence in India. Like the sex workers, actors in pornographic movies in India do it out of social and/or economic compulsions. This is particularly true for those involved in child pornography. Children are often unaware of the consequences of the activities that they are involved in. The students in schools are often unaware and/or tend to ignore this social backdrop within which pornography flourishes.

The recent ban on pornographic sites in our country was followed by debates in the media. The biggest argument is whether the court and/or the government has the right to act as a moral police on the citizens. Should citizens not have the right to make their own choices? The most prominent argument against pornography is the linkage established between watching pornography and engaging in sexual crimes. These debates have been addressed by many researchers as well as journalists. The following blog article can serve to start a discussion on the debate.

DEFENDING THE RIGHT TO WATCH VIOLENT PORN—HOW CAN THAT BE JUSTICE FOR APRIL JONES?

Mari Marcel Thekaekara

Did the Catholic priests who abused kids watch porn? Possibly not. Did dominant caste village men who rape Dalit women watch porn? I don't know. They didn't 40 years ago for sure. But does this prove something? I should not shoot my mouth off about things I don't really understand.

This much I do understand though. Porn has a lot to do with sexual violence. Reading about the abduction, abuse and murder of the five-year old April Jones in a recently published book by her parents Coral and Paul, it seems to me that there is a lesson we are determined to avoid.

By his own admission, pedophile killer Mark Bridger viewed explicit images of children being sexually abused hours before he kidnapped April from a street in the quiet Welsh town in which she lived. Other convicted pedophiles admit having done the same—their seized computers revealing this truth to police.

The pedophiles who raped a three-year-old girl in Delhi, after the infamous Nirbhaya rape of 13 December 2013, admitted to watching violent porn on their phones before shoving a bottle up the child's vagina. It's about power, frustration and violence. But they got the idea from the porn on their phones. Fifty years ago, men here did not know about violent porn. Children were safer.

Source: http://newint.org/blog/2015/04/10/porn-child-abuse/#sthash.7H0BuPAA.dpuf

---

During the discussion, the teacher should ensure that the students in the class do not feel judged for their activities. Further, the discussion should revolve around issues of making choices and taking responsibility for their actions, rather than only on the specific issue of sexual crime.

The above discussion would be suitable for all classes in secondary and senior secondary school. In senior secondary classes, teachers can also organise a debate in class about the notions of freedom and liberty and their interface with security concerns.

In younger classes, at the middle school level, debates and discussions may revolve around how Bollywood popularises a hero who eve teases. Popular Bollywood songs can also be used to analyse objectification of people and glorification of crimes. The following diary entry may also be used for initiating a discussion. Rajiv is a 17-year-old boy convicted for raping a young girl. His narration of the day is presented below:

I usually sleep late. By the time I wake up, my parents have already left for work. I am all alone in the house. I woke up late on that day as well. One of my friends called and we decided to watch some movies together. He brought them on his pen drive. His pen drive was full of adult films. We saw two or three of them. One of them showed a man behaving very violently with a woman. She seemed to be enjoying. I remember asking my friend how she enjoys being hurt. He was too busy watching the film to reply. He left after some time. I was all alone. One of my neighbour's daughter wanted some help with her homework. I asked her to come to my home. This was a routine thing. While explaining her homework, I started touching her. She didn't say anything for a while. I thought she must be enjoying. I was surprised that she could enjoy this even though she was only 10 years old. But she resisted when I tried to remove her clothes. I thought she wanted me to be aggressive. Like in the movie…

The following discussion questions may be used:

– Do you think what Rajiv did was natural?
– Do you think it was right for the court to send him to jail?
– What is his future after he is released from prison?
– How can we prevent young children and adolescents from watching adult films? Should we be stopping them?
– If you know of a friend who engages with adults media in print or video forms, what would you do?

SEXUALITY EDUCATION

Adolescents are full of energy. At the life stage that brings to them many new experiences and changes, they feel the need to explore and find their own identity. Many activities that they engage in as children do not interest them any longer. They are constantly looking for fresh avenues and exploring possibilities.

Puberty brings with it many overt and covert physical changes. Understanding their own bodies and the changes that they are experiencing is an important part of growing up. The school can take the initiative to organise seminars and workshops with students that go beyond just sex education. As has been discussed at the beginning of the chapter, sexuality education sessions need to start from primary school. The themes that need to be addressed across different classes have been presented in the table:

Primary School	Know Your Body
	– Digestive system
	– Excretory system
	– External parts

(Continued)

(Continued)

Primary School	**Respecting Your Body** – Maintaining privacy – How are boys and girls different? – Good touch, bad touch **Staying Safe** – Accompanying parents/teachers – Staying away from strangers – Child helpline and police numbers: 1098 and 100 **Sharing** – Who to contact when in trouble in school? – Do not hesitate to tell parents and/or teachers about being hurt
Middle School	**Puberty** – Understanding bodily changes in boys and girls – Support one another through the changes **Media** – Which role models to follow? – Developing healthy friendships between boys and girls is possible. **Breaking Silence** – Must stop being abused – Support one another and share with adults
Secondary School	**Reproduction** – Pregnancy requires more than physical readiness – Valuing relationships – Social values and marriage – Understanding gender roles and stereotypes **Experimentation** – How far is too far? – Is it okay if I feel the need to be sexually active? – Channellising energy to engage in other activities
Senior Secondary School	**Acting Responsible** – What can I do to prevent sexual crimes? – What can I do to stop my friend from becoming a victim or perpetrator? **Making Choices** – What will be the consequences if I am sexually active now? – Are there any consequences of pregnancy for boys? **Respecting Others** – Learning to deal with peer pressure – Understanding alternative sexuality

ON A CONCLUDING NOTE

The chapter focused on addressing issues related to sexuality and how they can be dealt with in the school. It is quite evident that the school and home have to work together to help children and adolescents deal with issues of sexuality. An important aspect to be recognised is that children and adolescents need to understand sexuality in both its physical as well as emotional terms. Further, it is by teaching respect for the opposite gender that children would learn to prevent being both victims as well as perpetrators.

11

Development of Self and Identity

The focus of this book has been on understanding the mental health concerns of school-going children and adolescents. Against the theoretical backdrop that was developed in the first section of the book, the second section addressed specific mental health concerns that are relevant to school-going children. Building confidence, faith in one's abilities and a positive sense of self have been recurring themes throughout the activities discussed. All of them contribute towards the development of self and identity.

Self and identity are often seen as synonyms and are used interchangeably. In the third chapter of this book, the process of identity development was discussed with reference to Erikson's work. To reiterate briefly, ego identity in Eriksonian terms refers to a sense of 'inner sameness and continuity' over a period of time. This sense must also be perceived by the significant others around the person. Here, focus is on developing an understanding of the individual as a composite whole. All activities and experiences of the individual contribute towards developing a sense of identity. The social context thus plays a significant role in this process. Bronfenbrenner's ecological approach has contributed to this understanding by explaining how the development of self of an individual takes place, in terms of its relation to the micro and macro contexts in which he/she lives and functions.

Self and Identity are often used synonymously. The reality is that while they are not synonymous, they are highly interwoven and draw extensively from each other. Self has more personal experiential dimensions which no doubt unfold in the sociocultural matrix in which the individual is situated, but these do not limit or completely determine what the individual feels about himself/herself. Further, self is influenced by the past experiences of the individual, those that are unfolding in the present and those which the individual envisions for himself/herself in the future. Dreams, goals and aspirations are an important part of self. Emotions, feelings and sentiments are important construals of the self. Thus, significant persons in an individual's life like his/her parents, teachers and friends and the nature of relations that the individual has with them become very important in the development of himself/herself. Identity, although inextricably interwoven with self, may be seen to have stronger social features and components that define a person. Everyone has a social identity (Jenkins 2008). This comes from the sociocultural context into which we are born. Personal experiences that unfold in this sociocultural context also give the individual a sense of personal identity. Identity is thus personal and social.

The debate on 'self' and 'identity' with clear definitions of them continues and is far from being resolved. Academic and populist literature thus continue to use the two terms either interchangeably or in the sense that holds meaning to the specific work. The present chapter focuses on developing attitudes and activities that can help to develop a healthy sense of self. The focus is more on the child rather than the technical differences and similarities between the two terms. The discussions in the sections that follow present the different personal and social factors that influence the development of identity. Taking cue from the works of identity theorists, it would be prudent to use these activities for children in the pre-adolescent and adolescent years.

UNDERSTANDING MYSELF

The present section focuses on helping children understand themselves. The activities in this section focus on helping children answer the Eriksonian question: 'Who am I?'. The main idea subsumed under this question is that in order to find a suitable answer, adolescents need to focus on understanding themselves through deeper reflection about their lives. Schools and home can provide opportunities to them for this. They can promote self-reflection in adolescents that would enable them to develop faith in themselves.

Perceptions about Self

The first step is to understand how one perceives himself/herself. A simple activity can be conducted to help adolescents to develop an understanding of this. Older, more expressive children can simply be asked to describe themselves (Figure 11.1).

Figure 11.1   Who am I?

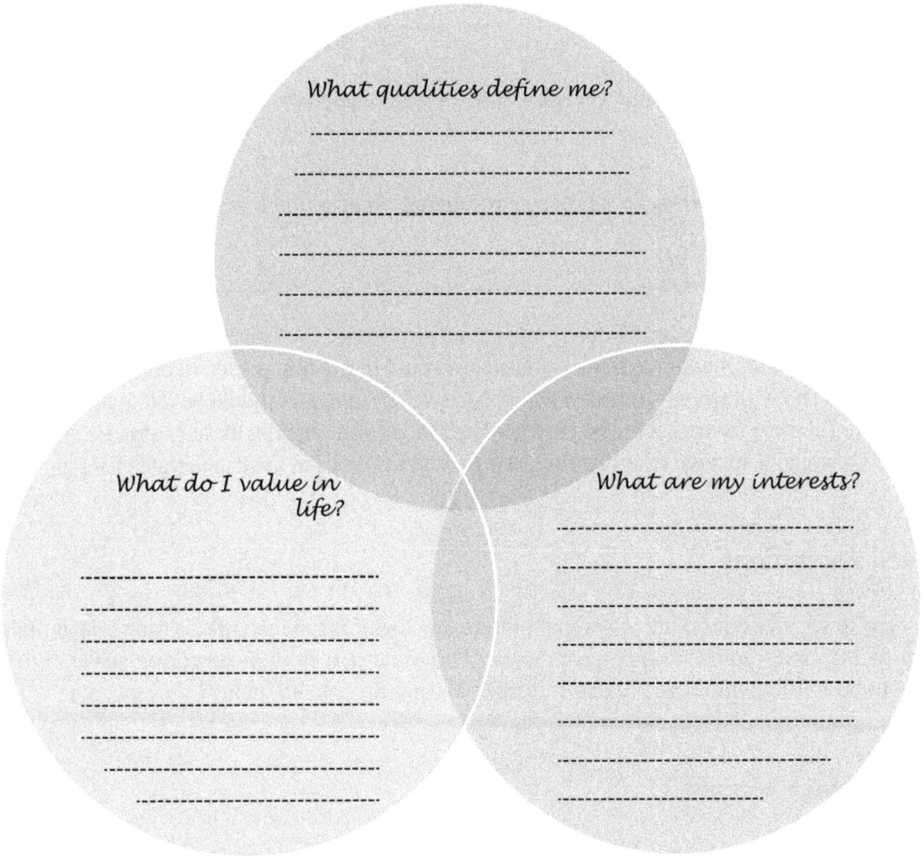

Source: Authors.

The intersection of the circles in Figure 11.1 shows that one's identity is a complex combination of all of these factors.

Younger students, and less expressive students, may require more clear questions to help them to arrive at an understanding of themselves. The format given below is useful for students from class six onwards to help them to discover themselves.

Who am I?
If you were to introduce yourself to someone who you have never met and want to befriend, what would you say?
It has been many days since you have not been alone at home. Your parents are away today and you are all alone. What would you like to do?
Think of your closest friend. What qualities do you like about him/her more than your other friends? What activities do you like to engage in with your friend?
If there was something that you could change about your physical body, what would it be and why?
If there was some quality that you could change in yourself, what would it be and why?

These formats should be filled individually and would also work best if discussed individually with the students. Ideally, the class teacher or the school counsellor would be the best person to discuss these. The choice of when, whether and with whom students want to discuss their thoughts should be left to them. Students can also be asked to fill these formats at the beginning of each academic session, for at least three or more successive years. This would help them to understand how their perceptions of themselves are changing over time.

Goals and Aspirations

Students tend to spend a considerable amount of time day dreaming. Much of this time is spent in thinking about the future. Goals and aspirations are thus an important part of their perceived sense of self. Often these dreams do not turn into reality when students have not thought about how they can reach their goals.

Career Guidance Sessions

Career guidance sessions should begin during middle school. Younger children can be provided a generic orientation to what it means to be a professional or an entrepreneur. It helps to share inspirational stories and biographies of successful people to inspire them into various professions. Two key aspects must be kept in mind when orienting students to various professions. First, care must be taken to provide a width of exposure. This means that students should be acquainted with career options that go beyond banker, lawyer, engineer, doctor, and the like. Second, stereotypes about professions, such as 'girls should be teachers, nurses, doctors' and 'boys should go into tough professions such as army, engineering, law' and so on need to be challenged. Role models of successful professionals in these areas should also be provided.

In senior classes, students would need individual guidance and support in choosing the specific career options that can be explored.

Making Choices

In addition to providing career guidance, teachers can help students in making choices. This form of support is particularly important in secondary classes after which they would have to choose which academic stream to pursue. Students must be helped to explore the options that they would have after they choose a particular stream.

Once they have chosen a particular career option, they can be asked to think backwards and decide the steps that they need to take to fulfil these goals (see Figure 11.2).

Figure 11.2   Goals and Aspirations

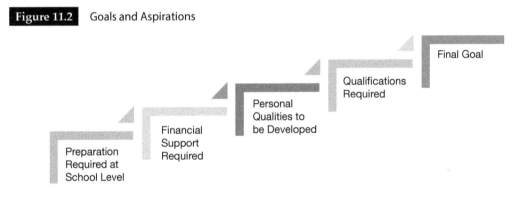

Source: Authors.

Locating Sources of Influence

Our goals and aspirations, our qualities and the things that we value are influenced by our experiences as well as the people around us. Our understanding of our selves is not limited to discovering what we believe in and what defines us. A complete understanding of our identity would involve identifying the roots of our values. These would also help us to locate fundamental changes in our attitudes and social settings that we need to make so that we can then take action. A further in-depth analysis would also provide us the opportunity to think about what these values translate into in our everyday lives. An example has been presented in Figure 11.3.

Figure 11.3 shows how the value of discipline has been imbibed by lessons at home and school. Everyday experiences at school and home can help a child to develop the notion of discipline. This

Figure 11.3 Sources of Influence

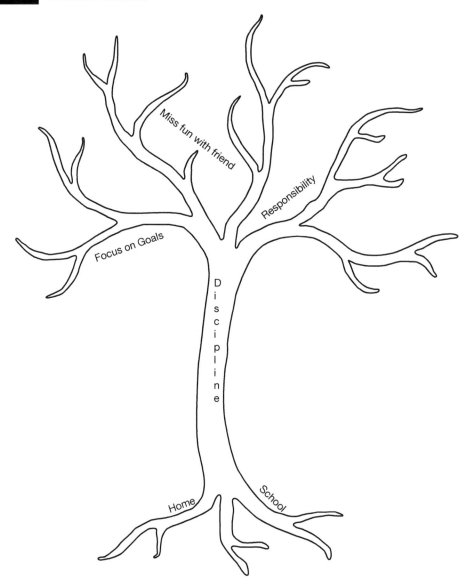

Source: Authors.

value in turn helps the child to take responsibility for his/her actions, and be more focused towards the goals that he/she wishes to achieve.

Blank formats of the tree can be shared with students to help them to reflect on the sources that have led them to develop certain values. Through discussion and reflection, they can be facilitated in understanding what they may wish to change. For instance, being overly disciplined may lead the child to miss out on the fun that his/her friends have. The child may thus think that it may be fruitful to balance excessive self-discipline by occasionally letting go of restrictions.

WHAT DO OTHERS THINK OF ME?

One's identity is not just shaped by how he/she perceives himself/herself. It is equally important to understand oneself in the context of what others think of us. In fact, the perception of others can help us to understand ourselves better. Part of the reason that adolescents feel misunderstood by others is because there is incongruence between how they see themselves and how others perceive them. An understanding of others' perceptions of them can be used to help them to reflect on this incongruence and work towards changing it. The activity given in Table 11.1 can be conducted to help students to identify this perception.

Table 11.1 can be given to the students.

Students should be allowed to modify the list of qualities as they desire. The teacher should help them to develop a list that is a healthy mix of positive and negative qualities. Once the list has been developed, students should be asked to make multiple copies of the list and distribute these to their family members, friends and others around them. Some of these can also be filled by people who do not know the students very well. This would help them to identify the perceptions of people about them who are close friends or casual acquaintances. A copy of this can also be filled up by the students themselves. They can mark the responses that different people have given to them on to the same sheet on which they have marked their own answers using different coloured pens. This would highlight the incongruences between what they think of themselves and what others think of them. The overlaps would also help them to reaffirm their faith in themselves.

The same activity sheet can be used to take their understanding a step further. Based on the incongruences, children can be asked to highlight the qualities that others have not marked but they would like to have in themselves. Those qualities that they would like to maintain further would also be highlighted. These highlighted qualities would mark their ideal self. This would lead them to compare their real and ideal self. Through personal discussion with the counsellor or teacher, they can be helped to move towards their ideal self from their real self.

Table 11.1   Knowing Myself through the Eyes of Others

A list of qualities has been given below. Encircle all qualities that you would associate with me.		
Helpful	Friendly	Artistic
Moody	Cheerful	Cooperative
Confident	Selfish	Dependable
Arrogant	Good sportsman	Caring
Good public speaker	Intelligent	Lazy
Creative	Loner	Unfriendly
Dirty	Humorous	Beautiful
Casual	Serious	Rude

Source: Authors.

Image Building

In the technology-ridden world that marks contemporary India, social networking sites play a major role. Most social networking sites allow adolescents to register with them at the age of 13 years or more.

However, many pre-teens lie about their age to register on websites. This is not just a means of communicating with their friends after-school, but also a way of making new friends. Being on social networking sites is seen as a way of becoming a part of the latest trends. A downside of social networking websites is that it leads people to build certain images of themselves that may not be true. Over a period of time, when they start getting appreciated for these qualities, they move further away from the real world. In order to maintain this false image, adolescents may start spending increasingly more time on the website rather than interacting with people in the real world. To add to the complexity, adolescents may also start to believe in this created image of self even when it is far from reality. This sort of image building must be prevented to help adolescents to stay in touch with their real selves.

Supportive Parenting

Adolescence is a time when the bonds between the parents and child also undergo a change. Both parents and children start to believe that they do not understand each other. This issue has already been discussed in detail in Chapter 9. It would be helpful if parents can be oriented by the school to deal with adolescents. This is the time when they start treating adolescents as grown-ups and expect them to partake of responsibilities at home. Yet, decision-making often remains in the hands of the parents. This creates a conflict for the adolescents who strive for greater independence. Parental expectations also place a lot of pressure on adolescents for academic achievement and a more serious approach to life. By asking parents to reconsider the importance that they attach to achievement and appropriate behaviour, parents can be asked to reflect on providing unconditional acceptance to their children. This helps adolescents to be more open to discussing their thoughts with their parents and ask for help in decision-making as well. Thus, the family can work together towards arriving at a consensus on important decisions.

RELIGIOUS AND COMMUNAL IDENTITY

An aspect that is significant in forming the identity of adolescents is their religious and communal background. Much of the religious values, cultural stereotypes and community-based perceptions that are formed by adolescents remain in the covert sphere. Children and adolescents pick up values, preferences and thought processes from the family and society in which they live. Often, these processes take many years and are never overtly discussed or acknowledged. It is obvious, for instance, that a child who is born in a Hindu family will also be a Hindu and develop the same religious habits as his/her parents, such as doing *pooja*, visiting temples and so on. Similarly, children are socialised into region-specific or community-based lifestyles and habits. These are transmitted in the kind of food eaten, style of clothes worn and languages spoken.

Developing Sensitivity

The heterogeneity in our country allows for pluralism or a mixture of cultures that a child is exposed to. This is particularly true for children living in urban settings where they are likely to engage with others from different religious and regional backgrounds. This exposure is important in building tolerance. However, in times of communal and/or religious conflict, people who have otherwise lived peacefully, tend to forget their relationships and begin to engage in violence against the other community. The notions of 'I' and the 'other' are developed in children as young as eight years (Gupta 2008).

It is important to therefore develop an attitude of sensitivity in children while they are still in school. The following excerpt and discussion questions can be used in middle school.

Hues of Identity

... My younger brother as a student of class two was beaten up by his classmates on being prodded and provoked by his class teacher. When school reopened after 1984 riots, the teacher dutifully explained to the children that Sikhs and Hindus were brethren and one community and should not fight. Whereas the real enemies were the Muslims. The children beat up the 'enemy' in front of the teacher. I still cannot come to terms with the fact that my parents did not confront or even report the incident to the authorities.

I remember a senior colleague's surprise on learning that I was a Muslim though I 'looked Indian' and comment in the selection committee that marks are given away in Aligarh Muslim University. These incidents fail to smear grey on the hues that I thought defined me as a person. These people were forgiven if not forgotten as being color blind or having a blinkered vision...

— Farooqui (2007)

Discussion Questions:

- What factors help us to form perceptions about others?
- How do you think the young boy in class two would have felt?
- Why did his friends beat him up? Should they have done so?
- What did the author's colleague mean when she said that she 'looked Indian'?
- How is 'looking Indian' different from looking like a Muslim?
- Has anyone of you ever faced similar incidents?
- Do we also form perceptions about others on the basis of their looks?
- How does religion influence who we are friends with?
- What other factors influence friendships?

Exercises such as the one mentioned above need to be regularly conducted to help children build tolerance and stronger bonds across heterogeneous religious, cultural and regional backgrounds.

Movie screenings of popular movies addressing religious and communal violence such as *Bombay* (1995), *Parzania* (2007), *Khuda Kay Liye* (2007), *Firaaq* (2008) and so on can also be organised. This can be followed up by discussion on tolerance, the effects of violence on society and the politicisation of religion. Movies such as *Dharm* (2007) can be used to discuss the relationships between Hindus and Muslims and to show how a staunch belief system can sometimes overpower our sense of humanity.

Friendships beyond Religion

In the light of the above discussion, a more focused discussion on how friendships get affected by incidents of communal violence can also be carried out. Friendship patterns during childhood seldom

get affected by religious backgrounds of students. In some families however, religious fundamental-
ism may dominate, preventing children from engaging with peers of other religions. The notion of 'I'
and the 'other' is so dominantly created that children form perceptions about their peers based on their
religious backgrounds. This can result in violence and aggression against one's own peers during times
of conflict. This has been addressed in Farooqui's article excerpted above. Movies such as *Rang De
Basanti* (2006) and *Kai Po Che* (2013) also address the theme of religion interweaving with friendship.

In this context, it is equally important to provide examples to students of friendships that go beyond
religious barriers. Numerous examples of extending help beyond religious boundaries can be shared
from the times of partition, Babri Masjid demolition, and riots in Gujarat and Mumbai. While these may
be difficult topics to address, it is important for a teacher to address them, lest students grow up with
strong communal sentiments. The following excerpt may be used to initiate discussion.

In the more recent past, Satish recalls playing football, cricket and kabaddi as a child with Muslim
boys of the neighbourhood. He visited their homes freely, as they did his, and was even friendly
with their womenfolk who did not observe any purdah from him. Accompanying his mother on
her rounds through the Muslim areas, he would carry the fruits and vegetables right inside the
houses and was never made to feel unwelcome. The understanding that existed between Hindus
and Muslims of the previous generations, Satish says, has disappeared in the younger one which
is a hot blooded lot. Whereas the older Muslims were tolerant, the young ones are aggressive and
are provoked to violence at the slightest of pretexts.

Kakar (2007)

Discussion Questions:

- Which 'earlier time' is being referred to here?
- Do you agree that communities have become more intolerant now?
- Do you see differences in lifestyles and behaviours of people belonging to different
  religions?
- What happens during times of communal conflict that turns people against each other
  during times of communal conflict?

The discussion in the classroom should allow students to think about both the homogeneity and heterogeneity present in their friends' circle. They should reflect upon the development of a mob culture or what
Kakar (2007) calls a 'crowd's identity' during instances of communal violence. The discussion must also
help students to think of ways of looking beyond religious stereotypes and prevent the formation of biases.

ON A CONCLUDING NOTE

The chapter discussed the different factors that influence identity. The school and home can both play an
important role in helping adolescents build a sense of identity. It also emphasised that parents and teachers
would have to be more tolerant as this is a phase in which adolescents would try out many different things
in their quest to develop a sense of identity. Identity development must be seen as a process and not an
end product. It should thus, not be expected for adolescents to arrive at a final decision during this phase.

Coping with Stress and Anxiety   12

Feelings of stress, pressure and anxiety are commonly experienced by everyone on a regular basis. Practicing psychologists report having patients as young as seven years old who need help in managing stress and anxiety. Common usage of these terms has led to the trivialisation of the experiences as routine and 'normal'. This leads to denial of the seriousness of the problem. If unchecked, stress and anxiety can lead to psychological problems, including clinical depression and emotional or nervous breakdown. In this chapter, we will first look at the meaning of stress and anxiety, demystifying its popular and clinical usage. This will be followed by identification of sources of stress in the lives of school-going children. Some common strategies that can be used for coping with stress will also be discussed.

DEMYSTIFYING STRESS AND ANXIETY

An average middle school student's daily routine involves getting up early in the morning and rushing for school. In households where both parents are working, the child would see and experience urgency in the charged home atmosphere where everyone is trying to finish home tasks and leave for work. This is followed by a packed school time. Afternoons and evenings are full of scheduled homework, tuitions and various activity classes that continue well into late evening. On an average day, a school-going child has little time and free space to be himself/herself. What this routine also highlights is that everyday life creates pressures and demands that need to be met. In other words, stress does not require any extraordinary event. Everyday tasks in themselves can be stressful. However, on most days, we are able to deal with this stress with ease. Familiarity with routine tasks helps to deal with the stress and demands without feeling overly anxious or inept. Stress, therefore, need not always be a deterrent from healthy functioning.

In simple terms, stress can be defined as a response of the individual to any demand that is placed on him/her. This response can be a thought or can involve physical action. In itself, this is not a problem. However, when the person has to address competing demands within a limited time frame or when these demands are accompanied by feelings of nervousness and anxiety, it can make one 'feel stressed'. Stress is thus not an external force but the response of the individual to such external forces. To reiterate, stress resides within the individual and not in external stimuli.

Anxiety refers to a feeling of unease or nervousness often resulting from an uncertain consequence of an event or situation. Anxiety is the anticipation of a future threat. It can have psychosomatic symptoms. Pacing to and fro, repeatedly tapping fingers or feet and nail biting are some behavioural manifestations. Somatic symptoms such as queasiness in the stomach, headaches, and the like, are also common complaints made by people experiencing anxiety. Rumination or overthinking or being preoccupied with thoughts of what is likely to happen in the future is also experienced by people with anxiety.

As you can see, stress and anxiety are not synonymous. However, they are frequently used together and can be closely interconnected. All stressful situations may not be accompanied with feelings of anxiety. A lack of awareness of one's own feelings can make one feel confused and stressed about the situation at hand.

Types of Stress

As has been mentioned earlier, stress may not always be harmful. It can also have a positive impact in many instances. Stress can be categorised on the basis of the impact it has on people. These are briefly discussed here.

Neustress

Earlier in the chapter, an average day in the life of a student was described. A student would go through most of these activities without experiencing any positive or negative impact. Thus, stress experienced on an everyday basis has no impact on us or is neutral. This is referred to as neustress. An average person is able to cope with everyday stressors effectively, and thus live a healthy life while experiencing neustress. It may be noted that when a person is unable to cope with stress, he/she will find these everyday life events also overly stressful. In such instances, these events will also not remain at a state of neustress.

Distress

As mentioned above, the experience of stress and not the situation in itself is what would make the stress harmful or helpful. Thus, when someone is able to cope with a situation, irrespective of how difficult it may be, it will not cause a negative impact or be threatening to the person's well-being. On the other hand, inability to cope with a situation will lead to a feeling of distress. Distress is experienced when the response to a challenge leads to too much or too low of an arousal. This is often manifested through irritability, churning or butterflies in the stomach, trembling hands, short temperedness and poor concentration. These are early warning signs that need to be checked and responded to in order to prevent major illnesses.

Positive Stress

Stress, surprisingly, can also have a positive impact. Some amount of stress can in fact be helpful in preparing for examinations, presentations, performances and new experiences. Positive stress can help in quickening of responses in the face of emergencies such as road accidents, helping a victim, playing tennis or squash, and the like. It also helps in outperforming oneself by pushing one's limits. It helps in preparing for deadlines as our body becomes more alert in the time of stress and works with maximum efficiency and productivity.

Psychological Disorders

If early warning signs of distress are ignored, it can lead to more serious consequences. For students, this may result in the loss of interest in school, underachievement in examinations, lower energy and enthusiasm, and even physical illness. It is important to note that one person's experience of distress can also affect others around him/her. Thus, where parents are undergoing distress, children are also likely to feel distressed. Children learn coping mechanisms from parents. At the same time, they are also affected by the atmosphere at home. An atmosphere charged by negative energy will also increase the chances of experiences of stress and anxiety for all family members. This will be more pronounced for children who may not have developed the coping skills to face stress and anxiety. This will increase the probability of developing psychological disorders such as social anxiety disorders, depression and paranoia.

SOURCES OF STRESS

The paragraphs above discussed how everyday life creates many demands on us which can lead to stress. However, our coping mechanisms allow us to deal with these pressures with ease. There can be many sources of stress and anxiety. These are broadly categorised into internal and external sources.

Internal Sources

Internal sources of stress refer to those factors that reside within the person itself. Stress is often induced due to one's own reactions and feelings that emerge in response to situations. Anger, frustration, sadness and other strong emotions tend to cloud thinking and reduced one's ability to deal effectively with situations. This leads to stress which will compound feelings further. In such a vicious cycle, it becomes difficult to address distress as the source of stress is not external but within the person. The person may not be able to identify the source of stress and thus will not be able to address it at all.

External Sources

External sources are those which reside outside of the individual. These are external, environmental factors that lead to distressing situations. In the lives of children and adolescents, there may be three main sources of stress. These have been discussed in the subsequent paragraphs.

Expectations of Excellence

One of the key sources of stress these days is academic pressure. Every child is expected to excel in academics. The pressure to not just be good but to be the best arises early in life. Increasingly, parents are enrolling children into preparatory classes for competitive examinations of engineering, medical, and the like from as early as class five and six. This creates a pressure on children to be the best in the class and to have clearly defined life goals from a young age. In addition, this also translates into every minute of the day being accounted for. School-going children are left with little free time and space to explore and be themselves. This competitive spirit spreads into non-academic spheres as well. There is a growing urge in middle class parents to raise children who are 'all-rounders' or doing well in everything. Thus, a child is expected to be good at oratory, performing arts, fine arts and sports in addition to academics. This leads to a host of classes that pre-schoolers start attending and continue well into college years. An expectation of excellence in every field is detrimental on two counts. First, it creates a pressure on the child to outperform everyone else and thus be constantly working. Second, it does not allow the child the time to engage in activities of interest and creates stress of engaging in tasks that the child may not like.

Family

A family is ideally expected to be a place of comfort and support that is often not available outside. It is a source of unconditional acceptance and has the potential to be the biggest de-stressor in everyone's life. However, it can also be a cause of stress. As was discussed in the previous paragraph, an expectation of excellence in all spheres can strain parent–child relationship and be stressful. This often results in children feeling unvalued and pressurised. Interpersonal relationships within the family can also be a cause of strain and stress for the child. Constant disagreements, arguments and fights at home can lead the child to feel insecure and affect academic performance as well. With growing cases of divorce, the child may also become a bone of contention in cases of separation. Changing family patterns, marked by a rise in both parents working and nuclear families, also has implications for the home atmosphere. If parents are not able to devote time to the child, he/she may not have anyone to share thoughts, feelings and ideas with. He/She may be left feeling lonely and uncared for.

Peers

Like the family, peers are also an important source of support to the child. However, the same relationships can be a source of stress. A competitive spirit stemming out of pressure to excel can dampen any friendship. In addition, peers can be a source of teasing, bullying and harassment. Schools, coaching classes, playgrounds and sometimes social networking sites can all be potential sites for harassment. An insensitive casual remark on the appearance, a joke about marks in an examination, a stutter on stage, falling in public or being picked up last for a sports team can all be potential sources of stress. Students may not be aware of the effect that these remarks may have. Caregivers in school and home settings will have to be watchful for any potential signs of distress in the child.

COPING WITH STRESS

Growing-up years are marked with developing life skills along with growth in physical and cognitive terms. Life skills include the ability to manage emotions and cope with stressors. Socialisation processes play an important role in learning the coping strategies. Observing others at home and school teaches a child the need and ways to manage emotions. The process is scaffolded by teachers and parents. Some of the common mechanisms for coping are discussed in the subsequent paragraphs.

Defence Mechanisms

Defence mechanisms are in-built in all of us to protect us from threatening situations. Using repression, rationalisation and sublimation are common ways in which people cope with stress. The concept of defence mechanisms was first propounded by Sigmund Freud and has been discussed in greater detail in Chapter 14. Defence mechanisms are unconscious processes and natural coping mechanisms. When a person is faced with a situation that is threatening to one's psychological well-being, the ego defence mechanisms are automatically employed to protect from a nervous or emotional breakdown.

Strategies

While defence mechanisms are employed automatically, we often also consciously use strategies that help us to cope with stress. Most of the strategies discussed here are commonly employed by everyone. It is important to note that the same strategy does not work every time or with every person. We all must have a repertoire of strategies that work for us in distressing situations. Parents and teachers should recognise that they are modelling behaviour to children and will have to teach these coping strategies to children.

Healthy Mechanisms

Coping strategies may be divided into healthy and unhealthy alternatives. Healthy strategies tend to provide relief that helps in dealing with the situation better. Some of these are discussed here.

Relaxation Techniques

Relaxation techniques include a series of activities that help soothe the nerves and physically relax the body. This helps in clearing out thinking and address the stressful situation more effectively. These include meditation and deep breathing exercises. However, an hour's good sleep can also be calming and help to deal with stress better.

Outlets for Expression

Finding an outlet for expression is one of the most important aspects of coping with stress. Talking about distress can provide cathartic relief even if the stressful situation is not addressed. Children must be encouraged to share their thoughts and feelings. These may be through creating regular spaces where children can engage with people they are comfortable with. In school, this can be accomplished through a regular mentor or tutor period once a week. At home, casual conversations over dinner every day or a weekly visit for lunch or dinner with one or both parents could work. Children may also be encouraged to write diaries or journals on a daily or weekly basis. They must be assured that these will not be read unless they tell someone to read it. Other forms of creative expression through painting, craft or writing poetry and stories can also be explored. Older children can also be encouraged to explore the world of blogs as a forum for sharing their creativity.

Healthy Habits

Stress induces hypersomnia or insomnia, overeating or loss of appetite and lethargy. These can be countered through healthy everyday habits. Unhealthy daily habits tend to add to stress. It is thus important that healthy habits be used to prevent and combat distress. Children should be encouraged to engage in physical activities on an everyday basis. This may include games, sports and dance or other performing arts. In addition, their food habits should also be monitored. Eating healthy foods and moderating junk food is important to maintain psychological well-being. Routinisation of sleep cycles is essential to maintaining healthy lifestyle. This includes six to eight hours of sleep on a daily basis. Further, as far as possible, nights should be reserved for sleeping and days for working. Late nights should be avoided. To encourage good sleep habits, routinisation of sleep through having sleep rituals, such as freshening up before sleeping and changing into comfortable clothes is important. Children and adolescents often sleep in their day clothes which may be uncomfortable for sleeping and can cause discomfort. This prevents deep sleep and relaxation.

Time Management

Children and adolescents also need to be taught how to manage their time between the different tasks that they are involved in. As has been discussed earlier, children in contemporary times are involved in multifarious activities. They need to balance their time among different activities as also be aware of what is on priority at what time. In helping children manage the time that they spend on the various activities, adults must also ensure that they are given flexibility to undertake tasks that they would like to engage in. Time schedules should also not be routinised to the extent of making them mechanistic. As far as possible, time schedules should be prepared in collaboration with children. Children should also be allowed the flexibility to change schedules to suit their moods wherever possible.

Taking Breaks

Another important aspect along with time management is to create space for taking breaks. Breaks from work are important on a daily basis. Developing a hobby that is relaxing and enjoyable for the child is important. This may include playing individual or group games, taking walks, going out with friends, painting, writing, listening to music, reading, watching television or Internet surfing.

At the same time, there will be times when children will need to take breaks from the routine tasks. Short vacations and family outings would be essential to break the monotony and provide respite from constantly being engaged in tasks. This will also provide the family with a time to bond together.

Motivation

When stress is induced due to overburdening and too much to do, it may help to motivate the child to meet set targets and deadlines. These may be set in consultation with the child on an everyday basis so that the child may receive encouragement regularly. Specific rewards for tasks accomplished will help the children to stay focused and engaged. Staying busy also helps in de-stressing by distracting from the stressor situation and preventing overthinking.

Unhealthy Mechanisms

Unhealthy mechanisms are those that do not address the situation and can also be harmful in the long run. These include escapism, overworking and substance abuse.

Escapism

Escapism refers to finding alternatives that help one escape from addressing the problem. In the face of a stressful situation, most people tend to not address the situation. This is particularly true when facing the situation involves discussion and confrontation. A situation that is also threatening to the psychological well-being will also be avoided. Temporarily escaping from the situation is important to bring clarity in thought but using this mechanism over a long time can be detrimental as it does not address the situation at all.

Overwork

In escaping from situations, many people tend to engage in many different activities. This can be a healthy mechanism when used in moderation. When too many tasks are taken up, the person may set unrealistic deadlines and become overworked. This can in fact add to the stress. This is also a form of escapism which does not help in solving the problem at hand.

Substance Abuse

In trying to avoid stress, children and adolescents tend to engage in substance abuse. This may begin early in life by inhaling intoxicating substances such as glue, correction fluid, petrol, smoking, drinking alcohol or taking drugs. Many children tend to learn these habits from home when they observe parents indulging in substance abuse. Observing peers and pressure from them can also be an initiation point. This soon leads to addiction before children realise the detrimental effects it has. This can be harmful both in the short run and long run.

ROLE OF SCHOOL AND HOME

Home and school can play an important role in addressing stress among students. Teacher and parents need to recognise their role as caregivers in helping children develop coping mechanisms. Teachers and parents must also recognise that they can be the source of stress for school-going children. They should thus reflect on their own activities while engaging with children. Having unrealistic expectations from children can lead to stress and anxiety for them.

Acknowledge Stress and Anxiety

The first step for teachers and parents is to acknowledge the existence of stress. Adults are often pre-occupied and stressed in their own lives and they often feel that children cannot experience stress and anxiety. Foremost is, thus, to acknowledge that children are also aware and experience stressors at home and school and feel stressed. The following simple activity can be undertaken with children to understand stress.

Ask children if they have ever faced any of the following situations and ask them to rate them according to what they find disturbing and stressful on a continuum from 1 to 10, where 10 is most stressful.

Situation	Rating
A friend is not talking to you because you did not share your tiffin with her.	
Your parents had an argument at home and asked you to sit in the other room.	
Your grandparent is in the hospital.	
You have lost your notebook and exam is just around the corner.	
You were given some money to buy something/pay for a school picnic. You have lost the money and do not know how to tell your parents about it.	
You accidentally broke an expensive showpiece or crockery at home.	
You overheard your father telling your mother that he has lost his job and he doesn't have any other source of income.	
Your friends have all purchased new clothes but you know your family can't afford to go shopping right now.	
You were selected for a competition but could not perform well and lost it. You don't know how your teachers or friends will react to it.	
You have scored low in an examination and the paper has to be signed by your parents.	
Your seven-year-old pet dog passed away after an illness.	

It is important here that parents and teachers ask students to mark only those situations that the child has been in. Imagining situations that the child has not yet experienced can in itself be distressing. For younger children, the teacher may also narrate a story of a child who feels stressed. This may be based on any of the situations mentioned above. After the story, the teacher may ask the students to share situations in which they feel stressed.

For older children and adolescents, they may be asked to list the situations in which they feel stressed:

Have you ever feel distressed? Have you ever seen any of your friends distressed? What are some of the reasons that lead to stress for you and your friends?

At home

_____
_____
_____
_____
_____

In school

_____

_____

_____

_____

_____

_____

With friends

_____

_____

_____

_____

_____

Online

_____

_____

_____

_____

_____

These activities are helpful in identifying causes of stressors for the school-going children. When children are able to anonymously share their stressors, teachers and parents would be amazed to see that many of the stress factors are similar for adults and children. Things that parents may be trying to hide from children would also find their ways of reaching children and add to their stress experience. In addition, interpersonal relationships are as much a source of stress for children as are studies. It is thus important that parents and teachers acknowledge that children experience stress as much as they do. Further, it is a general tendency to trivialise children's experiences. This may translate into belittling children about the amount of studying required in primary school, or laughing over fights between friends or siblings. As adults, we must be sensitive towards their concerns and pay attention to the genuine nature of stress that children experience.

Be Tolerant

Once teachers and parents have accepted that children experience stress, they must also demonstrate tolerance and patience towards the ensuing behaviour of children. Consider the following case:

Manish is in class eight. He has recently stopped completing his work and has started throwing tantrums when being questioned. He has occasionally demonstrated violent behaviour by throwing things around and trying to break the furniture. The teachers are concerned about his behaviour since he was previously a quiet child. Some teachers have written it off as a by-product of the onset of puberty. However, his class teacher feels that this has deeper reasons as it is not a consistent behaviour. She spoke to Manish separately and found out that his parents have recently been fighting a lot at home. They have decided to separate and are constantly arguing over who

Manish would stay with. He is even more disturbed since neither of the parents is ready to keep both him and his elder sister. He is perturbed that he would also have to part ways with his sister. Whenever there is an argument at home, he gets very disturbed and is unable to concentrate on school work. His parents have forbidden him from talking about it to his friends. Therefore, he ends up expressing his frustration through violence.

In this case, the stressor was the home environment and through the behaviour of the child in the school the teacher was able to reach the root cause of the problem. Manish's class teacher is likely to refer him to the school counsellor and if need be, she would also talk to his parents about the situation at home. If his sister studies in the same school, it would be appropriate for the counsellor to also inform her class teacher about the situation at her home. However, counselling is not likely to bring instant results. It would take time for the situation to settle at home and Manish would take time to adjust to the changing situation. While violence would not be accepted, teachers would have to show some tolerance towards his incomplete work and provide support in difficult times till he learns to cope with the stressor.

Create Opportunities for Channellising Energy

Bullying, aggression and violence are ways in which children release their suppressed energy. In times of stress, suppressed emotions, thoughts and feelings tend to create a state of arousal that needs to be satiated through activities which when not challenged can take socially undesirable turns. Teachers and parents would have to create opportunities for channellising energies of students in activities that help the students. This will require a tailor-made approach that is suited to the unique needs of the students. Teachers would have to speak personally to students to find alternatives that suit their interests and are able to keep them busy physically and mentally. This will help in preventing dwelling too much over events and situations unnecessarily.

Provide Space for Expression and Communication

Teachers and parents must learn to become active listeners. They should encourage children to share their concerns, however trivial they may seem. Children should be given time and attention and be encouraged to talk about things that are important to them. This will help prevent and alleviate stress and also give them the assurance of having someone dependable around. In times of distress, they would be able to share their concerns freely with adults and seek advice. Young children particularly may not be able to express through spoken words. Drawings, play, stories and other creative outlets should be carefully observed for any warning signs of stress and disturbance.

Organise Seminars and Talks

The school should make an active effort to organise seminars and talks for parents and children. Parents will have to be regularly reminded to not create undue pressure on children for performing well in school activities. Students will also benefit from seminars on relaxation therapies, time management skills, life skills of decision-making and emotion management. Talks and seminars also serve as forums for exchanging thoughts between parents, teachers and children.

ON A CONCLUDING NOTE

In this chapter we have demystified the notions of stress and anxiety. It is important that teachers recognise the positive and negative aspects of stress and acknowledge the presence of stress in the lives of children. In addition, the school and family will have to play an active role in helping children cope with stress. Most importantly, parents and teachers must make a conscious effort towards ensuring that schools and homes are not sources of stress for children.

13 Counselling Skills for Teachers and Parents

Section 1 of this book focused on developing an understanding of mental health and building perspective about various issues of relevance in the field of guidance, counselling and mental health. The chapters in this section also addressed the need to locate mental health within the context of home, school and community of the students. The second section focused on addressing the concerns raised in the first section and provided suggestive techniques and strategies that can be used by teachers, parents and caregivers. In the final chapter of this section, the focus is on the skills required to implement these strategies.

Throughout the book, the need to hire trained counsellors in schools has been emphasised. However, we must recognise that one or two counsellors are often not enough to address the needs and concerns of every student in the school. Thus, every teacher will have to take on the role of a counsellor for addressing the needs of the students on an everyday basis. Similarly, parents will benefit greatly from developing counselling skills. Engaging with children at home requires patience. Children require support and guidance in not just studies but also in personal and social adjustment. Developing counselling skills would thus be facilitative in parenting.

BASIC ASSUMPTIONS ABOUT COUNSELLING

In this section, we will talk about some of the basic assumptions that underlie all counselling processes. Counselling requires an engagement of at least two people. One is presumed to know more than the other. The process of counselling, although, is not based on knowledge as it is based on mutual trust and sharing of thoughts and feelings. This would help the counselee to take better decisions in life. This process requires the counsellor to show faith in the abilities of the counselee.

All counselling processes thus assume that human behaviour can be changed either from within or without or both. This approach emphasises that episodes and life events should not be taken as the end. It focuses on the ability of people to treat unpleasant situations and experiences as isolated incidents that are passing episodes in one's life. It is well within the abilities of the people to move on from such episodes and make amends if required. This process can begin from one's inner thoughts and reflections, and/or be scaffolded from external forces, such as an interaction with a counsellor.

In engaging effectively with challenges and opportunities, counselling processes assume the need and ability of human beings to be rational and reality oriented. This is essential in making decisions that are logically sound and contextualised in the settings in which one lives.

Most problems, difficulties and maladjustments are transient in nature and can be handled and dealt with. In other words, facing a difficulty or challenge should not be seen as a permanent roadblock. People can overcome these transient phases in life. The stigma attached to counselling is often because people believe that someone who is psychologically distressed can never recover. Counselling on the other hand, looks at these situations as temporary setbacks and not terminal illnesses.

Guidance and counselling are helping and facilitative activities that provide support in overcoming these difficulties. They are not a beginning of a dependent lifestyle. On the contrary, they are enabling functions that help to develop capacities for engaging with distress and disharmony later in life. Guidance helps individuals to discover their needs, assess their potentialities, develop their life schemes, formulate ways to achieve these schemes and proceed towards realising these schemes. The goal of guidance is not solving a particular individual's problem. Instead, it aims at empowering the individual to learn to solve his/her own problems. It helps individuals to develop better self-understanding, become more self-accepting and self-directed. Counselling is a more intensive form of guidance which helps individuals to move from dissatisfaction to satisfaction, pain to comfort, low self-esteem to high self-esteem and low social skills to better social adjustment. Counselling thus deals with one's emotions and experiences as well. In reality, guidance and counselling are only theoretically divided. They must aim at making the individual more competent and contented with his/her life situation.

CHARACTERISTICS REQUIRED FOR SUCCESSFUL COUNSELLING

In order to work with the assumptions detailed out above and meet the aims of guidance and counselling, the counsellor has to develop the characteristics that are important for this process. You may notice that some teachers are inherently endowed with these characteristics. However, with practise, these characteristics can be developed and sharpened.

Active Listening

In times of distress, people approach a counsellor only because they wish to be heard. They may not be hoping to get a quick answer or solution to their problem, but by expressing their discomfort, they feel relieved of stress. In a fast paced life, it is sometimes difficult to find someone who would lend us an empathetic ear. The counsellor serves an important role by listening to the counselee. Listening is not restricted to only sitting next to the person expressing his/her discontent. The counselee must feel that the counsellor is genuinely interested in listening to the difficulties expressed. Attention must be communicated through verbal and non-verbal means, through body language and eye contact.

Positive Regard

Positive regard refers to treating the other person with dignity and respect. The counsellor must adopt a non-judgemental stance. Irrespective of the conditions, thoughts, behaviours, habits and past experiences, the counsellor should accept the person as he/she is. This will be communicated through a genuine expression of concern.

Genuineness

The counsellor must be genuinely interested in helping the counselee. The relationship can be beneficial only if there is a commonality of interest. In school settings, if the student does not feel that the teacher genuinely wishes to help the student or has some ulterior motive towards helping him/her, the counselling process will not be fruitful. The counsellor must thus develop an authentic relationship with the counselee.

A Sense of Commitment

The person in the position of the counsellor should develop and demonstrate a sense of commitment towards the counselling process. Delaying or postponing counselling sessions, or showing preoccupation with other tasks while in conversation with the counselee act as indications that the counsellor is not interested in helping the counselee. Follow up meetings and frequent interactions are important if the sessions have to be successful.

Empathy

Empathy is the ability to feel the way the other person feels by putting oneself in a similar situation. An empathetic attitude differs from being sympathetic. Sympathy is expressed by feeling bad for someone else without being able to imagine oneself in a similar situation. It is remote and distant. An attitude of empathy is based on genuine care and represents sharing difficulties and meeting challenges together.

Open Mindedness

Open mindedness is particularly important in school settings between a teacher and a student. Students and teachers are often in disagreement over decisions about homework, excursions, uniform and other school policies. In addition, a classroom setting tends to define authority relationships in clear hierarchical terms. This creates a sense of otherness in the relationship. Age differences also lead to the generation gap between teachers and students. A teacher counselling a student would be successful only if he/she is able to listen to the other perspective with openness. This is equally true between parents and children. Where ideas, thoughts and feelings are dismissed as immature and childish without being given a patient listening, it leads to a fracture in the relationship, making counselling unsuccessful.

Ethic of Confidentiality

Counselling relationships are based on the ethic of confidentiality. Counsellors must adhere to this ethic and not disclose details of the events, discussions, thoughts and problems of the counselee. Teachers must be careful to not share details of the students with parents, peers or other teachers without the consent of the student. The student should trust the teacher to not disclose details with others, or else he/she will not share confidential details with the teacher. Only when there is a relationship of trust that the student will feel comfortable in sharing his thoughts and concerns with the teacher. It must be noted that once this trust is broken, even if it is in the interest of the child, the student may become more withdrawn and will not develop this trust again.

Facilitative Communication Skills

As has been described above, the process of counselling is dependent on communication between the counsellor and counselee. Most of counselling is dependent on the counselee's ability and willingness to share. The counsellor would have to develop skills of communication that help the counselee to share. Paraphrasing can be useful for helping the counselee to reaffirm thoughts and feelings. Positive verbal and non-verbal communication indicates interest and encourages the counselee to share in greater details. This includes maintaining an eye contact, smiling, interspersing conversation with leading words and gestures and a body language that reflects openness and acceptance.

Holistic Understanding of Human Development

A counsellor must be familiar with the stages of development in human life. This is helpful in understanding the needs, concerns and attitudes that are relevant to specific life stages. This is particularly useful in the context of gender-specific issues. It is also important that the counsellor understand the person in the context in which he/she lives and not apply an understanding of universal stages in a decontextualised fashion. Further, the counsellor should have a gender-fair attitude. In other words, the counsellor's own opinions should demonstrate sensitivity towards gender issues without being gender biased.

Relationship Building Skills

In addition to communication, relationship building skills would also include demonstrating patience towards the counselee. The counsellor will have to devote adequate time, show concern and sensitivity towards the counselee. With the right attitude, despite a busy schedule, the counsellor will be able to take out the time to engage effectively with the counselee. All of this will work towards building a relationship with the counselee, and encourage him/her to share inner thoughts freely.

Respect for Students' Inner Subjective Frame of Reference

The teacher as a counsellor must show respect for the students' inner frame of reference. Students' concerns are often dismissed as trivial and childish. This can be discouraging for the students. Students often use terms such as stress, tension, anxiety, depression, conflict, dilemmas, problems, worries, fears, apprehension and frustration. A teacher–counsellor must attempt to find out the subjective experience of the child. The difficulties will have to be understood from the point of view of the student and not of the adults.

STRATEGIES IN COUNSELLING AND GUIDANCE

The previous section focused on characteristics of a counsellor. The teacher, parent, counsellor or the caregiver can work towards developing these characteristics. This must be accompanied by strategies that can be used during counselling sessions. The strategies that are listed below cut across specific counselling techniques. These are also helpful in practising the counselling characteristics that have been listed above.

Reflection of Feeling

Reflection of feeling refers to mirroring the counselee's affect. It involves restating the feelings of the counselee as mentioned through the messages and tones conveyed by him/her. It provides validation to the counselee's feelings and emotions and provides reassurance to him/her. In younger students in school settings, it will also help children to express their feelings appropriately and discriminate between emotions. It encourages discussion and conveys understanding of the feelings of the counselee. By reflecting feelings back to the counselee, the counsellor expresses understanding and encourages conversation. This helps in exploring the problems in-depth.

Restatement of Content

Restatement of content is most commonly used in Rogerian therapy. It involves listening intently to the counselee and repeating the essence of the conversation. The basic purpose of restating content is to provide an opportunity for further clarification. It also tells the counselee that the counsellor has understood what the counselee has expressed. It also communicates to the counselee that the counsellor is only using what he/she has been told. The counsellor's bias will thus not enter the counselling process.

Paraphrasing

Paraphrasing and restatement of content are often used interchangeably. Paraphrasing differs from restatement in both the process as well as the intention. In restatement of content, the counsellor uses the same words or phrases as are used by the counselee. In contrast, in paraphrasing, the counsellor rephrases the counselee's statements. This is done through changing the words used by the counselee with the intention of bringing about greater clarity in thoughts. The client is thus able to understand his/her own thoughts better, rethink positions and develop fresh insights. This is appropriate to use when the feelings of the client are difficult to discuss further. Paraphrasing helps to bring clarity in what has been communicated, and move ahead rather than dwell on the same emotion or thought through reflection or reiteration.

Providing Optimum Conditions for Relationship Building

The previous section discussed the importance of relationship building in counselling. This requires development and provision of conditions that are conducive towards counselling relationships. This will include providing empathy, unconditional acceptance, positive regard and genuineness. In addition, counsellor must demonstrate congruence between words and actions while expressing concern.

SIMPLE GUIDANCE AND COUNSELLING TECHNIQUES

In this section, specific guidance and counselling techniques will be discussed which can be easily used by parents and teachers. While counsellors, teachers and parents will benefit from an understanding of the personality theories and psychotherapeutic schools of thought, these techniques also can be used independent of theoretical contexts.

Catharsis

Cathartic experiences are significant in helping a person to relieve stress and anxiety. This is particularly important for releasing emotions that have been repressed. Mere expression of thoughts, sharing of experiences or giving voice to fears and anxieties can provide a sense of release. It helps in removing the stifling feeling of being bottled up. School life is often packed with back-to-back activities. With both parents working and the pressure of jobs, leave little time for the parents to engage with children on a daily basis. Taking out time to allow the child to speak freely, and not within the restricted structures of the classroom, can be a liberating experience for the child. Parents and teachers can set aside some time every week during which children can speak freely. Allowing them to express without any restriction of what they can and cannot speak will enable them to free their minds and will give insights to both teachers and parents about the thought processes and feelings of students.

Rational Analysis

Rational analysis is based on Rational Emotive Behaviour Therapy developed by Ellis around 1955. It involves using logic and rationality to dispute irrational beliefs. A specific event or experience is discussed at length to uncover hidden beliefs that underlie the behaviour and thoughts. These hidden beliefs provide insights into thought processes that influence the behaviour across different situations. Initially, the counsellor and counselee may sit together to engage in analysis. The counselee can then be helped to reach a stage of independence in undertaking rational analysis by himself/herself. This would be an enabling experience for the counselee as well. Undertaking rational analysis would involve asking leading questions. For instance, the counsellor may ask the following:

- What were you thinking at the time of the incident?
- What are your feelings about the incident?
- Why did you act in the way you did?
- Are you convinced that your behaviour was appropriate? Or, How do you justify your behaviour?
- Do you think the other person was justified in his/her behaviour?
- What inconsistencies do you see in your thoughts and behaviour?

Questions such as these help the counselee to develop insights about his/her own behaviour and habits. Irrational beliefs may be disputed through self-reflection. One may ask:

- What is the basis of this feeling?
- Is this really true?

- Am I right in feeling like this?
- Are there other possibilities that exist?
- Am I overreacting to stimuli?

Other cognitive process may also be used for rational analysis and disputing irrational beliefs. These include debating and discriminating. A person can engage in self-debate and play devil's advocate with oneself. This will allow one to see different sides of the issue and gain fresh perspectives to the specific situation. Discrimination involves identifying and differentiating between rational and irrational beliefs. Irrational beliefs often involve using terms such as 'one must always' or 'one should'. This indicates that the behaviour is not based as much on rationality as it is on a belief that has not been thoroughly thought through. Debating may help to overcome these irrational beliefs. This is particularly useful in overcoming discriminatory attitudes and biases towards particular cultural and ethnic groups.

Recognising Feelings and Thoughts

The counselling process should aim to enable the counselee to recognise his/her feelings and thoughts and work towards developing a better sense of self. This involves being in touch with the reality and building a positive self-image. The counselling process should help one to recognise the life position one is in and stay rooted in the reality. Commonly used techniques include using an emotional balance sheet, preparing a privileges and problem sheet, and making a focus on positives list.

Emotional Balance Sheet

An emotional balance sheet involves listing one's positive and negative qualities as one's assets and liabilities. This should always be made in consultation with the counselee. Subsequently, the counselee can be helped to prepare these sheets with an increasing degree of independence. The counselee may only be able to think about negative aspects of himself/herself. These will have to be countered by the counsellor. When the counselee is feeling too low about oneself, the counsellor may help by listing some of the positive qualities. A simple format of an emotional balance sheet can be as follows:

Internal Qualities (Liabilities)	Internal Qualities (Assets)
Anger, Short-temperedness	Perfectionism
Overworked	Multitasking

Some qualities have been filled in the balance sheet above as examples. It should be noted that any of these qualities can be written as asset or liability. Being a perfectionist can be an asset or liability depending on the point of view of the person. The counsellor will have to help the counselee to locate his/her positive aspects rather than focus only on negatives. At the same time, identifying the liabilities can be helpful in locating the possible areas for improvement. In younger children, the teacher will have to help the child with a list of suggestive words that the child can classify. Older children will need less help in identifying one's qualities.

Privileges and Problems Sheet

While the emotional balance sheet is focused on looking inwards, a privileges and problems sheet is focused on the outside. When a person feels that it is not his/her own qualities but the circumstances that are leading to a lack of success or increasing difficulties in life, this serves as a useful tool for understanding one's life situation better. The following exercise may help in developing this sheet.

The passage given below is an extract from Malini Chib's *One Little Finger* (2011). Read the passage and fill in the table that follows from the perspective of the protagonist.

'I am told I revolted quite often. Maybe, I questioned my dreary life and why I could not run, play and explore my surroundings. I was pushed, wheedled, persuaded and coerced by my mother. Lots of bribes were used and I often got a chocolate bar if I did well.

The great thing is that although I could not do very much with my body, I understood all that happened around me. I even followed the stories my parents read to me. My father said I remembered each story so well that if he tried to skip a couple of pages to end the story quicker, I would know and start agitating and pointing to the book until he went back to the story. I could follow everything that people said to me though I could not respond.

Some people could not understand that although I did not speak, I could comprehend. These people had nothing to say to me. The children too could not understand why I did not play the usual games with them. They too left me alone. Mother recalls that at one birthday party, I was very depressed as everybody had left me alone. The hostess gave all the kids their going away presents of balloons, hats and whistles but left me out. She said she was sorry but she did not think I would be able to play with them properly. I think the worst thing that can happen to a child with disability is to leave them alone and not even talk to them.

When I went out, I became conscious of all the stares that I provoked, the hushed whisperings when I appeared, the unsolicited advice that was proffered. My mother writes that when I met strangers, or entered a room full of people, I began to put my head down, terribly conscious of myself and the fact that I was different from others. The thought that somebody may notice that I was present and ask something about me was mortifying.

However, I was fortunate I came from a privileged and well educated family. Both my grandfathers had been educated in England, and my great aunt was Lotika Sarkar—the first woman from India to have gone to Newnham College, Cambridge. My father and my uncle had both had their higher education at Cambridge as well'.

(5–7)

For younger children, a movie screening of *Frozen* (2013), *The Jungle Book* (2016), *Cinderella* (2015) or *Charlie and the Chocolate Factory* (2005) may also be held. They may then be asked to prepare a privileges and problem sheet for the protagonists in the movie.

Privileges and Problems Sheet for

....

Privileges	Problems

Once this task has been completed, the students may be asked to prepare a Privileges and Problems Sheet for themselves. The teacher will have to facilitate this process, particularly for younger children. Some possible answers may be difficulties in finances, family discord, supportive family, loving parents, good education or degrees, adequate infrastructure and so on.

Privileges and Problems Sheet for

....

Focus on Positives List

A focus on positives list works towards shifting the perspective of the counselee from only negative thoughts to positive thoughts. This also serves as a fruitful exercise when the person is facing a difficult situation. This is same as looking at a glass as half full or half empty. For instance, a child may have not done well in a stage activity in school. The child will be asked to look at the positive aspects of the situation:

– You were given a chance to participate.
– You were able to go on stage.
– It has helped you to recognise your difficulties and will be able to overcome them in subsequent opportunities.
– You have been able to identify your areas of interest.
– You remembered your lines, even though you were not able to win the competition.

The teacher's or parent's role in this exercise will be significant as the child may not be able to look at the positive aspects when overcome with emotions. The child may also be asked to revisit the event or experience after some time, once the initial emotional turmoil is over.

Negotiation Skills

Counselling processes can also be directed towards developing negotiation skills. Negotiation is important when there is an experience of conflict. Conflict may be experienced with someone else or with oneself. The counselling process can be geared towards developing the skills of negotiation so that conflict can be effectively resolved. It is important that the counsellor as well as the counselee recognise that the purpose of negotiation is not to arrive at a solution that suits everyone. In contrast, the focus is on arriving at an arrangement that would involve some amount of letting go from both sides. Through a process of accommodation, both parties will be asked to compromise a little. When taking decisions that lead to a mental conflict, children may be asked to weigh the outcomes, possibilities and the amount of time, money and effort invested in the task. They may also be required to see the effects of the outcomes on themselves. This in turn can help to take decisions that are best suited in the particular situation. This can only be useful when the client is able to look at the perspective of the other, without which a compromise will not be reached.

Thought Stopping and Channellisation

Thought stopping is also used as a cognitive strategy that helps to overcome undesirable thoughts that lead to maladjustment. In this process, the counselee is asked to watch one's thoughts and stop oneself from thinking negatively. This may be practised with the counsellor. The counsellor will ask the counselee to vocalise the thoughts about a particular issue. For instance, in school settings the student may be asked to imagine a test situation and ask to vocalise his/her thoughts and feelings right before examination. The counsellor will speak the word 'Stop' out loud whenever the counselee vocalises a negative thought or emotion. This will be an indication for the student to change the direction of his/her thoughts and emotions. The counsellor will slowly shift towards making the student more independent. The student will be asked to 'stop' himself/herself from thinking negatively. This will be first practised in front of the counsellor and subsequently by the student alone.

Thought stopping may need to be accompanied with channellisation. This is required particularly for clients who tend to overthink or are stressed about a future event. Channellisation involves a diversion of thoughts and at times actions. By channellising one's energies towards productive activities such as sports, fitness training, reading, painting and other activities that may be of interest, the counselee can prevent overthinking and stop the emergence of negative thoughts. The counselee may also engage in channellising one's thoughts towards ideas that are positive. The counsellor may have to initially help the counselee to think positively. Thus, when a counselee voices fears of failing an examination because of lack of preparation, the counsellor can say 'Stop! Why don't you instead think of the kind of questions you have prepared for and what if those were the ones that were asked?' or 'Stop! Why don't you think of the syllabus that you have already completed and the chapters that you can cover in the two hours that you still have left?' This can later be practised by the counselee independently.

Count Your Blessings

Counting one's blessings involves being grateful for what one has. This can involve the material possessions and the opportunities one has, or experiences one might have had. This is similar to focusing on positives but is not restricted to any one situation. While counting one's blessings, he/she is able to realise the tangible and intangible things that one has received. A sense of gratitude towards specific people, events or life in general can help to focus on the little things that we take for granted on an everyday basis. Being able to walk, use a vehicle, getting education, food on our plates, and having friends and family are simple essentials that never get acknowledged as significant aspects of one's life that make life beautiful. Counting one's blessings helps to find cheer and happiness daily rather than waiting for a big event to happen. A counsellor, teacher or parent can organise this as a one-time activity with the children or with a specific child needing help. In contrast, to develop it as a habit, the counsellor may use this activity at a fixed time daily to talk about what they are thankful for every day.

Assertive Training

Assertiveness training refers to developing one's abilities to express one's point of view at the right time. There is a thin line of difference between being assertive and aggressive and this must be taught to school-going children. This is particularly significant during adolescence when they develop habits that will continue throughout their lives. Assertiveness training involves knowledge of one's rights, duties and responsibilities. Some people would like to go out of their way to help others. This soon becomes a habit and they are taken for granted by others. This may be an unpleasant experience. To counter such attitudes of the person and others around him/her, the counselee needs to recognise his/her limits. A key question here is: 'How much time can I devote for others?' In answering this question, the counselee would also be expected to prioritise and take decisions about which tasks are more important. In contrast, there will be others who would not be able to express their needs and wants. The counselee needs to be trained to recognise their needs and wants and be able to express them to the right person, at the right forum. Both these exercises may require the counsellor to ask the counselee to list the things that they want but do not get because they have never asked for it. A key aspect of assertiveness training is to emphasise that assertion should not be done in the heat of the moment. In heightened emotional states, assertion may come across as aggression leading to disharmony and chaos. Using 'I statements' such as 'I feel …', 'I want …' or 'I think …' are important ways of asserting oneself. These are better than saying 'No' without suggesting alternatives. When inundated with work, it may help to ask for more time rather than take on deadlines that cannot be met. A combination of these may be used to meet the specific needs of the counselee.

Systematic Desensitisation

Systematic desensitisation is a behavioural technique that can be used to overcome fears and anxieties. In systematic desensitisation, a counselee who has a fear of a particular experience is exposed to successively greater anxiety producing situations. Each situation is first addressed in collaboration between the counsellor and the counselee and later independently. This technique also works well with children with special needs, particularly those with socio-emotional challenges. For instance, a child who has a fear of talking to strangers may be systematically desensitised through a trip to the market. This would involve:

- Discussing the trip to the market.
- Systematically going through the plan and the processes involved in going to the market, the possible people one is likely to meet and interact with.

- Following the plan, accompanied by the counsellor with a specific list of things to be brought, with minimal interaction with strangers. This may first require going near the market without actually entering the market place. At each step the counsellor will have to ask if the child is ready to take the next step.
- After several trips, the child may be asked to visit the market alone with the counsellor watching from a distance. This may be followed by the counselee visiting the market completely independently.

Minimisation of Stressors and Maximisation of Possibilities

This is a two-fold technique that works towards reducing the focus on problems, challenges and stressors on the one hand, and increasing focus on the possibilities of change, on the other. The counselee will be asked to list the stressors in his/her life. Each of these will be discussed in terms of the worst possible effects of each stressor. The question 'So what if it does happen?' is helpful in imagining the worst possible consequence and mentally being prepared for the difficulties. This also helps in the realisation that the consequences thought of are often not as bad as imagined. Simultaneously, the counsellor will help the counselee to identify the possibilities of change in situation. The counselee can then take a proactive stance and develop a plan for further action.

Life Skills Education

The counsellor can help the counselee to develop life skills such as problem solving, decision-making, developing leadership qualities, managing emotions, working with empathy and sensitivity towards others. Life skills education can be provided in a workshop mode by organising skill enhancing sessions. Students may also be given problem situations that will help them to analyse problems and arrive at possible situations. Discussing case studies helps to sharpen skills and prepare for future difficulties. The counsellor may choose to prepare cases that address themes that are of relevance to the children in specific developmental stages.

Role Playing and Role Reversal

Role playing and role reversal are important techniques to develop perspective taking abilities. A situation may be given to students to enact the role of the various characters involved in the situation. This enables preparation for facing a situation and learning possible ways of handling difficulties. Role reversal is used to help the counselee to understand the perspective of the other in the situation. For instance, a child may be asked to act out like his/her parent while the parent acts as the child. This enables both people involved to understand how the other person sees him/her.

Teaching Coping Strategies

Students would benefit greatly from learning coping strategies that help them to deal with everyday stressors. These should focus on healthy coping mechanisms such as engaging in interests and hobbies, rationalising, discussing the problems, maintaining diaries and so on. Unhealthy coping mechanisms such as substance abuse, self-harm and so on should be discouraged.

ON A CONCLUDING NOTE

In this chapter, the focus has been on encouraging caregivers, including parents and teachers, to take on the role of a counsellor. This will help in building better interpersonal relationships and enable the children to live healthier lives. Teachers and parents will benefit from using the techniques and strategies discussed above. The focus should be on facilitating students to learn these techniques so that they can use them independently later in life.

Psychotherapy and Mental Health

The first two sections focused on understanding the processes and practices that influence the mental health concerns that are of relevance to school-going children. These provide a peek into ground realities and are significant in informing practice in mental health and psychotherapy. Theoretical perspectives are equally important in the psychotherapeutic approaches to mental health. In fact, theoretical approaches are relevant only within the context of what can be seen as applicable in the field. It is thus hoped that the first two sections would provide the necessary insights to help a deeper understanding of therapeutic approaches.

In this section, the theories in the three forces of psychology have been discussed in the context of their therapeutic relevance. The first force began with Freudian psychoanalysis that focused on unconscious processes that bear significant influence on behaviour. This suffered from limitations in overemphasising sexual instincts and drives. Thus, followers of Freud broke away from this tradition and moved to a psychodynamic approach. The key contribution here is the recognition of an unconscious reservoir that influences behaviour. With a shift in psychology towards experimentation and validation, psychotherapy shifted in focus to understanding behaviour only through verifiable measures. In Behaviourism, thus, only what is overtly verifiable was given credence. This was supplemented by cognitive behavioural approach that recognised thought processes as significant in influencing human behaviour. Hence, this formed the second force in psychology. Psychologists soon realised that this was not enough to understand all of human behaviour. Shifting from this reductionist, mechanistic view of human beings, humanists moved towards a positive view of human beings as proactive beings that strive for growth and creativity. This has been discussed in Chapter 16. In practise, however, such therapy is rarely divided in watertight compartments. Therapists prefer to use an eclectic approach that works well with the clients. They also rely on alternative therapeutic practices which have been discussed in Chapter 17. The concluding chapter of this section and the book serves as a summarising chapter. The discussion in all the earlier seventeen chapters contributes towards an understanding of human nature and helps us to conceptualise a mentally healthy personality.

Theories and Therapies I: Psychodynamic Approaches to Therapy

14

Until the nineteenth century, persons with mental disorders were forcibly institutionalised. Little awareness about mental health, emotional difficulties and psychological disturbances resulted in inadequate professional help being available. Persons with mild to moderate difficulties were mostly ignored and left to fend for themselves. Those with severe difficulties were ostracised and forced to live in psychiatric institutions where methods of treatment were often inhuman and ineffective.

The treatment scenario changed with the advent of psychodynamic therapy, propounded by Freud in the early twentieth century. Subsequently, Skinner, Beck and Ellis were some of the other important theorists who made significant contributions to counselling and psychotherapy. In fact, psychoanalysis and behaviourism to which these theorists belonged were the first two forces in psychology. The third force, humanistic-existential psychotherapy emerged in the late 1960s with the work of Maslow, Rogers and Frankl.

In this chapter and those that follow, some significant theoretical and therapeutic approaches to understanding counselling which are relevant to education, will be discussed.

SIGMUND FREUD (1856–1939)

Freud is considered to be the father of psychoanalysis. All psychotherapeutic approaches, in fact, work in support of or against the theoretical constructs put forth by Freud. Radically different from the ideas of his times, Freud's theory was widely criticised. Although his ideas have been severely criticised, many of his contributions have provided the foundation for contemporary theories and practices in psychology and mental health.

Trained in medicine, Freud specialised in neurology. His early work made significant contributions to research in the area of brain and spinal cord. His interest in the works of Breuer introduced him to the use of hypnosis for treatment of emotional disorders. It was through Breuer's work that Freud developed an interest in and started working in the area of psychological disorders. His early experiments emphasised the importance of expression and free association. It was during the end of the nineteenth century that he first used the term 'psychoanalysis'. His early experiments had helped him to establish the significance of sexuality and sexual experiences in the lives of people. He particularly focused on infantile sexual experiences, early childhood experiences and sexual fantasies in his later works. Early childhood experiences are now recognised as significant by most clinicians and practitioners. Post World War I, Freud's interests in traumatic neurosis and treatment through psychoanalysis as an alternative to electric shocks also paved the way for furthering the understanding of post-traumatic stress disorder. Freud's contribution was also seminal in acknowledging that homosexuality is not a disorder or an illness.

To understand Freud's work, it is first important to understand his theory of personality. In presenting his understanding of human nature, he likened the human mind to a floating iceberg. From this he drew the analogy that the submerged portion of the iceberg is the deep, secret, personal chamber of every person's mind in which are stored his/her unfulfilled wishes and desires and negative life experiences that he/she wishes to wipe out of conscious awareness since they are painful, disturbing and anxiety evoking. He called this chamber the 'unconscious'. The portion that was visible in the case of the iceberg, he equated with the conscious chamber of the mind in which experiences were being lived and experienced continuously. Between the conscious and unconscious was a small overlapping region which he called the 'pre-conscious' from which some memories could be recovered. Collectively these constituted the topography of the mind. The Unconscious is the most important part in Freud's theory, particularly in the case of emotionally disturbed persons, as he believed that every disturbed person has a vast storehouse of painful, negative and repressed experiences, which he/she had to express, confront and deal with, if he/she had to be treated. In fact, unravelling the unconscious and promoting self-awareness of what was stored within it, was the main goal of psychoanalytic therapy (see Figure 14.1).

He also believed in the biological bases of human behaviour and thus the universality of psychosexual stages of development that all individuals undergo. These stages play a significant role in the individual's attempt to maintain a balance between his/her own sexual drives and socially acceptable behaviour. He acknowledged the role of environment only to the extent that it constituted the context in which children learnt the moral and social codes of acceptable behaviour in society, largely controlled by the superego.

Structure of Personality

Freud believed that the personality comprises of three systems, represented by the id, ego and superego. The id is completely unconscious, the ego partly conscious and partly unconscious and the superego more conscious and less unconscious. The three structures tend to overlap and often work together rather than operating as discrete entities.

The id is the biological component and works on the pleasure principle. It operates in close contact with the biological needs of the body, particularly hunger, thirst, sleep and sex, and seeks to satiate these needs whenever possible. The id is not controlled or subdued by the pressures of the external world. In simplest terms, it works towards avoiding pain and discomfort to the body and fulfilling the pleasurable needs and desires of the body. It is oblivious to notions of morality and constraints imposed by social relations since it is fully unconscious and operates entirely for pleasure. In order to fulfil its needs, the id relies on two primary strategies. These are reflex actions and primary processes. Automatic processes such as blinking and coughing are examples of reflex actions. Primary processes are those that help individuals to fulfil wishes through forming a mental image of the remedy. The most common example of these are dreams that act as the outlets of mental images, which in turn help to satiate needs and desires. It was for this important function that dreams perform that Freud gave great emphasis to understanding a person's dreams. At birth, we are only id. Since the id does not know reality and mere mental imagery is not enough to gratify instinctual needs, by the end of the first year of life, a portion of the id gets differentiated into the component called 'ego', which operates on the reality principle. For example, if a child is hungry and the id seeks gratification of the hunger, the ego helps to source the food.

| **Figure 14.1** | Freud's Theory at a Glance |

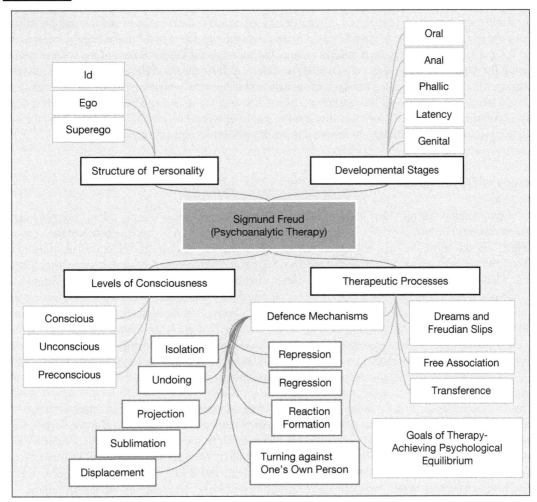

Source: Authors.

The ego also works to balance out the pressures of the impulsive, pleasure seeking id and the constraints put forth by the social and moral regulations of the superego, particularly on instincts related to sexual pleasure and aggression. It acts as a mediator between the id and superego. It postpones instinctual desires that cannot be gratified and simultaneously also encourages flexibility in moral decisions. It is the ego which balances out the internal and external pressures on a person. High ego strength ensures a greater sense of balance.

The superego works in sharp contrast to the functioning of the id. Like the ego, the child is not born with the superego. The superego develops as the child comes in contact with the outside world and the person learns to internalise the rules of the world. It works on the morality principle. A superego-dominated person is likely to be self-righteous, sacrificing and moralistic.

By the time an individual is five or six years of age, his/her personality has all the components: id, ego and superego. Id represents the biological aspect, ego the rationality and reality aspect and superego the social and moral aspect. All behaviour originates as a biological instinct in the id and through the principle of transfer of energy, the id transfers its pleasure wish through the 'libido' (the energy system) to the ego for gratification. The ego then transfers this to the superego for the fulfilment of the wish or desire. Basing the superego's response, the ego takes an action. If the superego refuses fulfilling the pleasure instinct of the id, which is often the case, especially with respect to sexual wishes and aggression, then a tussle which Freud called an 'intrapsychic tension' between the id and superego starts, which the ego has to control and handle. It does this through the use of ego defence mechanisms. Basically, the ego defence mechanisms help the ego to restore a sense of equilibrium and take care of the tension.

Stages of Development

Freud propounded that all individuals go through five life stages. These stages, called 'psychosexual', are considered to be universal. The term psychosexual was used by him because he believed that at every stage of life, the human being is vulnerable to sensorial excitation which he called 'sexual pleasure'. The organs and zones of sensorial excitation varied with age and developmental stage. He named them: Oral, Anal, Phallic, Latency and Genital. They are named after the erogenous zone where they are located.

The oral stage is the first stage that makes up the first year and a half of a child's life. During this stage, the mouth is the most important zone of a child's body. It is through sucking and eating that a child finds instinctual gratification. The mouth becomes the first erogenous zone for the child. Biting by the infant is a form of oral aggressiveness. 'Freud believed that developmental problems at this point could later manifest themselves in symbolic and sublimated forms through symptoms such as gullibility (swallowing anything), overeating, and argumentativeness (oral aggressiveness)' (Seligman and Reichenberg 2011, 43).

In the second stage, toilet training becomes the most important process of instinctual gratification. This includes the dimension of the physical pleasure of emptying the bowels as well as the social pleasure of impressing parents through bowel and bladder control. In the anal stage, the use of punitive and restrictive means to encourage children to learn control is likely to promote a controlling and compulsive personality type. This stage lasts up to the age of three years but is likely to have an influence on later life. Healthy parenting at this stage can lead to fostering creativity and reduce emotional difficulties.

From the age of three to five years, the child undergoes the phallic stage. Experiences during this stage are related to adult sexual relationships later on in life. During this stage, pleasure is associated with the genitals and experiences of masturbation and sexual fantasies. Freud also stated that children at this stage tend to develop sexual feelings towards the parent of the opposite gender. This is coupled with an unconscious wish of the child to kill the parent of the same gender. In boys, this is termed as the 'Oedipus complex'. It is the fear of retaliation by the father that leads the young boy to repress his feelings for his mother and identify with the father. The female parallel of this phenomenon is known as the 'Electra complex'. It is also during this stage that boys are likely to develop castration anxiety and girls are likely to develop penis envy. Contemporary thought, however, does not give credence to this aspect of Freud's theory and relegates it to a secondary position, along with many childhood experiences that are likely to impact a child. Theorists now also believe that irrespective of gender, children are likely to look towards their mothers as the first source of attachment.

The period between the ages of five and eleven years is considered the latency period and is a relatively quiet period. During this period, sexual desires tend to take a backseat with primary importance being given to social interests and relationships. The Oedipus and Electra complexes are resolved during this stage.

The final stage is the genital stage. Freud believes that this stage continues throughout the lifespan. It is during this stage that people tend to develop positive love and sexual relationships in the adult manner of heterosexual relationships as they are known and understood. In fact, it is the ability to engage in love and productive work that marks this life stage.

The psychosexual stages described above help us to understand the process of personality development in its dynamic form. Freud's theory has influenced several other personality theorists, the most significant among them being Erikson, whose work has been discussed in Chapter 3.

Implications for Psychotherapy

In this section, the key ideas of psychoanalytic therapy, which are relevant in counselling and dealing with children who are emotionally disturbed will be discussed.

Levels of Consciousness

As has already been discussed, Freud described the mind as being constituted of three levels of consciousness, namely, conscious, unconscious and pre-conscious. Two-thirds of the human personality remains at the unconscious level. Only the conscious element stays above the surface. The conscious comprises of the material that we are aware of and is available to us. The pre-conscious holds that information which is not a part of our awareness but is readily available and can be accessed. This includes information that we do not think of but is part of our memory and can easily be recalled. The unconscious is a reservoir of all those repressed drives, impulses and memories that are unfulfilled or too painful to be remembered. These are tucked away from our conscious mind into the unconscious for healthy living. The unconscious, Freud believed, held many more memories than the conscious and pre-conscious. These memories, when not addressed through therapy, continue to cause distressful experiences to the individual, as they may enter into the conscious, in distorted ways. Besides psychoanalysis, these memories can emerge into consciousness through dreams.

Dreams and Freudian Slips

Dreams and errors are ways in which the unconscious gets reflected in the conscious world. Freud believed that all dreams are meaningful and if interpreted through the symbols that they carry, may hold important meanings related to what is stored in the unconscious. Dreams are ways in which wishes are fulfilled, impulses are addressed and also help provide an outlet to those thoughts that cannot otherwise be brought into awareness.

Freudian slip is a term used to describe those errors, omissions or mistakes that hold latent meaning. They hold the potential for revealing secret desires and wishes.

Goals of Psychoanalysis

The analyst in this system works with the broad aim of ensuring efficient working of the ego and achieving psychological equilibrium. Further, he/she would encourage the client to maintain a balance between id impulses and superego restraint. Basically, the analyst helps the client to control immature impulses that can be harmful. Expression of thoughts and feelings through free association and catharsis, particularly those bottled up and repressed in the unconscious are also given importance, to expand self-awareness in the patient. Healthy use of defence mechanisms is encouraged.

In a typical therapy session relaxation followed by the patient lying down in a comfortable position on a couch is the beginning point. The analyst takes a backseat. The patient is encouraged to say and do whatever he/she wishes to do. The content of the patient's sharing is recorded and the analyst particularly notes the points of resistance in sharing, the shifts and fluctuations, gaps and inconsistencies and the opening and closing remarks in each session. All these are attempts at unravelling the unconscious.

Transference

One of the key components of therapy in psychoanalysis is that of transference. The client projects his/her feelings towards another person onto the therapist. This helps the client to express his deepest thoughts and emotions onto the therapist and successfully resolve any past issues that may have remained repressed so far. A successful use of transference would lead to strengthening of the ego through identifying and addressing root causes of the repressed feelings.

A contrasting concept is that of countertransference. In countertransference, the therapist projects his/her feelings in engagement with the client. While this can complicate therapeutic sessions and can be very emotionally draining for the therapist, trained therapists tend to use countertransference to assume the role of the person the client tends to project on him/her. In the resulting communication exchange, the client is able to address unresolved issues and reconcile any unaddressed differences in his/her mind.

Free Association

Free association is one of the most commonly used techniques for accessing repressed material by the therapist. In free association, the client is allowed to express freely whatever thoughts and emotions come to his/her mind. The therapist has to be careful in not using any form of censorship or judgement. Free association is often used to link thoughts and memories that we may not be aware, are interconnected. By identifying these blocks in association moving beyond them, the client and therapist are able to access sources of repressed anxiety and tension.

Defence Mechanisms

Everyone experiences tension and anxiety at some point in life. Freud believed that everyone has an innate tendency towards reduction of tension and anxiety. Anxieties tend to trigger defence mechanisms that help to deal with inner conflict, anxiety and painful emotions. While modern psychological studies tend to list over forty defence mechanisms, some of the defence mechanisms that Freud himself had put forth are discussed here.

Repression

In the process of repression, a thought or feeling which is threatening or distressful is pressed out of consciousness. Since it stays away from conscious mind, it will prevent painful experiences for the individual. This can however, lead to a distorted perception of reality. An example of this is not remembering details of an accident or an unpleasant experience on stage.

Regression

In regression, the person behaves in a manner that is indicative of a less mature age and stage in life. A young adolescent may throw a tantrum and walk out of the room when he/she is losing an argument, thereby displaying behaviour that is more appropriate for a child than an adolescent.

Reaction Formation

In reaction formation, the person tends to adopt attitudes and feelings that are diametrically opposite to what he/she is truly feeling. An example of this is saying that you are not angry and affected by someone else's behaviour when you are actually deeply hurt and very angry about it.

Isolation

The defence mechanism works by creating a disassociation between unpleasant thoughts and memories by creating a gap and preventing association with other thoughts. Freud gave the example of a person starting to talk about something and then taking a pause before moving on to talk about something else. The person thus blocks the unpleasant thought from being associated with other thoughts.

Undoing

In undoing a thought or feeling, the person tries to reverse an unpleasant thought or feeling that signifies an opposite feeling to the original thought. For instance, a person may buy a gift for someone he/she dislikes.

Projection

Projection refers to attributing unacceptable thoughts and or feelings to someone or something else. For instance, when a parent is angry, he may shout at the child saying that the child is shouting in anger.

Turning against One's Own Person

This is most commonly manifested in the form of self-harm or self-injury. The intention is to harm oneself, however, the person is not suicidal. Self-harm includes a variety of behaviour including cutting, burning, banging and so on.

Sublimation and Displacement

Displacement refers to channellising one's thoughts and actions onto something else. For instance, throwing and breaking objects in a fit of anger. Sublimation is a positive defence mechanism that involves displacement of energy into socially acceptable ways. For instance, in a fit of anger a child may choose to participate and practise aggressive sports such as boxing, football and the like.

Although Freudian psychoanalysis has had far reaching implications for various therapeutic approaches, it was seen as a lengthy and costly process, requiring specialised training. Having been based on individual case studies, there was also no visible evidence for its success as a therapy that could be applied on a large scale. In addition, it did not seem to benefit patients who had urgent concerns and it had limited applicability in out-of-clinic settings. So, although it is still in use, its form in contemporary times is very different. Very few features of the original system have been retained. For schools, the notions of catharsis, free association, use of defence mechanisms and developmental stages are important.

CARL JUNG (1875–1961)

Carl Jung was the pioneer of analytic psychology. At first, he worked with Freud extensively, and later moved away to propound his own theory. He shared a common interest with Freud in the relevance of the unconscious in influencing human personality. Jung's work eventually was influential not only in psychiatry but also in the fields of anthropology and religious studies. Born in Switzerland, Jung's own childhood experiences had a significant influence on his work later in life. His father was a pastor and so his experiences led him to explore the religious dimension of human life extensively.

The Human Psyche: Attitudes and Psychological Functions

Jung propounded that the human psyche has three levels: the conscious, the personal unconscious and the collective unconscious (see Figure 14.2).

Like Freud, he too believed that the conscious mind is only a small portion of our psyche. He believed that the ego is the centre of the conscious mind, and has considerable influence on the person's interaction with the environment. Ego is the reality awareness dimension of the conscious. In other words, the ego comprises of thoughts, feelings and memories that are within our realm of awareness. These help in forming a sense of identity. Within the internal and external manifestations of the ego are two noticeable attitudes: 'introversion' and 'extroversion'. Jung found that people tend to be either inwardly or outwardly oriented. While he did not view these orientations to be exclusive and discontinuous, he strongly believed that people tend to lean towards one of the two orientations. Introverts tend to be primarily interested in their own thoughts. They tend to be introspective and not much in contact with the

Figure 14.2   Jung's Theory at a Glance

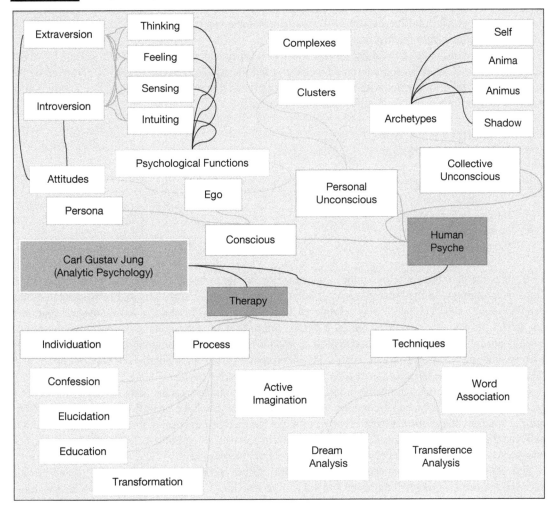

Source: Authors.

outside world. Extroverts are social and more aware of their social surroundings. They tend to engage more with the outside world.

Concurrent with attitudes are a set of psychological functions in every individual. These are:

i.   rational functions: thinking and feeling
ii. irrational functions: sensing and intuiting

Thinking and feeling are ways of forming judgements. The thinking function focuses on logic and objectivity to frame judgements. The feeling aspects tend to rely on value judgements and subjective criteria in making decisions and judgements. Feeling types are more prone to emotional aspects of experience.

Sensing refers to gathering details of perception on the basis of sensory experiences of touch, smell, taste, and the like. Intuiting depends on past experiences and unconscious processes while forming opinions. A strongly intuitive person will tend to add meaning to perceptions in a manner that this cannot be separated from the raw data itself.

Jung felt that only two of the functions are more developed and dominant in an individual. The function type indicates a person's strength and weakness and the style of activity generally preferred by the person. People tend to interact with the world through these functions. Accordingly, a combination of attitudes and functions puts forth eight personality types:

- Extraverted thinking type
- Introverted thinking type
- Extraverted feeling type
- Introverted feeling type
- Extraverted sensing type
- Introverted sensing type
- Extraverted intuiting type
- Introverted intuiting type

Besides the ego, the conscious mind also comprises of the persona. It is the mask that is worn that helps in engaging with the outside world. It helps to adapt to social situations and is influenced by the people we are with. The persona is considered to be inauthentic. In simpler terms, the persona does not reflect the thoughts and emotions of a person honestly. One's thoughts and emotions may not be socially acceptable and thus the persona protects the individual by providing an interface for interaction with the outside world. Persona or mask is the individual's system of adaptation or way of coping with real/social world. The persona can also be a mask of a 'collective psyche'.

The unconscious mind comprises a large part of the personality psyche. Jung agreed with Freud in accepting that the unconscious contains repressed materials that have an influence on the conscious mind. However, Jung differed from Freud in giving a positive connotation to the unconscious mind. He believed that the unconscious is the source of creativity, as well as emotional and spiritual growth. The unconscious comprises of the personal and the collective unconscious.

The contexts and content of the personal unconscious are specific to every individual. They include personal memories, thoughts, fantasies and subjective reactions to events and people, which are stored as clusters and complexes. These accumulations of associations sometimes may be of a traumatic nature and are likely to possess strong emotional content. Complexes are dynamic structures of the personality and comprise of feelings, thoughts and memories that are related to an archetype. The Freudian Oedipus complex is an example of how complexes are associated with archetypes of the mother and son relationship. Complexes generally comprise of a cluster of ideas and thoughts that revolve around a central theme. These are often emotionally charged.

The collective unconscious is a storehouse of latent memory traces, common to all people across the world. This predisposes people to react in particular ways to specific situations. Its contents are universal and historical, and largely comprise archetypes. Archetypes are primordial or predetermined images, thoughts and dispositions, which reflect part of man's cultural inheritance from the ancestral past. These are results of people's experiences throughout evolutionary history and are transmitted across generations. Important archetypes for studying personality and mental health include Self, Anima, Animus and Shadow.

The Self is a central archetype. It integrates the balancing of needs and messages of the conscious and unconscious. It emerges through dreams, symbols and perceptions. It is reflected in spiritual attitudes that mostly develop in the latter half of one's life. The Self expresses the unity of personality as a whole and encompasses both conscious and unconscious components.

The Anima represents the psychologically feminine aspect in the man. The Animus is masculine counterpart in a woman. Both these archetypes are part of the Self and have a significant influence on how we form our relationships with the other gender.

The Shadow represents the dark side of the individual. It largely comprises of those thoughts and feelings that are socially unacceptable. Shadow represents inferior/darker/negative traits of personality that individuals are usually reluctant to acknowledge. These are often morally objectionable and thus are mostly kept hidden from the conscious self as well as from others. The Persona and the Shadow work in contrast with each other. The Shadow hosts the desirable but socially unacceptable. The Persona represents what is considered socially appropriate and acceptable.

Individuation

Jung believed that a person aims towards a more honest living through a process of individuation. The person becomes more aware of his/her personal unconscious and lives in harmony with it. The Persona is slowly shed and gives place to the development of the Self. In fact, it is a process of self-realisation in which the worlds of the conscious and unconscious must be integrated. Jung's ideal of psychological health was conscious direction and guidance of the unconscious forces. The process of individuation can also be seen as coming to selfhood. It is an intrinsic tendency in all human beings. It is often described as the emergence of the undifferentiated self out of the unconscious.

In the process of individuation, the person first becomes aware of those aspects of the self which have been neglected. This is followed by reaching out into the unconscious and giving up those behaviours, values and thoughts that guided the first half of life. The unconscious is then confronted without any reservation or inhibitions. Dreams and fantasies are recognised and attended to. Creative imagination is exercised through painting, writing or some other form of expression. This is guided by a spontaneous flow of the unconscious and not by conscious, rational thought. Life goals may be reformulated and material, worldly goals are given up. This helps us to accept our Shadow and shed our Persona.

Having undergone this process, an individuated person would be more creative, free and spontaneous in his life. Living a more aware life would also mean that the person would be true to his thoughts, feelings and emotions. He/she is likely to have a high level of self-knowledge at both conscious and unconscious levels. There will be greater self-acceptance including one's own nature, with its strengths and weaknesses. While individuated persons may wear different personas, they do not confuse these roles with their true selves. All aspects of the personality are integrated and harmonised so that they can be expressed as an integrated whole. There will also be greater tolerance of human nature and greater acceptance of others.

Jungian Therapy

According to Jung, there are four stages of life: Childhood, Youth and Young Adulthood, Middle age and Old age. Therapeutic goals differ according to the individual's stage of life and particular circumstances. Therapy for people in early stages focuses more on attaining specific goals of adaptation, whereas goals for life's later stages focus more on realising the self. Analytic therapy usually follows a four stage path:

1. **Confession.** Confession refers to sharing secrets and revealing inhibited emotions. The patient shares his/her story, experiences and problems with the therapist. It restores the ego through a cathartic process, by giving went to material stored in the unconscious.
2. **Elucidation.** Here the therapist establishes a relationship with the client. Elucidation helps clients to gain insight into their personal unconscious and become more accepting of their shortcomings. Client's dreams are also analysed. Therapist points out projections and interprets what the client has shared. It also involves interpretation of transference.
3. **Education.** In this stage, insights are expanded and extended to social and behavioural aspects. In other words, education entails helping clients to draw out of themselves new and adaptive habits in order to replace their self-defeating habits.
4. **Transformation.** Transformation or change is only used, if necessary, in severe cases. The therapist helps the patient to work towards the process of individuation.

The relationship between the therapist and client involves a human dialogue with each client requiring individual understanding. Therapists and clients relate to each other at both conscious and unconscious levels. Some of the common therapeutic techniques that are used are: Active Imagination, Word Association, Dream Analysis and Transference Analysis.

Active Imagination

Active imagination refers to a conscious effort made to relax the control of ego and access the unconscious reservoir. Different techniques are employed by different individuals for active imagination. These include drawing, painting and other forms of self-expression.

Word Association

This is probably the most commonly used technique of analytic psychology. Here, both the word associated as well as the reaction time become important. Jung himself had strong intuitive powers and was able to interpret the meanings from the answers of his clients. Like in other techniques of therapy, the therapist's own abilities and personalities would play a significant role in the process.

Dream Analysis

Like Freud, Jung believed that potent material could be drawn from dreams that would help to understand the unconscious. He also undertook an analysis of the dreams retold by clients to uncover symbolic references to what is hidden in the unconscious.

Transference Analysis

In Jungian therapy, transference is used in the same context as in Freudian psychoanalytic therapy. This has been discussed earlier in this chapter. Jung believed that transference provides an opportunity to the therapist to analyse the details of exchange and to identify root causes of distress, anxiety and unhappiness. This also helps to identify emotions and feelings that may have remained bottled up and are expressed through episodes of transference.

Jung's work provides a rich understanding of human personality. His approach is well received by personologists. However, his theory does not suggest direct techniques that can be used for therapy. Jungian analytic psychology requires extensive training in the school of thought and is also a lengthy process, making it difficult to practise.

ALFRED ADLER (1870–1937)

Like Jung, Adler also initially worked with Freud and agreed with his ideas. However, over a period of time, he disagreed with Freudian determinism of biological and physiological constructs over psychological development. He eventually established his own personality theory and psychotherapeutic school called individual psychology. He particularly laid emphasis on social context, family dynamics and parenting process.

Adler was born in Austria. He had several bouts of illnesses during his childhood and wanted to become a physician. This later became an important influence on his theoretical constructs. Like Freud, Adler was trained in medicine. Freud recognised his talent in the early twentieth century and invited him to join the psychoanalytic school. The two worked together for several years. Adler disagreed with Freud about his beliefs about sexual impulses. He subsequently shifted his focus onto understanding the whole individual with reference to his internal world. His experiences with World War I also led him to strongly believe that people are motivated and driven by social interests and experiences.

Theoretical Constructs

Adler agreed with Freud in giving importance to early childhood years in a person's life. While he gave importance to biological factors, he also firmly believed that it is the self, which is of utmost importance in determining the future growth of the individual. He believed in the potential of the individual in purposefully choosing life paths, given a set of inherited characteristics (see Figure 14.3).

Feelings of Inferiority

Adler believed that all children develop feelings of inferiority when they see themselves in comparison with older siblings or with parents. He emphasised the point that how children are treated at this stage is significant in shaping their future. Children who are able to find outlets for expression and build positive self-esteem are able to overcome these feelings of inferiority. Children who are pampered and not allowed to overcome feelings of inferiority continue to depend on others in their adult lives. In contrast, children who are neglected or those who are discouraged from overcoming their inferiority feelings end up being discouraged and develop a sense of hopelessness.

Thus, it is important that children should be encouraged to strive towards overcoming feelings of inferiority through participation in creative pursuits.

Figure 14.3   Adler's Theory at a Glance

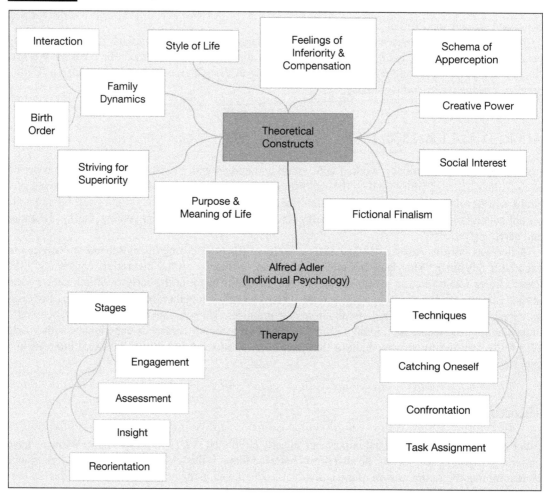

Family Dynamics and Birth Order

Adler gave importance to both family composition and birth order. He believed that not just the members in the family, but also the interactions that they have with each other hold significant influence on the child's life. The child himself is not a passive recipient but also an active participant in family life, constantly interacting with parents and siblings. He highlighted that it is the siblings who are the most different from us and who have the most important influence on us. The difference provides children with the opportunity to rethink their choices and the roles that they wish to lead in their lives.

He also gave equal importance to the birth order of children. The relative significance of specific order of birth has been discussed in the section below.

First Born

Adler believed that first born children are often high achieving. They tend to be well behaved and organised. They are strong leaders and responsible people. The birth of a younger sibling can make the elder one feel like a dethroned monarch as attention is showered on the next born. Successfully dealing with the birth of a sibling can lead to developing self-confidence.

Second Child

The second child attempts to cross the achievements of the first born. However, soon realising that he/she will not be able to outdo what the elder child has already accomplished, he/she tends to establish achievements in unconventional areas that the older one hasn't ventured into. The second born is thus more likely to take up unconventional career options in comparison to the first born who is likely to be more traditional. Second born individuals are also more expressive and friendly than first born individuals.

Middle Child

Middle children tend to feel sandwiched between the achievements of older children and the unconditional love and pampering received by younger children. While they usually enjoy many of the strengths of the second born, they may feel unloved and uncared for with families showering their love more on younger children. With positive parenting and encouragement, middle children can also be well-adjusted, friendly and high achieving.

Youngest Child

The youngest children are often pampered and spoiled by the rest of the family. Adler believed that they often expect others to take decisions for them and tend to assume lesser responsibility. Adler felt that they may also develop feelings of inferiority. They tend to find their own interest areas that are different from the rest of the family so that they can carve out their own niche without being compared to other children in the family.

Only Child

Only child tend to enjoy the lives of both the first born and the last born. They can be spoiled and pampered as they enjoy the privilege of being in an all adult atmosphere.

This may lead them to focus only on their own needs. They can also combine the high achieving status of the first born with the creativity and free spiritedness of younger children. They tend to mature early and deal well with adults around them. If parents are insecure, only children may end up adopting the worries of their parents.

However, these need to be treated with caution. People should not be stereotyped on the basis of their birth order. On the contrary, birth order should be taken as a component that can contribute towards a better understanding of the individual.

Striving for Superiority

Adler emphasised aggression as a means of overcoming challenges and taking initiative. Drawing from Nietzsche's concept of 'will to power', Alder refers to aggression as a means of fulfilling the urge for power. He elaborated that this may be the means to achieve a goal of superiority. People have an innate tendency to strive towards perfection. This striving for perfection is an important dimension of life towards which all individuals work. This goal of superiority can have both positive and negative connotations. Where the goals are rooted in social interests and welfare, these will take on positive connotation. Whereas where the goals are those of personal superiority, coupled with the attempt to dominate others, it may lead to the development of neurotic tendencies. Adler strongly advocated that people strive to maintain and develop a sense of self-worth.

Purpose of Life

Adler believed that people tend to work towards finding purpose and meaning in life. Without this sense of purpose, it may be difficult for adults to find a sense of achievement in life. He believed that often goals of life are decided during early childhood but tend to remain obscured from consciousness. It is these life-goals that guide and motivate us towards future career aspirations and choices. Life goals are influenced by feelings of inferiority and compensation. They serve to bridge this gap between the insecurities of childhood and abilities to overcome them in the future. Life goals tend to provide purpose and direction to our everyday activities.

Style of Life

Adler's work emphasised holism. In other words, he believed that people should be understood in their totality, that is, as a unified whole. One's style of life presents the unique way in which an individual chooses to pursue a life goal. He felt that an individual can be understood in his entirety if the life goal towards which all his energies are directed is identified. He reiterated that emotional problems and difficulties should not be seen in isolation but should be seen in the context of the larger life of the individual. In other words, it is the unified style of life that provides insights into the individual's psychology.

Schema of Apperception

Apperception refers to subjective interpretation of what is perceived. Schema of apperception refers to development of a sense of self and apperception of the world that influences behaviour. Adler said that our schema of apperception influences the way we perceive our surrounding. This is often self-reinforcing. For instance, when an adolescent believes that his parents are biased against him, any decision taken by the parent would be seen as deliberately contradictory to his wishes.

Creative Power

Perhaps Adler differed from Freud the most in his belief in the creativity of individuals. He believed that all human beings have creative potential that help them to set goals in life and work towards achieving them. Determining life goals, styles of life and schema of apperception are creative acts. Through these creative endeavours, Adler believed that people are in control of their own lives and destinies.

Social Interest

Adler saw a sense of continuity and solidarity as central to one's life. He felt that individuals tend to work towards not just their own personal interests, but also the interests of others. He gave importance to the social context in which the individual lives: family, community and humanity at large. He felt that by cooperating with others around us, individuals can truly overcome feelings of inferiority. A lack of cooperation with others can result in a neurotic life.

Fictional Finalism

He propounded that we all tend to set fictional goals that serve as ideals, giving greater meaning to life. These ideals keep on changing as life progresses. Although each of these ideals seems to present final goals, they also tend to change as life progresses. An example of fictional finalism is the belief that if I become the business head of this organisation, it will mean financial stability forever, thus solving all other problems. However, this is not a final goal that can actually provide a solution to all problems. Thus, once this is achieved, new goals are set that seem final but are only fictionally so. Nevertheless, these serve as important functions for giving direction to life.

Stages of Therapy

Adlerian therapy is best understood as a four phase process: engagement, assessment, insight and reorientation. The process has been briefly discussed in the subsequent paragraphs.

Engagement

In the first step, Adler advocates establishing a strong relationship between the client and the therapist. This is done by way of open communication that forms the basis of a warm and nurturing relationship. The therapist also tries to understand the client's own understanding of the problem and also the expectations that he/she has from the treatment. Here, the therapist focuses on the strengths of the client and his potentials and capabilities in dealing with the problems. It is through a relationship that is built on trust and shared understanding that clear goals for therapy are established.

Assessment

Adler suggested an in-depth analysis of the person's life and the problem faced. This is done through preliminary background information that helps in detailing out the person's life including family life, birth order and memories of early childhood. He believed that early childhood memories have a strong impact on present choices and attitudes. Subsequent interviews also focus on understanding the style of life of the individual. This includes religious beliefs, attitudes towards sexuality, social relationships and role models. The client is also asked to share his/her dreams.

Insight

In this phase, therapists adopt the stance of encouragement. At the same time, they put forth challenging options to the client. The therapist provides alternative views to the client and provides various interpretations. The client is encouraged to reflect on his/her own life and gain insights into the causes behind his/her behaviours and attitudes. The therapist encourages the client to rethink his/her beliefs, attitudes and behaviours.

Reorientation

In the final phase of the therapy, the client is encouraged to reorient their beliefs and behaviours. Once they have identified the potential problem areas in the first phase, they are able to reorient themselves to move towards new ideas and patterns of behaviours. The client and therapist are able to discuss future goals and make decisions about ways of strengthening social interests.

Some Therapeutic Techniques

Adlerian therapy can be implemented by using some simple therapeutic techniques. Some of the commonly used techniques include catching oneself, confrontation and task assignment.

Catching Oneself

In this technique, people are encouraged to be more conscious of their thoughts. This helps them to identify their repetitive and faulty thoughts. For instance, a person may be asked to become more conscious of the physical sensations experienced before he/she tends to get inappropriately angry. This will help to recognise physical signs of tension and help the person to prevent fits of anger.

Confrontation

In this step, the person is requested to explain a decision that seems to be in contradiction with what he/she has otherwise wanted to do. For instance, a child may be asked to recollect thoughts that led him to decide to go out with friends for a movie a day before the examination when he was otherwise worried about not doing well in examination.

Task Assignment

This is a commonly used strategy in which the therapist and the client together plan an activity that the client will be required to complete. Planning for tasks and committing to completing them serve the purpose of arriving at an agreement. They promote a sense of accomplishment and competence. Further, they also ensure that the person moves towards appropriate behaviours by designing appropriate tasks.

Adler's approach is much appreciated by contemporary psychotherapists and has had an influence on many theorists including May, Rogers and Frankl. However, there is little empirical evidence to support his claim of social interest being innate. Some of his ideas of fictional finalism and superiority have also not been validated.

ON A CONCLUDING NOTE

This chapter discussed the key concepts in the works of Freud, Jung and Adler, summarising the psychoanalytic tradition. While this approach has been severely criticised for the time it takes for therapy and a lack of empirical evidence, it is also the first force in psychology and must be acknowledged for having set the path for accepting psychological concerns as distinct from physical conditions that can be treated by medicine alone. In more ways than one, the psychoanalytic approach has set the pace and direction for all counselling and therapeutic approaches. It is called psychodynamic because it basically deals with knowing the inner dynamics and activities of the mind.

15 Theories and Therapies II: Behavioural and Cognitive Behavioural Therapies

The psychodynamic approaches to mental health and therapy were discussed in the previous chapter. They constituted the first force in psychology and dominated the first half of the twentieth century. The second force in psychology emerged in the 1960s although the psychologists who were part of it had already been in active experimentation and theorising since the 1940s. This approach focused on studying the behaviour of human beings as it was seen and observed. On account of its overarching emphasis on behaviour being the unit through which human action was understood, it was called the school of behaviourism. In the context of therapeutic approaches in mental health, behaviourism includes both behaviour therapy and behaviour modification therapy, as it later came to be known as cognitive behaviour therapy. These therapies will be described in detail with some suitable examples and illustrations in the present chapter.

To understand the rise of behaviourism, it is important to know what the limitations of psychoanalytic therapy were. Mainly, since it was time consuming and did not show immediate results, psychoanalytic therapy failed to gain popularity. Further, the therapy in psychoanalysis does not focus on visible change in behaviour, making its effects difficult to ascertain. In addition, what is held against it is that psychoanalysts rely on individual cases to study the effectiveness of therapy. Such an approach is not considered a reliable measure of judging the effectiveness or success of the therapy. What went against psychoanalytic therapy was that it focused extensively on the unconscious and on subjective therapeutic techniques, which were difficult to understand and appeared very abstract. Somewhere they mystified the understanding of human nature. Behaviourism rose as a response to these limitations of the psychoanalytic tradition. It focused on the here and now and on overt behaviour that could be seen and observed. It gained considerable momentum and became a strong and useful movement in psychology, influencing both learning as well as counselling and therapy. It continues to flourish till today.

UNDERSTANDING BEHAVIOURISM

In the context of psychotherapy, behaviourism is used as an umbrella term that includes three main movements, that is, classical conditioning, radical or operant conditioning and cognitive behaviour therapy (see Figure 15.1). Behaviour therapy is based on the principles of classical conditioning; behaviour modification therapy on the principles of operant conditioning; and cognitive behaviour therapy on the understanding of human behaviour that came from neo behaviourism. The former two together comprise behavioural counselling and therapy. Cognitive behaviour therapy is an independent therapeutic approach that also stems from behaviourism.

Figure 15.1   Behaviourism and its Types

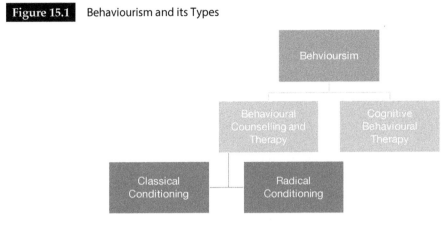

Source: Authors.

Classical Conditioning

Classical conditioning is also known as respondent conditioning. It explores the formation of stimulus and response (S–R) bonds, which become the characteristic way in which persons behave in situations where the same stimulus or some version of it are present. The main principles on which the S–R bond formation is based are association and contiguity. In the absence of these, extinction of the associative bond takes place. The formation of an S–R bond that leads to predictable behaviour is called conditioning. The process of conditioning leads to the same behaviour being shown, when the stimulus situation does not change substantively. The key proponents of this school were Pavlov, Watson and Raynor, as well as Wolpe and Hull. It shall be described more elaborately in the subsequent sections of the chapter.

Operant Conditioning

Also known as radical or instrumental conditioning, operant conditioning is based on the idea that individuals live and operate in the environment in which they are situated. Often the stimulus is not clear and it is difficult to identify the S–R bond. Yet responses are made. In this situation, the consequences of the response made determine the behaviour of the individual. If the consequences are pleasant and rewarding, the behaviour will be repeated or get reinforced. Likewise, if the consequences are unpleasant, the behaviour will not get reinforced or repeated. This approach rests on the assumption that the external environment is what induces people to make responses. It is called response–reinforcement (R–R) psychology. The key psychologists who promoted this approach were Thorndike and Skinner. Their ideas and principles are discussed in the sections that follow.

In practical terms, the principles of classical and operant conditioning are not applied in a purist manner. A combination of the two is generally used. They are often referred to as **Radical Behaviourism**.

Cognitive Behaviour Therapy

Arriving at a blend of behaviour, social learning and cognitive theories, psychologists such as Ellis, Beck, Lazarus and Kazdin developed cognitive behaviour therapy (CBT). Within this tradition, the person is given importance as a thinking and rational being, capable of taking decisions and solving problems. Each individual is seen to respond differently to the same stimuli owing to variation in cognition. Thus, CBT recognises individual differences on the account of cognition, which behaviour therapy does not.

In the sections that follow, both behavioural counselling and therapy and CBT shall be discussed.

BEHAVIOURAL COUNSELLING AND THERAPY

Behavioural counselling and therapy work on the principles of behaviourism in which the belief is that it is the behaviour of organisms, not mental phenomena that determine their learning, attitudes and habits (see Figure 15.2). They rest on the assumption that personality development is environmentally determined and individual differences are derived from variations in environmental experiences. The notion of dualism is rejected. In fact, the notions of mind–body, body–spirit, and body–soul are considered as having no scientific validity in the development, prediction and control of human behaviour. Further, the view that is promoted is that, although personality development has certain genetic limitations, which are fixed, the effects of environmentally generated stimuli play the dominant role. In other words, the individual's behaviour is either a response to a given stimuli or a response which is reinforced externally.

Figure 15.2   Behavioural Counselling and Therapy at a Glance

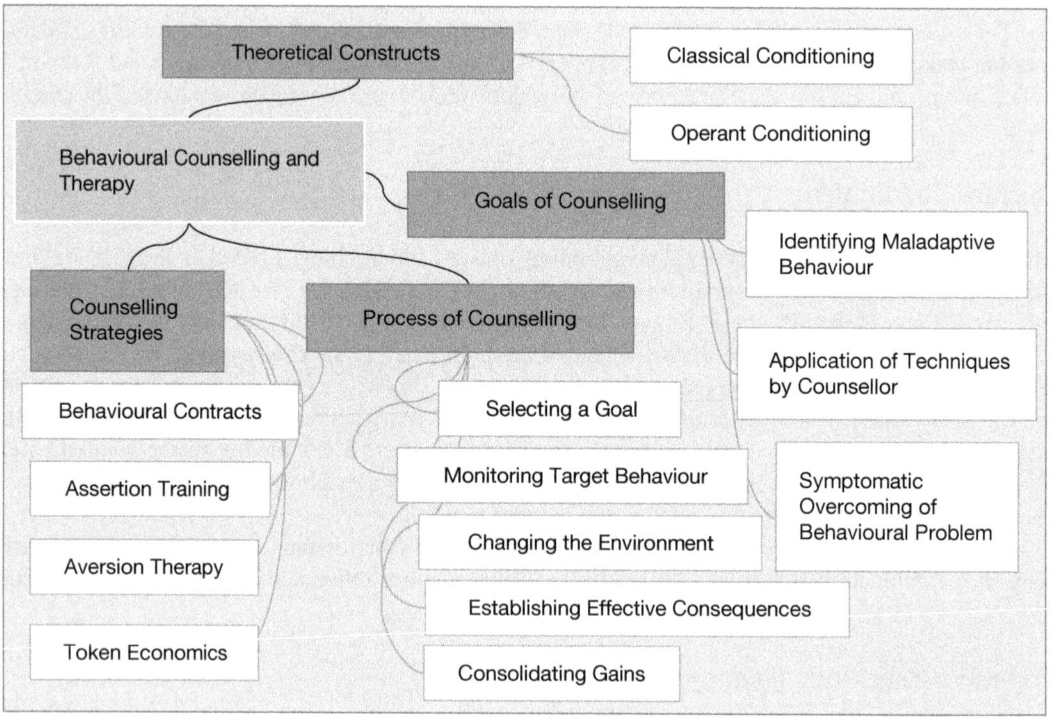

Source: Authors.

Theoretical Constructs

The theoretical formulations of this approach are influenced by two strands: classical conditioning and operant conditioning.

Classical Conditioning

Classical conditioning, as was discussed earlier, rests on the bond between stimulus and response, popularly known as S–R bonds. In any given situation, an individual receives stimuli from the environment and responds to it. This is best illustrated through the famous Pavlovian experiment that has been conducted on a dog. The dog salivated whenever food was given to it. Slowly, Pavlov conditioned the dog to associate the arrival of food with that of the ringing of a bell. However, the bell ring alone was not a sufficient stimulus for the dog to respond with salivation. Each time the bell was rung, it was observed that the dog began to salivate, even before food was offered to it.

Thus, an unconditioned stimulus (food) elicited an unconditioned response (salivation). This was followed by the association of the conditioned stimulus (ringing of bell) with the unconditioned stimulus, which led to conditioning of the unconditioned stimulus. Subsequent experiments revealed that the ringing of the bell alone led the dog to salivate. Here, a conditioned response (salivation) was elicited from the conditioned stimulus.

Conditioning, as has already been mentioned, is based on the principles of **contiguity** and **association**. In the experiment described above, the dog was seen to form an *association* between the ringing of the bell and food being offered. This led it to salivate even at the sound of the bell alone. Pavlov observed that this association was only possible when the two stimuli were presented in close succession. This is also known as **temporal contiguity**.

Over a period of time, if a conditioned stimulus is presented in isolation from an unconditioned stimulus, it is likely that the conditioned response will not be present or will become extinct. This process is known as **extinction**. Research by Pavlov also showed that the response does not vanish completely. There were several times that the dog responded to the bell ring after a time lag from the earlier experiment. This is known as **spontaneous recovery**.

Two other important principles of classical condition are discrimination and generalisation. **Discrimination** is the process in which the individual makes distinction between various kinds of unconditioned stimuli. The dog in the Pavlovian experiment would respond to a certain kind of bell and not to all sounds of bells ringing. In contrast, **generalisation** occurs when all similar stimuli are responded to similarly, that is, the dog responds with salivation to the ringing of any bell. A common example of this would be the response of the child to the sound of his parents' car coming to pick him up from the day care centre. Initially, the child will respond with eagerness to the sounds of all cars or horns of cars. Slowly, the child learns to discriminate between the sounds of cars and responds only to the sound associated with his parents' arrival.

Operant Conditioning

Operant conditioning, in contrast to classical conditioning, does not rest on the premise of a stimulus eliciting a response from the organism. It rests on the belief that the organism act upon the environment. In other words, the response is *emitted* and not *elicited*. The emitted responses that receive positive reinforcement are strengthened. And, the responses that receive negative reinforcement are weakened or not repeated. Thus, behaviour is based on response–reinforcement or R–R bonds.

Reinforcement can take many forms. **Positive reinforcement** refers to the presentation of a desirable experience subsequent to behaviour. This strengthens the behaviour and increases the chances of repetition. In contrast, **negative reinforcement** involves presentation of an undesirable experience subsequent to particular behaviour. This reduces the chances of the repetition of that behaviour. Punishment, the third consequence, basically breaks the behaviour. Punishment can take the form of presentation punishment and removal punishment. **Presentation punishment** involves providing a negative experience in response to some behaviour. In **removal punishment**, a positive experience is prevented in response to some behaviour. This may be summarised as shown in Table 15.1.

Another important concept is that of **schedules of reinforcement**. A schedule indicates a list or set of behaviours that will be reinforced. Continuous reinforcement involves reinforcing every behaviour. In this case, sometimes the reinforcer stops being effective because the individual knows that every response will be reinforced. Instead, partial reinforcement can be used which involves scheduling reinforcement. Schedules of reinforcement are divided into ratio and interval schedules. In a fixed ratio schedule, every nth response is reinforced. For instance, the teacher decides to reinforce every fifth answer that she receives in class. In a variable ratio schedule, the reinforcement will still be dependent on the frequency of responses. However, the number will not be fixed or predictable. In a similar manner, in a fixed interval schedule, the criterion of time instead of frequency of responses is used for providing reinforcement. Thus, in a fixed interval schedule, reinforcement will be provided after a pre-decided time interval. The teacher may, for instance, choose to divide the class time into 10 equal parts. So, in a 30-minutes class, she would provide reinforcement after every 3 minutes. In a variable interval schedule, the time interval will not be fixed, but vary between reinforcements. In a modular approach, various schedules of reinforcements may be used to suit the needs of the situation.

Another common method used in behaviourism is that of **shaping**. Shaping, or the method of successive approximation, refers to providing reinforcement at various steps of the process rather than only rewarding the final successful behaviour. For instance, instead of reinforcing only when scoring a basket, a child may be reinforced for correct technique, appropriate dribbling, timing and closer to target shoots while playing basketball. This shifts the focus from the final 'product' to the process of behaviour. **Modelling**, which is based on the principle of imitation, is another common technique that is used. Here, an appropriate behaviour is demonstrated to the child. When the child observes that behaviour is being reinforced positively, he/she learns to repeat the same behaviour.

When the same amount of a reinforcer loses its effect in encouraging behaviour, it is referred to as **satiation**. Regularly using the same reinforcer brings in an element of routinisation that loses its value in reinforcement. For instance, a child who gets a bowl of ice-cream every day after an hour of studying will consider it a routine and would either demand increase in quantity or ask for variation in flavours

Table 15.1 Types of Punishments and Reinforcements

	Pleasant Experience	**Unpleasant Experience**
Presentation	Positive Reinforcement (E.g., providing an extra hour for playing after completing studies.)	Presentation Punishment (E.g., giving someone extra homework for disrupting the class.)
Removal	Removal Punishment (E.g., disallowing a child to play with a friend for leaving food unfinished.)	Negative Reinforcement (E.g., allowing a child to not eat vegetables he does not like for lunch that day, after having scored well in examination.)

Source: Authors.

for it to continue to be a reinforcer. In contrast, if the reward has not been used in the recent past, it will create a sense of **deprivation**, thus increasing its value as a reinforcer.

Goals of Counselling

On the basis of the theoretical postulates given above, the following goals of counselling in behavioural counselling and therapy emerge:

- Identification of maladaptive behaviour/s and assessing their nature and intensity.
- Dealing directly with each of these behaviours through application of experimental techniques by the counsellor.
- Providing symptomatic relief and overcoming the behavioural problem.

Behavioural counselling and therapy represents a directive approach in which the counsellor plays a significant role. The counselling process is guided by the counsellor, with specific directions being given for changing the behaviour of the counselee. The model of counselling is interventionist, with the counsellor suggesting what and how possible changes in behaviour can be made. In contemporary behavioural therapy, however, a collaborative rather than an interventionist approach is used. The counsellor and client together decide the course of action that would help bring about adequate change in behaviour.

So, in this system, the focus of the therapy is on the behaviour itself and not on the factors that have led to this behaviour. It does not focus on either identifying or changing the causes that have led to maladaptive behaviour or maladjustment.

The counsellor–client rapport is based on accurate listening, concern, caring and acceptance. Understanding the client as a unique person is an important process input. Reinforcers will thus be based on the needs of the individual client rather than a 'one size fits all' approach.

Applications of Behavioural Counselling

Behavioural counselling is one of the most commonly used techniques of counselling and therapy in contemporary times. It is used in family counselling for parenting and child management and in business and industry. It is also used extensively in education for managing several problems like developmental disabilities, childhood autism and schizophrenia. It is further seen to be effective in management of personal problems and encourages the use of self-management techniques. It is applicable equally for gerontology and behaviour modification with individuals from diverse cultures. It is commonly and successfully used in cases of clinically diagnosed psychological disorders.

In a regular classroom, behavioural counselling can play a significant role. Some of the applications are presented below.

- Getting a behaviour to occur more often with positive and negative reinforcement and punishment.

    Positive reinforcement: 'Rahul, finish your work quickly and then you can go out and play'.

    Negative Reinforcement: 'Rahul, if you don't finish your work quickly, you will not be allowed to go out and play'.

    Punishment: 'Rahul, you are dreadful, you don't do your work properly. Now stay at home. No playing for you for one week'.

- Developing and maintaining behaviour with conditioned reinforcement

  'Okay students, here is how you can be considered for a prefectorial position'. The teacher will then spell out the conditions which need to be followed. Reinforcers will be provided when conditions are fulfilled.

- Doing the right thing at the right time and place: stimulus discrimination and generalisation.

  'Now students, please work at your desks'.

- Getting a new behaviour to occur through shaping.

  'Teaching a student to shed the nervousness and become more confident by providing several and varying opportunities to perform'.

- Getting a new sequence of behaviours to occur with behavioural chaining.

  'We need to build up systematically on your Maths related problems. Let's see how we can make you more confident and happy about Maths'.

- Establishing a desirable behaviour by using escape and avoidance conditioning.

  'That's bad for your health. Don't do it'.

- Decreasing a behaviour with extinction.

  'Ignoring a distracting behaviour in class and not providing attention to the disruption'.

- Developing behavioural persistence through the use of intermittent reinforcement.

  Improving a student's spellings in Hindi: 'Let's see how many words you can spell correctly. Let's beat yesterday's record'.

- Using types of intermittent reinforcement to decrease undesirable behaviour.

  Reducing talkativeness, shyness, non-cooperative behaviour and so on.

- Using S–R mediation and reinforcement mechanisms to

  o   teach rules,
  o   construct appropriate goals,
  o   provide guidance,
  o   provide situational inducement and
  o   modelling.

Process of Counselling

The process of counselling involves the five steps that are mentioned here. Steps 1 and 2 lead to behavioural change. Steps 3, 4 and 5 lead to sustainability of the change.

Step 1. Selecting a goal/target behaviour: The goals should be decided one at a time and not as one overarching goal. They should be measurable, attainable and positive. They should clearly spell out the desired level of expectation for performance and the time frame within which it should be achieved.

Step 2. Monitoring target behaviour: Using baseline assessment, the existing status should be recorded. A record of the process should also be maintained.

Step 3. Changing the setting events/environment: Here, situations which inhibit the progress towards achievement of the target behaviour may be altered/changed so that it is easier for the person to emit desirable behaviour.

Step 4. Establishing effective consequences: A record of the process towards achievement and change of the target behaviour should be maintained. Threatening situations should be removed by providing appropriate reinforcers to encourage desirable behaviour and discouraging undesirable behaviour. In-built into the process, there should be many reinforcers which the person values.

Step 5. Consolidating gains: What has been achieved should be evaluated and maintained. Self-management to areas that need improvement should be prescribed.

Counselling Strategies in Contemporary Behavioural Counselling

Counselling strategies are based on overt behavioural changes. It requires the collaborative effort of counsellor and client, where the counsellor's role is that of a facilitator or mentor, with consistent emphasis on self-management. Agency has to be provided to the client in the course of counselling by building up specific programmes.

Behavioural Contracts

Behavioural contracts are developed in a collaborative effort between the counsellor and the client. The client enters into an agreement with one or more persons to perform or attain specific pre-determined responses or goals.

Certain guidelines can be kept in mind for effective development and implementation of behavioural contracts. These are as follows:

- Select one or two behaviours that need to be changed.
- Describe those behaviours so that they can be observed and measured.
- Identify rewards that will sustain the changing process at various junctures.
- Rewards should be immediate.
- Initial contract should be based on shaping (successive approximation principle).
- Rewards should be frequent and in small amounts.
- Locate people who can help to observe the process and contribute by giving rewards.
- If goals are not achieved, rewrite/reformulate the contract.
- Keep the contract sustained for the maintenance of the behaviour.

The contract is usually maintained in writing and signed by both the parties. A follow up is organised regularly to ensure that the contract is fulfilled. Further, the reward or reinforcer should be decided in consultation with the client.

Role Playing

The technique of role playing is intended for expanding client awareness and displaying alternative behaviours to the client. It has been effectively used by behavioural counsellors for career counselling and behaviour rehearsal, as it helps in preparing for an upcoming task or situation that the client is nervous or anxious about.

Assertion Training

The purpose of assertion training is to empower clients to actively initiate and carry out desires, choices and behaviours. It helps in teaching clients alternatives to passive, helpless, dependent and stifled ways of dealing with life situations. The techniques used to achieve assertion goals are modelling and role playing. Passive, aggressive and assertive situations from the life context of the client are used to demonstrate model behaviour that helps the client to develop assertiveness. This is followed by progressive and successive reward on the achievement of steps of target goals and reinforcement for maintaining new assertive behaviour.

Aversion Therapy

Based on the principles of deconditioning and reconditioning, that is, replacing the maladaptive response with a more desirable one by using aversion, this form of therapy employs procedures such as electric shock, stimulus satiation and unpleasant mental and visual imagery to inhibit unwanted behaviour. This was traditionally used for managing substance misuse problems and is no longer practised on ethical grounds.

Token Economies

Token economy is a systematic procedure in which tokens are given as immediate tangible reinforcers for appropriate behaviours. They can be encashed later for incentives and privileges such as shopping in school canteen, local shops, malls and so on.

Behavioural counselling and therapy has been found to be successful in bringing about behavioural modification, particularly in reducing anxiety and dealing with stress. However, as a school of thought, it has several limitations. It fails to give recognition or cognisance to the ability of the individual in thinking and rationalising situations and behaviour. Early behavioural theories rose as a response to psychodynamic theories. However, the school of behavioural counselling was not insulated from the developments in the field of psychology. The 1960s and 1970s were marked by a cognitive revolution in psychology which influenced psychotherapy as well. The combination of behaviourism and cognitive theories led to the development of CBT, which is discussed in the subsequent section.

COGNITIVE BEHAVIOUR THERAPY

CBT emerged in the 1960s and is still a dominant movement among practitioners. They find it an effective tool for treating common psychological disorders, including behavioural problems. It is a directive form of counselling and therapy that focuses on understanding the influence of thoughts on behaviour. Some of its key proponents are Albert Ellis, Aaron Beck, Donal Meichenbaum, Arnold Lazarus and Alan Kazdin. All cognitive behavioural therapies rest on three basic assumptions (see Figure 15.3). First, behaviour is influenced by thoughts or cognitive activity. Second, these thoughts can both be monitored and modified. Third, change in cognitive activity can effectively bring about a change in behaviour, leading to desirable behaviour. Thus, if thoughts are negative or dysfunctional, they can result in negative conditions of anxiety, depression and self-destructive behaviour.

Figure 15.3   CBT at a Glance

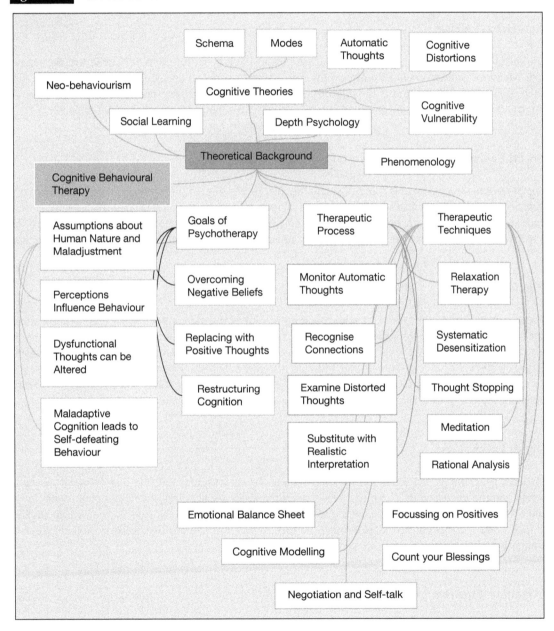

Source: Authors.

Theoretical Background

CBT emerged from the principles of neo-behaviourism and social learning. It is widely influenced by the theoretical ideas of phenomenology, depth psychology and cognitive theories.

Neo-Behaviourism

Building on the works of classical behaviourists such as Pavlov, neo-behaviourists believed that behaviour cannot be understood in its entirety but only in terms of stimuli and reactions. Neo-behaviourists, such as Tolman, Skinner and Hull believed that learning is a cognitive process. Thus, on the basis of information gathered from the environment, behaviour tends to be purposeful and goal directed.

Social Learning

Social learning emphasises the role of the environment in learning. In this view, learning occurs through observation and may not result in a change in behaviour. It is the expectation of reinforcement that influences cognition and, in turn, behaviour. For example, the observation of another child being rewarded for a particular behaviour develops an expectation of reward for similar behaviour in the child observing this.

Phenomenology

Phenomenological studies focus on understanding the subjective perceptions of an individual towards specific experiences. In psychotherapy, a phenomenological approach would work towards understanding the person's experiences not as an outsider but in the way the person feels and thinks about them. Based on this view, which posits that the individual's view of self and personal world are central to how he/she behaves, CBT focuses on understanding the individual's perceptions and attempts to identify potential sources of discomfort in thoughts, leading to dysfunctional behaviour.

Depth Psychology

In depth psychology, the focus is on understanding the unconscious and the link between the conscious and the unconscious. Cognitive behavioural therapies are also influenced by depth psychology, since they also focus on an individual's internal frame of reference and the sources from which his/her thoughts and feelings emerge. It is through the identification of sources that a change in behaviour is attempted to be achieved.

Cognitive Theories

Cognitive theories aim to understand thought processes and how they influence behaviour. They presume that thoughts are the primary determinants of emotions and behaviour. They reject the reductionist behaviourist postulate of stimulus and response as determinants of behaviour.

CBT is anchored in constructs like schemas, modes, cognitive vulnerability, automatic thoughts and cognitive distortions that are drawn from cognitive theories.

Schemas

Schemas are patterns of thoughts that organise information into categories and attempt to study the interrelationship within and between the various categories. Cognitive behaviour therapists believe that schemas form the core beliefs that guide behaviour and, thus, play a central role in psychological problems. Therapy aims at altering maladaptive schemas by highlighting inconsistencies in thought patterns and developing new schemas that help in adaptation.

Modes

A mode is a temporary state of mind that we tend to experience occasionally. A mode is a cluster of schemas that tend to act together. When a person finds a situation threatening or disturbing, an associated schema mode is activated. Schema modes influence coping styles and are classified into four categories, that is, child mode (vulnerable, angry, impulsive/undisciplined and happy child), dysfunctional coping modes (compliant surrenderer, detached protector and overcompensator), dysfunctional parent modes (punitive and demanding parent) and healthy adult mode (Young, Klosko and Weishaar 2003). A patient would develop any of these modes depending on the perceived experiences of stress. For instance, a stressful situation can act as a trigger for the activation of one of these modes. If the impulsive child mode is activated, the person may behave in the manner of a careless child. Reckless driving, substance misuse, self-harm such as injuring oneself, gambling and fits of rage are examples of impulsive child mode. The goal of therapy is to have long lasting activation of the healthy adult mode. The healthy adult is comfortable in making decisions and solving problems, thinks before acting and forms healthy relationships.

Automatic Thoughts

Automatic thoughts tend to appear almost simultaneously with the experience of an event or situation itself. An example of an automatic thought is the experience of anxiety and fear in response to the thought of being in danger when we see an out of control vehicle coming towards us. At times, however, automatic thoughts are not rational. For instance, the feeling of anxiety emanating from the thought of being in trouble as the principal has asked you to come to the office. Here, the thought of being in trouble has occurred automatically, irrespective of any previous action that may lead a person to believe that he/she is in trouble. In other words, the person jumps to conclusions without adequate evidence for the same. Through CBT, the person would be encouraged to check such thoughts and redirect them towards adaptive behaviour.

Cognitive Distortions

Patterns of thoughts that are not based in reality are known as cognitive distortions. Simply put, our mind convinces us to believe in something that is not really true. Such distorted thoughts serve to reinforce negative thoughts and feelings. A teacher who continues to believe that a student is deliberately disobedient or rude towards her would find every behaviour of the child directed towards her, annoying her, although the child may not be intending so. Self-fulfilling prophecies are also often a result of cognitive distortions. For instance, someone who believes that he/she always fails whenever he/she tries something new may end up failing because he/she has not put in his best in this new endeavour since he/she already felt he/she would not succeed in it. Cognitive distortions are often irrational and exaggerated.

Cognitive Vulnerability

A pattern of thought that is negative, irrational, incorrect or distorted may predispose a person to develop psychological problems. This is known as cognitive vulnerability. Vulnerability would exist before symptoms of a psychological problem appear. It increases the probability of a maladaptive response, which in turn increases the likelihood of the development of psychological disorders.

Sources of Cognitive Distortion, Vulnerability and Automatic Thoughts

Cognitive vulnerability, automatic thoughts and distortions result from a variety of sources that include inaccurate perceptions and beliefs. Biases in perceptions occur when we lose objectivity in observing people, situations or events. Stereotypes, cultural biases and prejudices often stem from biased perceptions. For instance, the bias that a student from an underprivileged background is more likely to have stolen cash than a student from a financially stronger family background stems from an existing bias and not the specific situation at hand. People may also be selective in their perception and only pay attention to that which supports exiting beliefs. Stimuli that cause discomfort or need realignment of thoughts are often ignored.

Overgeneralisation is another source of cognitive distortion. Overgeneralisation occurs when a generalised opinion is formed on the basis of a non-representative sample. For instance, after failing once in the examination, a student may develop the belief that he/she would never pass in that subject. Or on the basis of one failed performance on stage, a student believes that he/she is not good at performing arts. In personalisation, a person attaches blame and guilt for an undesirable outcome or situation to himself/herself, even when he/she has no control over the situation. An example of this is a mother who feels she is solely responsible for a child's poor performance in school and believes that she is a bad mother. While a parent's role is pertinent in the education of his/her children, blaming oneself without finding the cause of a situation is maladaptive. Magnifying refers to exaggerating something to an irrational level. This is reflected in the oft used idiom, 'make a mountain out of a molehill'. Minimising is the opposite of magnifying. Here, a person would minimise the benefits accruing to him or her and not look at the positive aspects of something. Beck put forth the notion of arbitrary inferencing as the tendency to draw out conclusions in the absence of evidence or on the basis of insufficient evidence. An example of this is a teenager who believes that she is not pretty because of not being selected for the lead role in the school play.

CBT thus works on the postulates and ideas, put forth by other theoretical perspectives. These form the basis of the assumptions about human nature and maladaptation, discussed in the section that follows.

Basic Assumptions about Human Nature and Maladjustment

Unlike behaviour therapy, CBT gives credence to thoughts and ideas of individuals. Recognising the person as a whole, it supports the notion that a person's total functioning includes cognition (thinking), affection (feeling) and action (behaviour).

It believes in the potential of humans to think rationally. At the same time, it acknowledges the possibility of irrational thinking in people. Instead of focusing on the external environment, it places the locus of control internally in the person himself/herself. In other words, humans tend to generate their own difficulties. Thus, a lot of problems that are manifested in behaviour are due to cognitive processes that may be faulty or maladaptive.

Therapy rests on the assumption that humans have the capacity to understand their own irrational thinking. When they change their irrational dysfunctional thinking, they return to their earlier state of adjustment and well-being. Many individuals form self-defeating habits. The power to overcome dysfunctional thinking and self-defeating habits lies very much with the individual. Perceptions can be altered/changed, restructured and reformulated.

Maladaptive cognitions lead to maladaptive, self-defeating behaviours. Adaptive, self-enhancing behaviours can be acquired by the client to generate positive, self-enhancing thoughts. Self-help books target developing such thought patterns and habits that help a person to achieve his/her goals. Clients can be taught to shift from covert self-defeating thoughts and attitudes to self-enhancing thoughts and behaviours. Someone who believes in his/her ability to influence the behaviours and patterns of others is more likely to be able to convince others in a process of negotiation and discussion. In contrast, someone with a low self-esteem may not be able to convince others about his/her point of view.

Goals of Psychotherapy

Based on the discussion above, the goals of psychotherapy in CBT may be summarised as follows:

- Overcoming negative beliefs, thoughts, attitudes, images and self-dialogue that are generated internally. Initially the therapist works towards identifying the negative thoughts that are leading to maladaptation. The therapist then helps the patient to overcome these thought patterns which are at the source of other psychological problems.
- Replacing them with positive thoughts, beliefs and images. The second goal of psychotherapy is to replace negative thoughts with optimistic and rational thoughts and beliefs. These may be situation specific and alter the patient's perception towards a specific situation or person.
- Restructuring of the client's thinking, coping ability and behaviour. The third goal of psychotherapy is to bring about a change in cognition in order to replace the negativity and maladaptation with positive thoughts and adaptive patterns of thoughts and behaviour.

Therapeutic Process

Based on the goals of therapy described above, the process of therapy would require the counsellor to help the client to identify and monitor negative thoughts. Automatic thoughts would have to be reassessed for their rationality, supported by evidence-based inferences. The client would also be helped to substitute biased perceptions. In the long run, the process would make the client independent in identifying biased thought processes. These have been summarised in the flowchart given in Figure 15.4.

Figure 15.4 Therapeutic Process in CBT

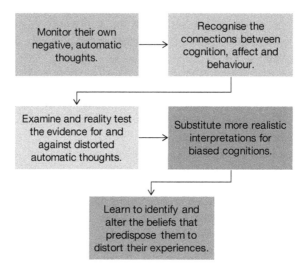

Source: Authors.

The therapist uses several process techniques as part of therapy to help the client move towards the final goal of developing adaptive cognitive structures and thought patterns. These include the following:

• Asking clients to provide reasons for a particular thought, idea and behaviour. This helps the client to identify inconsistencies and irrationality in their own thoughts and ideas with reference to the specific situation at hand. Accepting that their thoughts are not rational would help clients to move towards positive, rational thoughts.

• Using a whiteboard for clarification, making connections through flowcharts, establishing linkages, engaging in listing. Using this technique would help the client to recognise patterns in thoughts and establish the interconnections between thoughts, feelings and action. This in turn helps to establish a cause–effect relationship. Establishing interconnections is also an important technique to identify missing connections, overgeneralisations and arbitrary inferences.

• The therapist can help the client to move from faulty logic to consistent patterns of thoughts by asking questions, such as, Where is the evidence? Where is the logic? Are there other ways of perceiving the situation? What do I have to lose? What do I have to gain? What would be the worst thing that could happen? What can I learn from this experience? What is the evidence in favour of my interpretation? What evidence is contrary to my interpretation? Is there an alternative understanding or view point which I can build upon?

• A table that helps to categorise thoughts may help the client to identify cognitive distortions.

Situation causing negative emotions	Automatic thoughts which arise	Types of distortions in these thoughts

• The technique of decatastrophizing is used to help clients imagine the worst case scenario. This helps in cognitive restructuring that helps to address cognitive distortions, particularly magnifying, discussed earlier. In answering the question 'what if', the client is helped to establish that the worst case scenario is not as threatening or life altering as it appears. An example of this is to help a child to understand that going on stage and not performing well may not have as bad consequences as it appears to him/her at present.

- Reattribution involves alternative causes of events. This works well in cases of personalisation by helping the client to think of other reasons that may have led to the problems.
- Redefining the problem or situation involves negotiating with the client in identifying the source of the problem. Often the problem situation may be misinterpreted by the client and may not be rooted in reality. Here, redefining the problem situation would be essential. For instance, a child not performing well in mathematics may be attributing his low performance to inability while the root cause may be the inadequacy of the amount of time spent on studies.
- Decentring from one's own ideas, rigidities and fixations is important to understand that there are alternative ways of thought and perception that vary from one's own. This is important to understand maladaptive behaviour for clients who tend to think that their thoughts are central to the way everyone thinks and behaves.
- Refashioning beliefs and expectations. This requires the therapist to assist the client in rethinking existing beliefs about a particular situation or person. This would help the client to reassess his/her expectations and explore alternative ways of thinking.

Therapeutic Techniques

Therapeutic techniques used for helping clients in CBT primarily focus on cognitive restructuring. This focuses on disputing irrational and maladaptive thoughts and replacing them with rational thoughts through a process of restructuring ways of thinking and believing. Several techniques are used to achieve such restructuring. Some of these are discussed below.

Relaxation Training and Therapy

Problems such as stress, anxiety and physiological problems that do not have medical causes can be addressed through relaxation therapy. The therapeutic technique essentially involves relaxation of muscles and the whole body. This may be undertaken through guided techniques for deep breathing and muscle clenching and release. This is followed by mental relaxation by attempting to let go of distracting thoughts. External sources of cognitive stimuli are blocked. Once relaxation from anxiety is achieved, it is followed by training for prolonged usage of self-relaxation techniques to control stress in various situations.

Systematic Desensitisation

Systematic desensitisation involves exposing the client to increasingly intense sources of anxiety while coupling it with relaxation therapy. This enables the client to move towards overcoming anxiety in a step by step manner. An example is to help a child overcome stage fear by first asking the child to speak to the teacher from his/her seat. This is followed by asking the child to stand up and address the whole class first from the seat and later facing the whole class. Subsequently, the child may be provided opportunities to speak in the assembly, in front of the whole school and at interschool level.

Thought Stopping

Thought stopping works on the principle that if irrational and maladaptive thoughts are repeatedly interrupted, their frequency will eventually be reduced. Initially, the therapist would verbally stop the client whenever an unwanted thought is expressed. Later the client is asked to practise thought stopping several times a day. Verbalising the word 'stop' whenever a distressing thought comes to mind has been found to be an effective way of dealing with anxiety causing cognitive patterns.

Meditation

Meditation is a therapeutic technique that facilitates the client in focusing on an external or internal stimulus that helps to prevent a focus on aversive stimuli. It helps clients to make a conscious effort to focus on happy thoughts that help them to enhance their sense of self and overcome self-defeating thoughts.

Rational Analysis

The process of rational analysis involves identifying the processes through which irrational thoughts have developed and learning how they can be overcome. The first step involves identifying the source experience that led to the development of the irrational thought. This is followed by an analysis of the thought that was developed and feelings that are associated with it. Subsequently, the client can identify the inconsistencies and replace irrational beliefs with rational thoughts.

Focussing on Positives

This process involves asking the client to look at the positive aspects of any situation rather than the negative aspects. For instance, someone who has scored low in examinations can be asked to focus instead on having passed the examinations and moved on to the next class. Focus can also be shifted towards looking at examinations as a learning experience and identifying areas that require more work.

Count Your Blessings

In an extension to focusing on positives, counting your blessings would not just refer to one experience or situation. Instead, it focuses on developing a macro perspective towards life and being thankful for everything that is good and smooth. On a particularly rough day, clients can even be asked to develop appreciation for a smooth travel journey, having a job or having a home.

Negotiation and Self-talk

Self-talk refers to the process of acknowledging your own thoughts and talking to yourself about objectively looking at a situation and recognising the feelings that emerged as reactions to a distressing situation. People end up spending a lot of time dwelling over negative effects of an event or experience.

However, through self-talk, they can negotiate with themselves and avoid spending too much time only on the negatives. This involves trying to develop an objective third person account of the situation and reassessing one's own reactions to it.

Cognitive Modelling

Cognitive modelling involves both overt and covert strategies that aim to change the client's beliefs and attitudes towards a situation. The therapist may role model the client in a distressing situation, thereby demonstrating to the client what should be done to tackle the situation. This is followed by step-by-step instructions, to be carried out by the client in a modelling situation. The client eventually learns to instruct self while facing the situation in real life. In covert modelling, clients are assisted in envisioning a model or foreseeing themselves successfully handling a situation. This helps in developing a positive sense of self and faith in one's abilities to meet desired goals.

Emotional Balance Sheet

In an emotional balance sheet, the therapist helps the client to note down all the thoughts and feelings associated with a situation or person. These are categorised into gains and losses, like in a traditional balance sheet. This helps the client to identify what is pulling him/her down and what can help to focus on the positive aspects. The client can also be encouraged to use the same task for various situations that he/she finds difficult to address.

Applications and Usage

CBT is commonly used for the treatment of human problems related to dysfunctional thought patterns. It moves away from behaviourism in expanding its focus to thoughts, along with giving credence to manifestation of problematic behaviour. It has also been used for treating generalised anxiety, addiction (including alcohol addiction), severe emotional disturbance and anti-social behaviour. In educational settings, the therapeutic approach of CBT is used for addressing concerns of negative body image, bulimia, non-compliance in assigned tasks (e.g., homework), and attention deficiency and hyperactivity disorder.

ON A CONCLUDING NOTE

As has been mentioned earlier, the behavioural and cognitive behavioural therapies hold significant influence in contemporary psychotherapeutic practices as well. Producing immediate results that are observable and measurable helps the client and the counsellor to maintain the direction and pace of therapy. However, this suffers from obvious limitations of being reductionist and mechanistic. It disregards individual differences in emotions, wants and choices. These were addressed by the third force in psychology which will be discussed in the next chapter.

16 Theories and Therapies III: Humanistic Approaches to Therapy

The mid-twentieth century was marked by two dominant forces in psychology: psychoanalysis, known as the first force, and behaviourism, known as the second force. Psychoanalysis, as was discussed in Chapter 14, made many contributions to understanding human nature but it was not without its limitations. These largely arose from the excessive emphasis in the Freudian system on the unconscious processes and sexual motives underlying behaviour. Although the neo-Freudians, through their own writings changed the scene somewhat, the need for an approach which was objective, more representative of the population in its scale and where prediction and control of human behaviour were possible, became the need of the time. With this was born the school of behaviourism, also known as the second force of psychology. Behaviourism remained the dominant school of psychology for a long time and, in fact, continues to be important and widely prevalent till date, particularly in the case of children, persons with special needs and the emotionally disturbed. Chapter 15 clearly illustrated how these groups were addressed through various therapies that belong to the behaviourist school of thought. However, a strong limitation that it carries is that it does not address the mental processes adequately. Even with the advent of the cognitive school of thought, this approach remained highly mechanistic and somewhat dehumanised. In fact, it was in response to the mystification of human nature in psychoanalysis and the quest to re-humanise its understanding, after what behaviourism had done to it that the humanistic school of thought arose in psychology. Humanism places emphasis on human potential and rests on the assumption that people try to strive towards achieving perfection and work towards recognising their full potential. The approach drifts away from behaviourism in attempting to study the whole person and does not just focus on the visible actions or behaviour of the person. It celebrates subjectivity and individual differences and accepts diversity and uniqueness of every individual, rather than looking at these as limitations.

The key proponents of Humanism began their work in the 1940s. Maslow's humanistic approach, with its focus on needs, and Rogers' phenomenological approach are central to this school of thought.

ABRAHAM MASLOW (1908–1970)

Maslow was born to Russian–Jewish parents in New York, USA, in the early twentieth century. He was a bright student throughout school and college but could not accept pursuing law as a career option, although his father wished it for him. He chose to study psychology in college and was drawn towards Watson's behaviourism. He eventually worked with Thorndike, Adler, Fromm and Horney. He was strongly influenced by the works of the Gestalt psychologist Wetheimer and the cultural anthropologist Benedict. During his graduation days, he was convinced of Freud's emphasis on the role of sexuality in influencing human behaviour. Later, there came a shift in his understanding of social and personality psychology. This happened in the post-World War II period, marked by the various influences that he engaged with from different schools of thought within psychology. Although, he is known as one

Figure 16.1   Maslow at a Glance

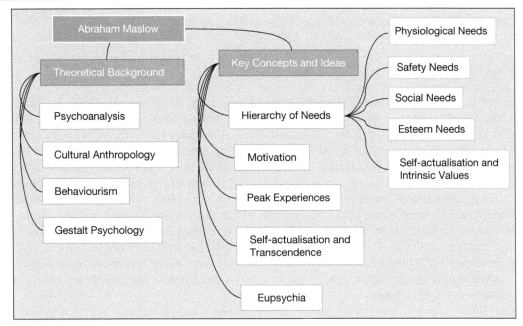

Source: Authors.

of the pioneers of humanistic psychology, Maslow himself disliked the label, stating that labels were restrictive.

Theoretical Background

Malsow's work, as has been described in Figure 16.1, was influenced by a number of psychologists. In studying psychopathology, he relied on the psychoanalytic tradition in its attempt to unravel the unconscious. However, he felt that this had little application in understanding everyday human behaviour. He felt that somewhere the view about the human nature was lopsided and presented only the limitations of human beings. His understanding of social anthropology led him to believe that human behaviour is influenced by the cultural contexts in which it unfolds. He thus believed that studying social and cultural patterns is important to understand human behaviour. Inspired by the works of Wetheimer and Goldstein, he emphasised the need to understand a person as a unified whole. Maslow's notion of self-actualisation has been drawn from the work of Goldstein, who believed that tension release is only important to people who are unwell. A healthy person would work towards tension increase in moving towards self-actualisation.

Key Concepts and Ideas

Maslow is known for his contribution towards understanding human needs and how they drive people to work and behave. Unlike psychoanalysis, his work focuses on how people function on everyday basis and is not restricted to pathological illnesses. In contrast to behaviourism, Maslow emphasised that it is not just the external environment but also the inner drives that motivate people to work. Some of his key concepts and ideas have been discussed in the subsequent paragraphs.

Hierarchy of Needs

Maslow floated what is known as a hierarchy of needs, which was discussed in fair detail in Chapter 3. This hierarchy flowed from basic physiological needs at the base of the pyramidal structure floated by him to the higher order need for self-actualisation, at the apex (see Figure 16.2). He believed that basic needs that are physiological in nature, such as hunger and thirst, must be met before higher order needs emerge. Deprivation of these needs would lead to problems. This was followed by the need for safety and security in terms of having permanence of shelter and affiliation with one's family, educational institution, workplace and so on. An orderly schedule and rhythm in life also provided fulfilment of the safety and security needs. Once a person feels safe and stable, the social and emotional needs for love, belonging, affiliation, recognition and so on through family and friends, emerge. Up to this level, the entire set of needs is called deficiency needs. Maslow used the term deficiency to highlight that non-fulfilment of any of these needs would continue to motivate the individual to find ways of fulfilling them. It is only when the deficiency needs are satiated that the higher order needs emerge.

The higher order needs which are called the growth needs include esteem, beauty, aesthetic and cognitive needs and the need for self-actualisation. Esteem needs are those that lead to developing self-respect and recognition from others for the work done by an individual. The beauty, aesthetic and cognitive needs are those which keep the individual happy and intrinsically motivated by the sheer joy and fulfilment of what they are doing. The highest need is the need for self-actualisation, in which the individual works towards developing his/her capacity to the fullest level of inner joy and contentment. Here, the individual serves to fulfil the function, he/she was born to fulfil. A painter would thus strive towards painting the best picture he can, not for appreciation from the world but because he is capable of painting to his full capacity. A teacher would continue to engage with full flourish because the act of teaching gives her meaning and joy in life. She is not teaching for awards, appreciation or fulfilment of her work profile. The higher order needs are also called 'being' needs, as fulfilment of them is important in helping a person live a full life and not just exist. In 1969, Maslow expanded this need hierarchy to include a higher stage, which he called the stage of meta-needs. He believed that in an individual who is already self-actualising, the existing five stages of the need hierarchy do not act as adequate motivating factors. Thus meta-needs consisting of intrinsic values, such as truth, goodness and justice are what drive the individual's work, behaviour and engagement.

Maslow's theory is more often depicted in a five stage pyramidal structure. The lower order needs are broad-based since all individuals experience these. The peaked top represents that it is only a few who reach the higher order needs.

Motivation

To explain the dynamics of how and why people work and behave, Maslow used the concept of motivation, stemming from need fulfilment. To simply state, it functioned on the basis that it is the dominant

Figure 16.2   Maslow's Hierarchy of Needs

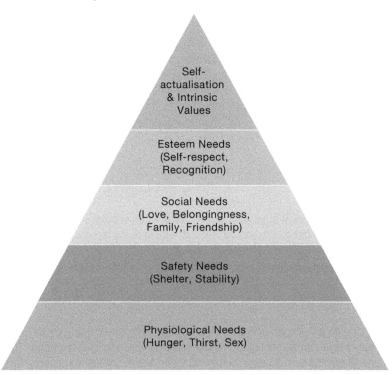

need at a given point of time that drives a person to work or behave in a particular way. What is significant about Maslow and makes him different from other need theorists is that while most of them work only at understanding behaviour orientations that flow from dealing with deficiency needs, Maslow also propounded the role of higher level needs. In his theory he explained that at the basic level deficiency needs motivate people to work. These are followed by the emergence of higher order needs. A lower need acts as a drive or motivating force till the time it is not at least partly fulfilled. However, once a lower order need is fulfilled, a higher order need emerges. Lower order needs lead to deficiency motivation. But, once these needs are fulfilled, people are still motivated by other needs. These include curiosity, interest and a search for enjoyment. So the spectrum of motivation may include seeking a positively valued goal, such as job recognition, a pleasure trip, a sense of joy in serving humanity or even a work of art. At still higher levels, motivation is derived from self-actualising and fulfilling one's intrinsic values.

Self-actualisation and Peak Experiences

A unique contribution of Maslow is the concept of peak experiences. He defined these as moments of joy and excitement that hold significance in the person's life. These are unique to every individual. In peak experiences, people tend to feel an intense emotional surge or feel overwhelmed. These maybe moments which hold emotional significance or provide insight into an alternative way of life.

Exposure to life changing art or music is also often considered to be a peak experience. All individuals have some peak experiences in life. However, people who are self-actualising tend to have many such experiences. Self-actualisers are psychologically healthy individuals who are productive and make significant contributions to the work that they undertake. They may not have experiences of transcendence. Maslow places people with transcendent experiences as hierarchically above the self-actualisers in need hierarchy. Those who are driven by intrinsic values tend to have many transcendent experiences in which there is an experience of limitlessness. Those who transcend have a clear vision of their own as well as others' abilities. Maslow highlighted that although experiences of transcendence have a spiritual angle, the characteristic is not restricted to creative pursuits and alternative lifestyles alone. He said he found many self-actualisers who were also transcending among businessmen and managers.

In his final work, Maslow propounded eight characteristics of people who were self-actualising. These include:

- Concentration reflected through a heightened sense of awareness of the events and surroundings.
- Making choices that lead to growth of the individual by being open to new experiences rather than only staying restricted in the comfort of safety.
- Self-awareness about one's inner nature, abilities and preferences and designing one's life around these.
- Honesty and responsibility towards one's actions and not being overly concerned about social image.
- Trusting one's own judgement in making life choices rather than being driven by social pressures.
- Self-development in order to be able to make use of one's talents and abilities.
- Having peak experiences and using them to develop better self-awareness and clarity in thought.
- Recognising one's ego defences and limiting their usage.

Maslow highlighted that self-actualisation is not a goal to be reached but a process that leads towards a more fulfilling life.

Notion of Eupsychia

Maslow coined the term Eupsychia to refer to an ideal society that would comprise of individuals who would work towards leading fulfilling lives. Members of such a society will be driven to work towards seeking personal fulfilment and would be self-actualisers. He highlighted however, that a society can only provide the environment that fosters actualising and need not produce self-actualisers. In organisations and societies, a Eupsychian attitude would encourage commitment towards work, and provide openness for experimentation and concomitantly personal development.

Applications to Counselling

While there are no specific techniques of counselling and therapy that Maslow suggested and there is little work that talks about his work in psychotherapy, his ideas have been widely recognised as being relevant even in contemporary times, where the approach is towards understanding the person as an integrated whole. In fact, it was with the efforts of Maslow and Rogers' work that the basic premises underlying human nature, which are so important in guidance and counselling, changed. The growth potential of the individual began to get recognised; their lived, subjective experiences became important in trying to understand them and their own goals and aspirations became significant in knowing and recognising their uniqueness. Maslow's theory has immense implications for understanding motivation and can be used in management as well as education. The first step in counselling would be to recognise the unfulfilled needs that create dissatisfaction and help individuals towards fulfilling them. In institutional settings like those of home and school, many examples and illustrations can be cited. In many upper class homes there is adequate material fulfilment, but there may be deprivation in social and emotional needs. For instance, if parents are professionally very busy, with very little time to spend with their children, the emotional needs of the children may remain unsatisfied and their behaviour towards their parents may reflect this. Similarly, if a child is hungry or sleep deprived, there is no point coercing him to study because he will have almost no concentration until his basic needs are met. There are many examples of similar kind. Analysing the preponderant needs that operate at a given point of time in a child's life and finding enabling ways for their fulfilment are thus the role of the counsellor, parent or teacher. The facilitative role of caregivers and teachers is a major contribution of Maslow's theory.

However, his theory is critiqued on two grounds. First, his work did not suggest any methods and strategies for counselling and therapy and is thus limited in its scope. Second, although his theory focuses on a hierarchy of needs, research has shown that these needs do not always arise in the same order as were suggested by him. They are often marked by overlaps. Some people also tend to actualise before lower order needs are met. Yet his contributions outweigh the limitations of his work and he is acknowledged as a very important personality theorist and thinker in mental health. He helped to re-humanise humans after the mechanistic approach of behaviourism, where man was equated with animals. Further, his approach established all the positive aspects of human nature and reposed faith in the human capability. Somewhere implicit in these assumptions were the seeds of self-directed counselling or what came to be known eventually as the growth dynamic or non-directive approach to guidance and counselling.

CARL ROGERS (1902–1987)

Rogers was born in Chicago to an engineer father and was the fourth of six children. He was an early reader and was known for being an intelligent and disciplined student. His childhood years were marked by the predominant influence of religion in his home and environment, essentially Christian practices. He was widely read and reflective about what he read. As a result, many latent questions about religion arose in his mind. These were answered when he travelled to China in his early young adulthood. The visit to China in fact was a life changing experience for him. He decided what his life and professional commitments would be. He was clear that he wanted to be in a helping profession. He eventually became a professor at the University of Chicago and established a counselling centre there. His work was greatly influenced by existentialism and phenomenology.

Key Concepts and Ideas

Rogers' ideas are based on the insights and learning that emerged from his interaction with his clients while working as a counsellor. His theory is rooted in the belief that people have an innate tendency to

Figure 16.3   Rogers' Person-centred Approach at a Glance

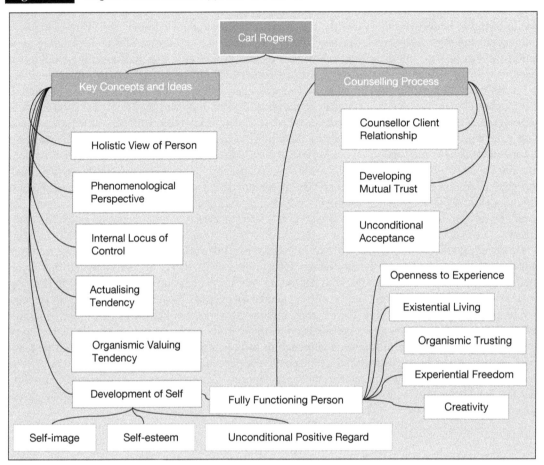

Source: Authors.

move towards growth. This is a natural propensity, common to all human beings. He also subscribed to the view advanced by the phenomenological approach, wherein the belief was that every person is unique and has his/her own subjective reality, flowing from his/her life experiences (see Figure 16.3). So like Maslow, he had distinctly humanistic leanings in which a person's experiences and inner potential for growth formed the core of his assumptions. Some of the key concepts and ideas from his approach are discussed below.

Holistic View of the Person

Rogers emphasised that the person be understood as a whole. This was in contrast to both the psycho-dynamic and behavioural approaches. He did not focus on dividing the structure of self into conscious and unconscious processes. Neither did he agree to the reductionist approach of understanding a person only with reference to his behaviour. He felt that the person must be understood holistically. One's internal frame of reference is influenced by experiences, feelings, emotions and behaviour. Thus, it is interplay of all of these that contributes to the person as a whole rather than a sum of various fragments. The notion of holism was also inspired by a belief in the organic continuity between the past and present experiences of a person and his goals and aspirations for the future.

Phenomenological Perspective

The phenomenological perspective emphasises understanding oneself from an internal frame of reference. In this approach, the person's psychological reality or perceptions of the world around him/her are given more importance than the objective reality. Each person constructs his/her own inner world which gives insight into his/her personal meaning to the events around him/her. This determines his/her beliefs, behaviour and relationships. Also, one's phenomenological field influences one's future experiences. This explains why each person perceives the same situation differently. A student while confronting her teacher with a difficult question in the class may view it as the starting point of an important classroom discussion, while the teacher may view it as a challenge to her authority. Likewise, when children question some of their parents' decisions in the hope that a dialogue will follow with them, most often it does not happen, as parents see this as questioning of their point of view. They are unable to see the intent and perspective of their child. Rogers believed that it was important that the client's inner frame of reference be given primacy in therapy and external opinions, and not be imposed upon him/her.

Internal Locus of Control

In sharp contrast to behavioural approaches, the person-centred approach to therapy emphasises the internal locus of control in understanding behaviour. Rogers acknowledged historicity by accepting that the past, present and future must be seen in continuity to understand experiences and perceptions. He focused on the present and the future, emphasising that man is not a hapless victim of what has already happened in the past but is proactive and 'in control' of his behaviour. So, without undermining the influence of early childhood experiences, Rogers believed that an internal locus of control translates into the ability of the person to direct his life towards fulfilling his actualising tendency, rather than giving in to the past.

Actualising Tendency

The actualising tendency refers to 'the inherent tendency of the organism to develop all its capacities in ways which serve to maintain or enhance the person' (Rogers 1959, cited in Weiner, Stricker and Widiger 2003). It is an active process and accounts for the person initiating, exploring, producing change in the environment, playing or even creating. In other words, a person strives towards growth and fulfilment. The tendency moves from fulfilment of physiological needs towards self-sufficiency and finally towards enhancing autonomy. Rogers believed that this actualising tendency was the driving force for every living being.

The tendency does not lead to tension reduction. Rather, it leads to tension increase. A person would perform to his/her full capacity when he/she feels dissatisfied with the current state of being. Thus, it will be an increase in tension that would lead a person to strive towards improvement and perfection. It eventually culminates in the process of becoming fully functioning, manifested as leading a more satisfying and enriched life (striving). The concept of a fully functioning person will be discussed in greater detail subsequently in the chapter.

Organismic Valuing Process

In working towards becoming a fully functioning person, Rogers propounded that people make use of their innate ability to know the processes that are more important or relevant for them. In other words, the organismic valuing process refers to the evaluation of life experiences in terms of how well they serve the actualising tendency. Positive experiences which promote the actualising tendency begin to get valued. Experiences which hinder or block the actualising tendencies are valued negatively. A person thus tends to control his/her life experiences and actions on the basis of this 'inner voice' that tells them what is helping them to move towards becoming a fully functioning person. There is a movement towards experiential self-control and internal locus of control.

This tendency is evident from early childhood itself. In fact, Rogers argued that people learn to trust others more than they trust themselves as they grow up. This can be counterproductive as a trust on others can move one away from the actualising tendency. In Rogerian terms, 'conditions of worth' assigned by others lead to developing similar conditions of self-worth.

Self and Process of Development of Self

In Rogers' person-centred approach, the development of self is central to the therapeutic process. One's self-concept comprises of image one has of self, with reference to the different roles played. It is an organised way in which one views himself/herself. Experiences, values, beliefs and personal meanings serve towards maintaining and enhancing the sense of self. It also includes the way in which one relates to others. In contemporary psychology, this is referred to as the relational self. A related concept is that of self-esteem. Self-esteem involves attaching value to the sense of self. In Rogers' work, it is also sometimes referred to as self-worth. A positive self-esteem refers to holding a positive sense of who we are and what we do. In contrast, devaluing one's characteristics involves negative self-esteem or feelings of being unworthy.

Another important notion is that of the ideal self. Our ideal self refers to who we strive to be. It includes aims of life and ambitions and since aims and ambitions keep on changing, our ideal self is a dynamic concept. The closer one's self-concept is to the ideal self, the higher is the chance to move towards becoming a fully functioning person. A total state of congruence is rarely ever achieved. However, a person would continually strive towards achieving this congruence.

The process of the development of self moves towards creating a perfect congruence between the self-image and the ideal self (see Figure 16.4). However, this is only possible when the child receives positive regard from others. Developing a positive self-esteem necessitates the fulfilment of the need for appreciation and acceptance. This is the need for positive regard. Socialisation experiences, however, often tend to place conditions of positive regard. In other words, a child is considered worthy of love and positive regard only if certain conditions are met. These may refer to being expected to behave in a certain way, score particular marks or excel in specific activities. This can be detrimental to the development of a positive sense of self. Over time, these conditions begin to be adopted by children and become conditions of positive self-regard. The child thus learns to value himself/herself only if and when these conditions are fulfilled. As was mentioned earlier, this can take the child away from his/her

| **Figure 16.4** | Congruence between Ideal Self and Self-image |

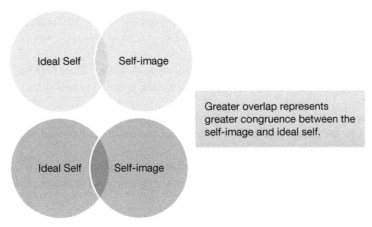

Source: Authors.

organismic valuing process. To ensure that the sense of self is developed, caregivers must provide the child with unconditional positive regard that fosters feelings of love and acceptance.

Psychopathology

Psychopathology develops when incongruence is experienced between self and experience. A child may find an experience organismically valuable, but the same experience may not be appreciated by others. A common example is when a child who is happiest in creative pursuits or sports is being told to focus on academics. A person cannot develop feelings of positive self-regard unless congruence is achieved between organismic experiences and positive regard from significant others. Incongruence, when it emerges, is dealt with at first, through the use of defence mechanisms. These mechanisms include perceptual distortion, rationalisation or denial. These have already been discussed in greater detail in the chapter on psychodynamic approaches to therapy. A breakdown in defences can lead to psychopathology.

Fully Functioning Person

The concept of a fully functioning person in Rogers' theory is akin to the notion of a self-actualised person in Maslow's theory. In Rogers' view, a fully functioning person is described as one who recognises his/her capacities and talents. This acceptance of his/her capacities and talents helps the person to perform to his/her full potential. His concept of a fully functioning person is also a reflection of what and whom he considers to be mentally healthy. He gave the following personality dimensions that reflect authenticity and congruence and constitute the characteristics of a mentally healthy person.

1. Openness to Experience:
    A fully functioning person feels free and is ready to try out new experiences. He/she does not feel stifled and is spontaneous in accepting new challenges and undertaking fresh adventures.

2. Existential Living:
   This refers to living in the moment. A fully functioning person would not dwell too much on what has already happened, nor plan too much about the future. He believes in living fully and richly in each moment of existence, as it comes.
3. Organismic Trust:
   This refers to the person's ability to consult and abide by his/her inner feelings, as the major basis for making choices in life. This helps in furthering the actualising tendency.
4. Freedom:
   Rogers' emphasises the feeling of being free in the context of having an internal locus of control. In other words, the being and not the environment is in control of the person's experiences.
5. Creativity:
   Here, creativity is not restricted to great inventions or innovations alone. It refers to the feeling of doing something new, thinking out of the box and going beyond the mundane.

Basic Assumptions about Human Nature

On the basis of the key ideas discussed above, the basic assumptions about human nature that the Rogerian approach rests upon are briefly discussed here. To begin with, he views the human being as a rational being, who is influenced by socialisation process, is forward-moving and realistic. Anti-social and negative emotions like jealousy, hostility and so on are reactions to the frustration of basic impulses like love, belongingness or security, which he saw as the basic needs of all human beings. He emphasised the inherent goodness of human beings and perceived them as cooperative, constructive and trustworthy. Believing in the actualising tendency, human beings learn to regulate their own actions and balance their needs. Thus, they have the potential to move away from a state of maladjustment to a state of psychological adjustment. Subjective experiences and acceptance of associated feelings are central to this process of adjustment.

Processes of Maladjustment

Maladjustment occurs due to a distortion or denial of an individual's perception of his/her experience which is incongruent with the person's self-structure. Incongruence between the real and the perceived self leads to tension and internal confusion. This is addressed through distortion of one's sense of self and defence mechanisms such as rationalisation, fantasy, compensation, projection and paranoid idea-tion. When defences break or become inadequate, anxiety, threat and disorganisation result. Rogers described anxiety to exist on a continuum from mild to severe. However, unlike the psychoanalytic tradition, he did not give categories such as neuroses and psychoses.

Counselling Process

The counselling process in Rogers' system was originally called client-centred therapy, but was later renamed, person-centred therapy. He felt that since his concern was with the person, client sounded too official, legal and formal. So, he went for a change. Like the rest of the theory, person-centred therapy operates on the assumption that if facilitative conditions are provided to a person facing emotional difficulties and a relationship of trust and positive regard is built between the therapist/counsellor and the person seeking help, the latter will be able to find ways out of his/her difficulties and also learn to deal with them. He/she would eventually be able to lead a more self-directed life.

The starting point of therapy requires recognition on the part of the therapist/counsellor that the person is in a state of incongruence, feeling vulnerable and anxious. The therapist/counsellor, in contrast is in a congruent state. He/she experiences and demonstrates unconditional positive regard and empathy towards the person. Through empathic understanding he/she communicates to the person that he/she understands his/her internal frame of experience. Nowhere are conditions imposed. Rather, a lot of time and effort is devoted towards building up facilitative conditions for counselling, as also the relationship between the counsellor/therapist and the person. Progress in the counselling process is focused on the counsellor/therapist–person/counselee relationship through the expression of empathy, genuineness, positive regard and unconditional acceptance. These are the responsibilities of the therapist/counsellor.

In person-centred counselling, it is expected that the person/counselee will experience a loosening of feelings during the counselling process. A change in the manner of experiencing and a shift from incongruence to congruence will also be experienced. A receptive person/counselee is likely to feel more comfortable in communicating more openly about himself/herself when the conditions of counselling are made conducive. He/she may also experience a change in the way he/she perceives his/her problems and how he/she relates to them. By the end of the process, the client would experience a change in the way he/she relates to the world.

Goals of Person-centred Therapy

On the basis of the discussion above, the goals of person-centred therapy include helping the person to be more congruent and more open to his/her experiences. The process would facilitate the development of more realistic perceptions. Through better psychological adjustment, it is expected that the person would become more effective in problem solving. As a result of the increased congruence between self and experience, his/her vulnerability to threat will be reduced. His/her perception of the ideal self will also become more realistic. He/she will begin to have an increased degree of positive self-regard, perceive others more realistically and accurately and experience greater acceptance of others.

Counsellor's Characteristics in the Person-centred Approach

Counsellors have a very significant role to play in the counselling process. Since the approach focuses on the subjective reality of the person, counsellor must not impose any external values or standards on to that person. For this, counsellors have to continuously endeavour to be genuine in their relationship with their counselees, listen actively to them and communicate their empathy. Through the tone of voice, words and non-verbal behaviour, counsellors should be able to assure the counselee of acceptance of the person he/she is. In other words, counsellors have to attempt to communicate unconditional positive regard towards their counselees. Understanding may be communicated through non-verbal cues of acceptance and appreciation, through restatement of content, reflection of feeling and paraphrasing the counselee's ideas and experiences. The counselees must be assured of trust in their abilities to be more responsible and self-directing. Finally, counsellors must create an environment that encourages and nurtures them to experiment with new behaviours.

Counselling Strategies

The person-centred approach to counselling is a non-directive approach that focuses on processes and providing experiences that help to create a safe and helpful environment in which the counselee can achieve congruence. The counsellor can use a number of strategies that work towards facilitating empathic understanding, such as attending to the client's expression, restatement of content and feeling and by appropriate non-verbal communication such as posture, body movements, gestures, silence and voice quality. Genuineness can be communicated by giving free space to the person and bringing naturalness and spontaneity to the counselling sessions. Through a consistent approach in the counselling sessions and an attitude of mutual sharing, the counsellor and the counselee can build a relationship of trust. Paying attention to a person's concerns and feelings, active listening, developing a non-evaluative attitude towards the client, according dignity and worth to him/her, situating understanding in the client's frame of reference and building up the client's potential and self-direction will help towards developing unconditional positive regard.

Rogers' person-centred approach is considered to be one of the most accessible and comprehensive treatment systems. With its focus on understanding the person as a whole, it shifted the perspective of psychotherapy to a positive view of human nature. It is frequently used in combination with other therapeutic approaches. However, the approach has been found to have limited success in cultures where expression of emotions is not encouraged. Some individuals also feel uncomfortable in expressing their emotions and so the therapist/counsellor is expected to modify techniques and strategies to suit individual needs. It has been found to be particularly effective with adolescents and young adults and as an attitudinal stance, across age groups.

ON A CONCLUDING NOTE

The chapter presented humanist schools of thought that focused on the inner frame of reference of the person rather than only on over behaviour or cover unconscious processes as in behaviourism and psychodynamic therapy. Humanistic therapy suffers from the limitation of being time consuming and subjective, thus providing little empirical evidence of effectiveness.

The three chapters on theories and therapeutic approaches have focused on the founding ideas of psychotherapy and mental health. The next chapter will present an overview of some therapeutic techniques used by practicing counsellors and psychologists.

Alternative Practices in Psychotherapy

The previous three chapters focused on describing the therapeutic approaches drawn from the main forces of psychology, that is, psychoanalysis, behaviourism and humanism. While each of these were distinct in their characteristics and features, in the real therapeutic situation it is seen that most psychotherapists, even if they belong to a particular school of thought, tend to use an eclectic approach, focusing more on the practices that work well for the patient rather than on maintaining theoretical purity. Keeping in mind the practice of psychotherapy in this chapter, the focus is on presenting some of the popular alternative practices in psychotherapy. It may be noted that there are many therapeutic practices which are followed in contemporary times, often drawn from the classical traditions but simultaneously new practices and adaptations keep on emerging from time to time. Most therapists develop their approach based on their own professional and personal experiences and thus each of them may have a unique working style. Contemporary popular practices include spiritual practices, alternative healing, emotion therapy, family therapy, interpersonal therapy, play therapy, group therapy and transactional analysis, among others. In this chapter, the therapies that are popularly used with school age children have been discussed.

PLAY THERAPY

Understanding Play

The word play is often used to refer to any activity that results in enjoyment. Engaging in play is presumed not to have any purpose other than the child's enjoyment and pleasure and so is often dismissed as being a superfluous activity. In reality, play is a very significant part of a child's life but somehow it is given little credence by parents and teachers alike. Observing children at play brings to light the insights that play holds about children's lives, thoughts and feelings. The discussion that follows will focus on understanding what constitutes play and reflect on the importance of play in a child's life.

The following excerpt from Garvey (1990, 2) highlights the nebulous nature of play and the associated difficulty in defining play.

> An infant shaking a rattle again and again, a kitten chasing its tail, a group of boys absorbed in a game of marbles, a girl preparing an elaborate feast for the inhabitants of a doll's house, a toddler gleefully running from its mother, girls skipping rope to a rhymed chant, a child finger painting, two monkeys taking turns at attaching and fleeing, a little boy spanking and scolding his stuffed bear—are all these events play? What characteristics do they have in common? Is there any feature unique to play? Is play in childhood related to adult play? To the play of young animals?

Garvey brings to light the wide scope and variety of activities that constitute play. Play is seen as an instinctive activity. Scholars believe that playful behaviour of young ones imitates the behaviours of adults. This is visible across species. Play is thus seen as directed towards building skills that are necessary for life. Another common characteristic of play is the lack of purpose and experience of thrill and enjoyment. Spencer argued that this is necessary for spending surplus energy that accumulates as part of normal functioning. Stanley Hall proposed the recapitulation theory of play in which he expressed the view that the change in forms of play across developmental stages reflected the course of evolution across time. Contemporary theories of play have revised these theories of instinctive preparation, surplus energy consumption and recapitulation. Pretence in play, for instance, is seen as expression of hidden worries and fears. In such an approach, play takes the form of cathartic release.

Types of Play

Whitebread (2012) has elaborated on the types of play. He divided play into five categories. These build upon Piagetian categories of sensorimotor play, symbolic-representational play and games.

Physical Play

This includes exercises such as jumping, climbing, dancing, skipping, bike riding and fine motor practice through colouring, cutting, clay modelling, and manipulating action and construction of toys. Research evidence shows that this helps in the development of the whole body and improves hand–eye coordination. Post pre-school years, physical exercise is also combined with tumbling, jostling and wrestling. This is generally undertaken with family and close friends and is known to help create close emotional and social bonds. Differentiating between such play and aggression also helps to develop social and emotional skills. Further, engaging in play that promotes fine motor skills helps to develop abilities of concentration and perseveration.

Play with Objects

This relates to the Piagetian concept of viewing children as little scientists exploring the world. Grasping anything within reach is observed in infants. As motor skills develop, children like to throw things, rotate them, bite them and hit with them, while engaging in sensorimotor play. This is followed by attempts at sorting and classifying objects according to size, colour and number. Building blocks and other construction toys are important as children grow older. These are supplemented by skills of storytelling, imagination and problem solving.

Symbolic Play

Symbolic systems include language, numbers, visual symbols and music, among others. These form an important part of play as children attempt to master these skills and knowledge. Play helps to experiment with symbols through sounds, jokes, tones, riddles, drawings, rhymes and songs. It helps to understand diagrams, read maps and deal with proportions. Drama and role play also help to develop performing abilities, confidence and social engagement.

Games with Rules

Children tend to invent rules for games. Often these are ways of learning social adjustment and developing maturity through sharing, taking turns, listening to one another, developing perspective and building leadership qualities.

Importance of Play

We must recognise the importance of play in children's lives. During infancy, play is important in developing motor skills in children and facilitating their cognitive development. It is also acknowledged as an important experience for children in developing their language and communication skills. Further, play serves as a concrete, natural outlet for a child's fantasy and imagination and helps to promote spontaneity and decision-making skills in them, through choices of play that they have to make. Through the rules and structures that play activities carry, play serves as an important socialisation agent, helping children to engage with others around them. It also allows for developing physical movement and a sense of balance and helps to foster creativity. Physical play actually promotes the development of dexterity in the task at hand. In allowing children to explore the world around them, play fosters cognitive and emotional development. For instance, it helps children to overcome fears and prepare for adult roles. In free play, children can be encouraged to take their own decisions, work at their own pace and identify areas of interest. In schools, play can be a source of academic learning, foster readiness for learning and develop problem solving skills.

THERAPEUTIC USE OF PLAY

Play as discussed above has tremendous potential as a learning resource. Considering that play is seen as an outlet for expressing covert thoughts and feelings, it can be used for uncovering the different socio-emotional layers in children's lives and understanding them better. As a therapeutic tool, play is generally used for analysis during the early and middle childhood years. Expressing one's feelings through play provides a natural, free flowing outlet that is non-judgemental for children. It is often used successfully with children who have been labelled as 'problematic' at school or at home. Behavioural issues, including indiscipline and disruptive behaviour, are often addressed through play.

Play therapy is used to communicate with the child and help him/her to overcome psychosocial challenges, promote better social adjustment and address emotions stemming out of traumatic experiences. It is also used sometimes as a diagnostic tool. By observing children at play with doll houses, dolls, animals and so on, the underlying causes of disturbed behaviour may be identified. Free play has also sometimes been used to identify and detail out experiences of sexual abuse. Play therapy can in addition, be used for desensitisation that helps in overcoming fears.

Process of Therapy

Therapeutic sessions last from thirty to forty five minutes in which the child may play individually, in pairs or in groups. The therapeutic use of play requires, first and foremost, creating an environment that fosters free play. It should be a physically and emotionally safe environment where the child is free from inhibitions. The child should not feel threatened or judged. In general, medication is not used in this form of therapy.

The therapist may play along with the child or let the child play alone. Observations are sometimes shared with the child after the session. During play, the therapist may engage with the child, providing him/her with undivided attention. This helps him/her to cope with difficulties by talking about them, or playing them out and expressing, or releasing the stored up problem or tension.

Types of Play Therapy

Play therapy can broadly be classified into two types: directive and non-directive. In non-directive play therapy, the child is given free space to explore and is encouraged to use play to find solutions to his/her problems. In directive play therapy, the therapist provides the structure in which the child is expected to play. The therapist provides guidance through the play to help the child deal with his/her behavioural difficulties. Non-directive play therapy has its roots in the psychodynamic tradition where play is considered a form of cathartic expression and release. In directive play therapy, overt behavioural concerns and cognitive reconstruction are given more prominence.

A common technique used in non-directive play therapy is Sand Tray Therapy. Developed by Lowenfeld in 1929 and revised by Kalff in 1980, the technique provides a sand tray and some objects to the patient. This is followed by complete, unstructured free play by the patient. It is sometimes also used for family therapy. The therapist only observes the entire process and does not intrude through guidance, direction or talking. Analysis involves noting the non-verbal play, choice of objects and restrictions imposed on the objects.

Using Freudian techniques, toys are used for non-directive play therapy. This involves providing access to toys such as animals, dolls, puppets, colours, cars and so on to the children. Free play with toys allow children to express feelings that they are not able to verbalise. This helps in cathartic expression and allows children to develop deeper insights into their consciousness.

Axline (1969) gave eight principles of non-directive play therapy that guide the therapist:

1. Establish rapport by developing a warm and friendly relationship with the child.
2. Accept the child unconditionally.
3. Develop a sense of 'permissiveness' so that the child feels comfortable to express freely.
4. Recognise the child's feelings and reflect them back to the child to help him/her to gain insight.
5. Demonstrate respect and faith in the child's abilities to make choices and solve his/her own problems.
6. Let the child lead the way and direct the conversation and play.
7. Allow the therapeutic process to progress and grow at its own pace.
8. Establish only those limitations that are essential to anchoring the therapy in given situations.

Directive methods tend to have the therapist engage actively in playing with the child. Instead of letting the child choose the direction of play, the therapist will intervene and suggest objects to create or play with. Storytelling is also commonly used in directive play therapy. Therapists often choose stories that have an underlying purpose and narrate them to children to bring about behaviour modification. While engaging in doll and puppet activities, children are given themes and character sketches that they can work with. Directive therapy is also commonly used with trauma victims to allow them to talk along with engaging in playing in the sand. The therapist can additionally use toys and dolls to demonstrate cognitive strategies that can be used by the child.

Effectiveness of play therapy is dependent on a number of factors. The number of sessions of play engaged in has a strong bearing on the effectiveness of the therapy. In general, more sessions have shown to have greater efficacy. Children in crisis, in hospitals and in post-trauma settings, have been found to respond well to treatment through play.

Implications for School-going Children

The previous section has discussed the use of play for therapeutic purposes. However, play also needs recognition as an important part of a child's everyday life. Children must be allowed to engage in free play from a young age. Teachers and parents should recognise their role as followers in free play exercises so that children can take the lead. Such participation provides deep insights into the way children think. In her study on understanding children's play at the pre-primary level, Gupta (2012) found that children display gendered behaviour in their choices as early as pre-school level. One of the episodes she has described in her work is reproduced here:

Class: K.G.

Corner: Dolls House

The play episode that I observed involved seven girls. In the dolls' house, together they decided to play 'Shopping–Shopping'. The game began with assigning roles to themselves and dressing themselves with *dupatta*s (long scarves). They also carried a purse each and in their purse, they put in toy plates which they pretended to be cash. While they were deciding their roles, a few of them sat on the floor and started playing with the dolls. Out of seven, only three were actively participating in the dialogues and leading the play while the others were following them and enjoying themselves. Since they were playing shopping–shopping, so they pretended the two windows of the dolls' house to be shopping counters. The window on the right was assumed to be the delivery counter and the window on left was the shop counter. Two girls were inside the dolls' house while the rest were outside near the two windows of this corner. While deciding the characters that they were to enact, some evidence of conflicts were observed but were resolved by them through mutual consent. One girl said to another:

Girl 1: '*Tu mausi hai*' (You are the aunt)

Girl 2: '*Nahi mein mummy hoon*' (No, I am the mother)

Girl 1: '*Nahi, mein mummy hoon, itni sari mummy nahin hoti hain*' (No, I am the mother. There are not so many mothers)

While the two girls were deciding who will be what, another girl went on the window (shop counter) and start shouting,

Girl 3: '*Kis kis ko lahanga kharidana hai aa jao*' (All those who want to purchase *lehenga*s, please come)

As soon as the girl on window made the call, all the girls went to the counter. Some of them were carrying dolls with them.

Girl 2: '*Maine apni beti ke liye bahut chamchamane wali saree lee hai*' (I have purchased a very bright saree for my daughter)

Girl 1: '*Aap ke pass safyed chamchamane wali saree hai*' (Do you have a bright white colour saree?)

Girl 3: '*Nahi safyed nahi hai, laal, hari, neeli hai. De doon kya*' (No, there is no white saree. Red, green, blue are there. Should I give you?)

Girl 1: '*Nahi, ab mujhe* ear rings *do*' (No, now give me ear rings)

'*Aur ab mujhe chahiye apne bacche ke liye choodi*' (Now I want bangles for my child)

'*Kitne rupye huye*' (What is the total amount?)

Girl 3: '100'

Girl 3: '*Kisko lahanga chahiye to le lo*' (Who want *lahanga*s?)

Girl 4: '*Mujhe chahiye, mujhe chahiye*' (I want, I want)

'*Ye wala do*' (Give me this one)

The girl then left the counter without paying the amount to the girl at the counter to which the girl at counter said,

Girl 3: 'Hello madam, *paise*'

Girl 4: '*kitne ka hai*' (How much does it cost?)

Girl 3: '1 Re'

When the girl pretended to close the shop, the girl at the counter said

Girl 3: '*Darwaaza bannd mat karo, ye hamare customer hain*' (Don't shut the doors, these are our customers)

Girl 3: '*Kisko lahanga chahiye le lo*' (*Who wants lahanga*s?)

'*Sab samaan milta hai is dukaan par*'

Girl 5: 'Frock milti hai'

Suddenly all girls start shouting

'*mujhe 6 do*'

'*mujhe 5 do*'

Girl 3: '*Ek ek mango mein zyada nahi de paongi*' (Ask one by one, I can't give so many frocks at a time)

Soon the wind up bell rang and the girl at the shop counter said to the customer girls

Girl 3: 'Shop *band hone wali hai* please *aap kal le lijiyega*' (The shop is about to close, please you purchase what you want tomorrow)

All the girls then came inside the dolls' house and started arranging the corner back into its original form. The time spent here was 15 to 20 minutes.

The episode highlights how children's play can be representative of their everyday life experiences. The play setting provides a space for interpersonal relationships, communication and building life skills. Play thus can be a useful resource for teachers and parents to build bonds with children, develop their confidence by using reinforcement and allow for space to explore the world.

GROUP COUNSELLING AND THERAPY

Sometimes therapy works better when employed in group settings rather than on an individual basis. Where a small group of students share a common problem, they may be better helped through a common counselling or therapeutic settings. Group therapy may be based on cognitive behavioural techniques, interpersonal therapeutic techniques or psychodynamic techniques. Although it is used for developing life skills such as anger management, mindfulness and relaxation techniques, it is most frequently used for fostering and maintaining healthy interpersonal relationships. To develop free expression, focus is given to art, music and dance as therapeutic techniques. Group counselling and therapeutic sessions may be conducted by one or more therapists along with a preselected group. It is believed that members of the group are also likely to benefit from interacting with each other and they may not benefit as much from individual therapy.

In group therapy, members are encouraged to talk to each other and share events of their lives with honesty. A common problem helps members to bond together and share in a comfortable manner. Support groups help to overcome a sense of loneliness. Commonalities help to find support and face challenges together. Group therapy settings thus become safe spaces, where new techniques can be experimented with to bring about changes in one's life. Listening to others also helps to build perspective and a sense of empathy. This is particularly useful for people with low self-esteem, those dealing with loss, trauma, anxiety and depression.

A group suitable for therapy comprises of 8 to 15 participants with a shared problem. Historically, group therapy was set up for providing sensitivity training in military settings. Feedback, role play and problem solving were used for building insights about each other and themselves.

Group therapy works through self-help groups, support groups and psychotherapeutic groups. Self-help groups comprise of people who have similar problems. They are not led by a professional therapist. An example of a self-help group is people dealing with a life threatening disease. They may come together to share their concerns, emotions, fears and experiences. Support groups are organised by professionals. A group with a common symptom, for instance substance misuse and addiction, may be led by a therapist to work together through the process of de-addiction. In working together in a group, the clients are able to share the challenges and difficulties they are facing in implementing the techniques and in turn providing emotional support to each other.

Process of Group Counselling and Therapy

Each group counselling and therapy group will follow its own course. Much of the processes followed depend on the group leader. Most groups tend to follow the processes detailed out below.

Pre-group Phase

The process of group counselling and therapy starts with a pre-group phase. This serves as an orientation to all the members. The group leader provides details of the purpose of the group, introduces all the group members to one another and gives an outline of the kind of processes the group will follow. This will help group members to decide whether they wish to continue with the group or not.

Individual Sharing

In the next step, each member of the group shares the personal goal that has brought the member to the group. This helps members to know one another better in their personal journeys towards growth. Personal goals also help the leader to decide on the course of action in the group so that the needs of all group members are met.

Developing Relationships Based on Trust

A group can work well as long as group members, including the leader, share a relationship based on mutual trust. Members must abide by confidentiality and respect other members' concerns and struggles. The therapist or the group leader will have to play an active role in helping group members to know one another and develop strong bonds. Further, these relationships must be maintained throughout the therapeutic process.

Focusing on the Problems

A group of people with different goals, perspectives and orientations can lose focus. The therapist has to ensure that all members of the group focus on the immediate problems at hand and work towards addressing these. Therapy sessions can otherwise become discussion sessions that may not lead anywhere and tend to stagnate.

Overcoming Resistance

Group members may initially be resistant to changes suggested by the therapist or the leader. They may feel uncomfortable in trying out new changes and implementing suggested experimental strategies. They may feel inhibited in sharing their difficulties, fears and challenges faced. The therapist would have to build an environment that is comfortable and helpful in overcoming inhibitions and resistance.

Expressing Inner Turmoil and Feelings

The next step is for group members to share their inner thoughts and feelings. The group leader must encourage individual members to participate in sharing their thoughts and emotions. Some members may be more expressive than others. The therapist would have to facilitate the silent members into sharing their inner turmoil and cope with distressful thoughts and feelings.

Exiting from the Group

The therapeutic process can be a strong support for people dealing with stressful situations. However, groups cannot last forever. When a majority of the group members have overcome the problem situation, the group may be disbanded. Alternately, the group can keep on learning with members leaving and new members joining in. However, just as initiation into the group can be difficult, moving out of the group can also be equally difficult. The therapist must help individual members to begin dealing with the issue on an individual basis and reduce dependence on the group. This may require follow up with individual members.

Role of the Group Therapist

As is evident from the process described above, the group therapist has a significant role to play in the therapeutic process. In the beginning of the section, we described that a group therapy session may not always be led by a professional therapist. In such cases, the group leader will ensure the smooth conduct of the therapy sessions. In the paragraphs that follow, the word 'leader' will be used to represent both a leader and a therapist.

The group leader has to play a pivotal role in initiating and promoting interaction. He/she will have to structure the group in a manner that the group members feel comfortable in sharing their thoughts and experiences. Communication within the group should not be dominated by only a few members. The leader must model appropriate behaviour in involving everyone in the group, sharing anxieties and fears and relating to others.

The leader would also have to engage with members in helping them to achieve their personal goals through group processes. The members should be able to connect to group processes and learn to benefit from them. They should also understand group dynamics, so that they can relate to other members and help each other through the process of counselling.

Group leaders will have to be active listeners. They will have to work with receptivity and be conscious of the verbal and non-verbal communication of the members. This will help them to guide the group members towards better understanding of one another and make them feel cared for. Members will also feel safe and comfortable in sharing their innermost thoughts.

At the organisational level, group leaders will have to set time limits, establish group rules and ensure smooth conduct of the group meetings. This involves ensuring that all members feel safe and are aware of their responsibilities towards the group and other members.

Implications of Group Therapy and Counselling

Group therapy is found to be most effective in combination with individual therapy. In educational settings this can work in isolation as well. It provides the benefit of addressing a common problem in one session and reaching a larger number of students. In school settings, group counselling and therapy can be used in single sessions that help to prevent and address issues that are associated with developmental stages. This may include building concentration, gender sensitivity, decision-making skills, anger management, interpersonal relationships, career counselling and sensitivity training among others. The sessions can be conducted by the school counsellor or the class teacher also. In addition, the counsellor and teacher may choose to invite experts to address specific concerns of students.

TRANSACTIONAL ANALYSIS

Eric Berne (1910–1970) was a Canadian psychologist who propounded the theory of transactional analysis to explain human behaviour. Building on Freudian notions, Berne believed that insights into people's behaviour can be developed by observing their social interactions. He was among the first psychologists to apply game theory to psychology. Game theory uses mathematical models to understand decision-making in situations of conflict as well as cooperation. In brief, using this theory, the psychologist attempts to identify the ego state of the person and uses it as a basis for understanding behaviour. It is used as a theory of personality, an approach to understanding social interaction and a method of therapy.

Understanding Personality and Human Nature

Berne propagated the notion that all humans can be understood in terms of ego states. Ego states are patterns of feeling, thinking and behaviour. Each human being exhibits three kinds of ego states, that is, parent, adult and child. At a given moment of time, in a social situation, an individual will exhibit any one of these states. One of these states is usually predominant. The three states are depicted in Figure 17.1.

Figure 17.1 Ego States in Transactional Analysis

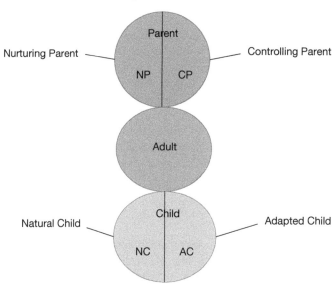

Source: Authors.

Parent Ego State

The parent state is a set of feelings, thoughts, attitudes and behaviours which resemble those of parental figures. These are subdivided into two states: the Controlling Parent and the Nurturing Parent. The controlling parent assumes a stance that is inhibiting and restrictive. The nurturing parent is supportive and enhances growth. The function of the parent state is to diminish anxiety by making certain decisions automatic and to conserve energy.

Adult Ego State

In the adult ego state, the person autonomously and objectively appraises reality and makes judgements. The characteristics of an adult ego state include organisation, adaptability and intelligence.

Child Ego State

The child ego state is a set of feelings, thoughts, attitudes and behaviour patterns which are relics of an individual's childhood. In other words, hidden inside everyone is the little boy/girl who thinks, feels, acts and responds in the way he/she did as a young child. The child state can also be divided into two states: Natural Child and Adapted Child.

Transactional analysis assumes a positive view of human nature. It rests on the belief that all humans are born with the capacity to be happy and at peace with themselves and others. In transactional analysis, this is popularly stated as 'I am OK, You're OK'. Berne (1966) stated, 'Every human being is born a prince or princess; early experiences convince some that they are frogs and the rest of pathological development follows from this'. All human beings possess the complete neurological apparatus for being reality oriented. This is what Berne called 'adult functioning'. All humans have a built-in drive to both mental and physical health.

Key Concepts

Dominant Ego State

The ego state which is most connected with psychic energy will be dominant at that time. Humans are motivated principally by three hungers: stimulus, recognition and structure. Stimulus hunger here refers to the need to interact, communicate and relate to others. Recognition hunger refers to having reciprocal interactions and relationships in which others acknowledge and recognise the individual. Structure hunger refers to the need for order, system and organisation for continuity in one's existence.

Strokes

Berne also put forth the concept of a stroke. A stroke is the basic unit of interaction. Strokes may be physical, verbal or non-verbal, but constitute the ways of communication or transaction with others. All humans thus have a need to be stroked. Strokes or social interactions can take any of the following forms:

1. Withdrawal: This is a state of an absence of overt communication with each other.
2. Rituals: This represents stylised signs of mutual recognition. These are generally brief and do not lead to interaction. For example, greeting each other through a few words or non-verbal gestures.
3. Activities: This refers to interacting for a common task. The relationships are matter of fact and restricted to the task at hand.
4. Pastimes: This refers to superficial conversations over general topics such as politics, the weather and so on.

5. Games: Interactions here take two levels. At the first level, the interaction is overt and of a social nature. At the second level, the interaction is at the covert, individual level.

6. Intimacy: The relationship is bilateral, candid and game free. It involves mutual sharing and does not involve exploitation. This generally satisfies stimulus, recognition and structure hungers.

Types of Transactions

Transactions or interactions of an interpersonal kind happen through an exchange of strokes. These strokes are exchanged between persons' ego states with one another. Transaction analysis involves diagnosing the ego state from which the stimulus stroke has come and which ego state of the other individual it is directed to. For example, Parent to Parent, Parent to Adult, Parent to Child, and so on. It also involves identifying whether the response stroke comes from the same ego state to which the stimulus stroke was targeted. This results in three kinds of transactions:

1. Complementary Transactions: In complementary transactions, people receive a response from the ego state that they have addressed. For example, a conversation between a teacher and student, where their position decorum is maintained.

2. Crossed Transactions: In crossed transactions, the response to the stimulus usually comes from an ego state which is different from the one addressed. It may reach an ego state which did not send the original stimulus. Communication thus breaks down.

3. Ulterior Transactions: In ulterior transactions, communication is disguised. In other words, under socially acceptable communication, an individual engages in an underlying socially more risky communication. For example, a teacher gives an ultimatum to the student to complete his work, the student disregards it as repeated warning from the teacher. In reality, the teacher and student have a complete mistrust of each other. The teacher may be biased against the student and the student may be demotivated towards work.

Life Scripts and Life Positions

Script is a life plan in which persons structure their time, their interactions, goals and so on. These are based on the decisions made in the childhood, primarily mediated through parents. Scripts determine people's destinies including their approach to relationships and to tasks. Scripts lead people to have an illusion of personal autonomy when in fact they are carrying out, often unthinkingly, the directives of the scripts. Sometimes people may question their scripts and feel the need to rewrite them. They have an identity crisis or moratorium which typically triggers this off. Mental health may be inferred from the life positions held by an individual. A healthy personality holds the life position 'I am OK, You're OK'. Life positions of 'I'm OK, You're not OK' and 'I'm not OK, You're OK' reflect neurosis. Finally, 'I'm not OK, You're not OK' represents psychosis.

Applications of Transactional Analysis

Therapy in transactional analysis would be aimed at helping the clients write their own life scripts rather than following scripts that have been written for them. It thus will focus on bringing autonomy. Therapy emphasises the recognition that the power to change and make decisions rests within the client himself/herself.

Transactional analysis has immense use for school teachers. It can help them to understand communication better and thus enable them to direct conversations with students by engaging with the right ego state.

Transactional analysis is an important therapeutic tool and has an advantage of acknowledging the capacity of the client to change. The second strength of transactional analysis lies in equipping the clients with an understanding of the theory. This translates into building their capacity for handling problems that may arise post-therapy. However, the therapeutic approach suffers from the limitation of being used at a superficial level, with the focus only remaining on the jargon. In addition, there is little empirical research to support the theoretical foundations of transactional analysis.

YOGA

In psychotherapy, yoga is seen as a technique of relaxation. In literal terms, the word yoga means to join or unite. The practise of yoga is aimed at self-realisation. Yoga is often seen as a method or technique that helps to achieve the union of the personal self with the ultimate, spiritual self. Yoga thus embraces both the philosophical roots to which it belongs, as well as the physical practice form that it assumes. It is a way of recognising and utilising one's inner potentials. It taps into one's whole being, encompassing physical, mental, emotional and spiritual aspects.

The concept of Spirit or *purusha* is central to the philosophy of Yoga. *Purusha* refers to pure consciousness. In other words it is the spirit that is limitless. When manifested in the individual, the *purusha* takes the form of the self. Self represents eternal existence and unbound happiness. However, humans remain unaware of this till the time they attain self-realisation. The goal of yoga, therefore, is seeking the source or the self within oneself.

Creation or *prakriti* is governed by three *guna*s or characteristics of *tamas, rajas* and *sattva. Tamas* represents inertia, *rajas* represents activity and *sattva* represents clarity. Individuals aim to reach a balance between these three. However, one of the three tends to dominate. Yogic practices aim at calming the mind. Thought processes are represented through *chitta* or mind. Awareness of the self is possible only when there is a balance between the three *guna*s and the body and mind are still and calm. Desires, ego, ignorance and fear act as obstacles to the path of enlightenment or self-realisation. Abnormal behaviour is a manifestation of the domination of the *guna*s of *rajas* and *tamas*. As has been mentioned earlier, all three *guna*s are present in every individual. Normality and abnormality are thus seen on a continuum and refer to variation in degrees of presence of the three *guna*s.

Techniques of Yoga

Techniques of yoga focus on the all-round development of body and mind. However, individual techniques may tend to focus on any one aspect rather than all of the aspects simultaneously. These include:

Health and Hygiene

In yogic practices, the first and foremost focus is often on maintaining physical strength and bodily fitness. This includes exercises as well as dietary control to develop a balance between the three *guna*s.

Realisation of Powers of the Mind

By developing powers of focus and concentration, the individual is able to tap into one's inner potential. This will help in achieving emotional and mental peace and calm. Yogic practices thus help in broadening the mind and recognising the powers of the mind in accomplishing tasks that seemed hitherto beyond reach.

Samadhi

One of the main aims of yoga is to reach *samadhi* or the union of the soul with the Supreme Being. It is thus a method of self-realisation. Focus in such techniques is on spiritual development and achieving a higher state of consciousness. This leads to happiness and contentment.

Yoga for Personality Development

The techniques described above serve important purposes in personality development. Through dietary regulation and exercise, the person can achieve detoxification and purification of the body. In contemporary times, where everyday life is fraught with addictions of the body, this can be particularly useful. Addictions would include dietary addictions to junk food, as well as addictive habits such as social networking. It can also help to develop resistance to and de-addiction from substance abuse.

Yoga provides a moral code of conduct that helps an individual to live a better adjusted life. By practising the life of a yogi, a person would live with honesty and truthfulness. A *sattvic* life or a life of purity will help in living an authentic life with little inner turmoil and conflict.

Yogic practices advocate control over senses as well as one's ego. Control over senses helps in ensuring that individuals respond to situations rather than reacting. By becoming more aware of one's ego and exercising control over it, one is also able to reduce conflicts and attain greater peace within and without.

Meditation and concentration also help to develop greater awareness of self and the world around us. This helps to also elevate consciousness to a higher level and eventually attain self-realisation.

Benefits of Yoga

Yogic practice has several benefits. It encourages optimism and faith in one's abilities. It helps to overcome negative attitudes such as ignorance or *avidya,* ego or *asmita,* attachment and jealousy or *raag–dwesh.* It helps to connect to oneself better by attempting to reach the inner consciousness. It relieves tension and anxiety and helps to channellise one's energies. It is rejuvenating physically and spiritually. It encourages controlled behaviour by choosing response to stimuli or environment. Through greater awareness of self, it helps to manage stress.

Implications for Schools

Schools can organise regular sessions that would help children to tap into yogic practices to move towards development of all aspects of their personality. This may be done through organising short yoga sessions in the daily morning assembly. Alternatively, this may be offered as an option in various physical education activities such as aerobics, sports and athletics. Organising workshops on a regular basis can also help to teach techniques of yoga to children. Teachers and parents will find that encouraging the practise of yoga among students will help them to cope with academic stress and deal with emotional turmoil during adolescence. Relaxation techniques and *asana*s that promote concentration are helpful in improving performance and build confidence.

ON A CONCLUDING NOTE

Alternate therapeutic practices vary largely according to the belief systems of the therapists and the training that they have undergone. Most therapists tend to follow an integrated approach, relying on techniques that provide for immediate benefits and also contribute towards psychological well-being in the longer run. The therapeutic practices discussed in this chapter have practical utility and focus on immediate benefits. While these are best practised under the supervision of a trained therapist, many of these practices can be applied by everyone. An understanding of these therapeutic techniques would help teachers to engage more effectively with school children.

18 Understanding Human Nature

In the previous chapters we discussed different theoretical approaches to understanding personality and psychotherapy. In the present chapter the focus is on understanding human nature as it is seen by the different schools of thought in psychology. The theoretical approaches provide anchorage to guidance, counselling and therapeutic practices. They also influence our understanding of human nature which in turn impacts everyday practices and belief systems.

The theoretical approaches to psychotherapy run parallel to the historical evolution and developments in the field of psychology. To briefly reiterate, the first force of psychology is represented by psychodynamic theories that focus on unravelling the unconscious to understand human personality. Freud's pioneering work focused on sexual, libidinal energy as the driving force of human behaviour. Jung and Adler carried his work forward, deviating from some of his ideas and propounding their own theories: analytic psychology and individual psychology, respectively. The second force of psychology emerged with the domination of scientific validation and experimentation in psychology. Shifting the focus from the unconscious to overt behaviour, behaviourism and cognitive behaviourism emerged as prominent therapeutic alternatives to psychodynamic techniques. While these proved to be effective techniques that worked towards changing patterns of behaviour as well as thoughts, they dehumanised the individual and gave little credence to the person. Humanism thus emerged as an alternative to the reductionist, mechanistic approach of behaviourism. The third force, dominated by the works of Maslow and Rogers, attempted to understand human needs and motivation and the development of self from the subjective perspective of the individual.

In this backdrop, the chapter will begin by developing a framework for understanding human nature and then discuss human nature in the context of the three forces of psychology.

ASPECTS OF HUMAN NATURE

Several theorists contributed to the trajectory of development in personality theories. Each theorist worked with a set of fundamental assumptions about human nature. These assumptions guided the vision of the theorist about the structure of personality and the notions of mental health and psychological well-being propounded by him or her. In this section, we will look at the fundamental questions that each theorist answers when addressing the concept of human nature. This will provide the framework within which the three forces of psychology will be revisited in the subsequent section. Hjelle and Ziegler (1992, 20) had developed a framework for the analysis of personality theories on the basis of the basic assumptions they hold about human nature. These were categorised into 'relatively continuous, bipolar dimensions' that provided a grid like structure within which personality theories could be placed. The dimensions that they had used are:

1. Freedom–Determinism
2. Rationality–Irrationality
3. Holism–Elementalism
4. Constitutionalism–Environmentalism
5. Changeability–Unchangeability
6. Subjectivity–Objectivity
7. Proactivity–Reactivity
8. Homeostasis–Heterostasis
9. Knowability–Unknowability

These categories serve as a useful tool if theories are to be analysed comparatively, in terms of their respective positions across these dimensions. As the authors stated, 'A major reason for treating these nine assumptions separately is that they permit relevant distinctions to be made among personality theorists. Certain assumptions are more salient than others in a given personality theory; the strength that each assumptions carries varies from theory to theory' (29). Further, it is difficult to peg the position of a personality theorist at any one point on the continuum. The categories thus are limiting and restrictive. An alternative approach, which is followed here, is to identify the fundamental questions that personality theorists address. It is important to recognise that theories may not take 'a position' in answering these questions and are thus not understood in comparison of another or in contrast to each other. Instead, the purpose here is to understand each theory in terms of the explanation it offers as a way of addressing the fundamental questions raised about key aspects of human nature. Each theory can and should be studied as a standalone theory that provides a unique way of understanding human personality. The questions discussed below, and the understanding of personality theories discussed so far, also serve the purpose of helping teachers, parents and caregivers to reflect on their own opinions and beliefs about human nature. This in turn can provide insights into our practises that are anchored in beliefs.

FACTORS INFLUENCING HUMAN NATURE

The first aspect in understanding human nature is to identify the factors that influence human nature. The fundamental question to be addressed here is: Is human nature a consequence of constitutional factors or environmental factors or both? One's feelings, beliefs and perceptions can be influenced by the person's innate tendencies to react to situations in a particular way. This accounts for the individual differences in the way people address situations. In contrast, some theorists opine that it is not constitutional but environmental factors that influence human nature. Early childhood experiences, stress factors and family dynamics are some of the external or environmental factors that influence human nature. Still other theorists are of the opinion that human nature is influenced by a combination of internal and external factors.

COMPREHENDING HUMAN NATURE

Human beings are considered the most complex of all living beings. The differences in the way people think and behave add to the complexity of biological structure. Jokes about the incomprehensibility of human behaviour, rationality and thought process are common. The fundamental question asked is: Is man completely knowledgeable or are there some private zones and experiences which are unknowable?

Theorists that focus on the overt aspects of human nature would believe in the knowability of human nature. On the other hand, those who believe that over behaviour is influenced by covert thoughts and feelings advocate the presence of the unconscious that is never fully comprehensible and yet exerts profound influence on the conscious. For the latter, human nature will never be entirely comprehensible or knowable.

STRUCTURE OF PERSONALITY

Theorists understand individuals in two distinct ways. The fundamental question here is: Is man better understood as a unified, integrated whole or a summation of parts? This is different from reducing the focus to any one aspect of the personality. In both views, a person is seen as comprising of many different facets: physical, emotional, cognitive and psychological. However, in the latter view, an understanding of each of these aspects individually is seen to provide an understanding of the person. In the former view, the person is not seen as a sum of parts. Instead, all these facets are seen as parts of an integrated whole which do not have any meaning in isolation. In yet another view, each of these aspects can be understood individually but in relation to each other.

SENSE OF CONTROL

Another important aspect of human nature is the sense of control that an individual has. A belief in ability of individuals to exercise control over one's actions puts the person incharge of one's future activities and life direction. In contrast, a deterministic view would look at the person in terms of the external forces that exert influence on the person. Thus, the family one is born in, life experiences, and socio-economic and cultural aspects would hold bearing over the kind of personality one develops. The key question addressed here is: Does man have free will or is he a victim of deterministic forces?

THOUGHT PROCESSES

Cognition and thought processes of individuals influence one's behaviours, actions and relationships with others. In understanding thought processes, theorists may presume that human beings are basically rational. This enables one to use rationality as a means of maintaining psychological well-being. A presumption of irrationality would give credence to behaviour and relationships being influenced by emotions, feelings and thoughts that are not rooted in rationality. The fundamental question to be answered here is: Is man basically rational? Does he retain his propensity to be rational? Ability to maintain rationality orientation will influence one's ability to maintain balance and psychological well-being.

EXPERIENCE AND PERCEPTION

In understanding human experience and perception, theorists presume an understanding of humans as thinking beings. Giving credence to individual differences, theorists recognise that the perception of the same phenomenon can vary for every individual. Each person thus forms a subjective perception of the world around him or her. This forms the subjective realm of reference which is important for understanding that person. In contrast, theorists argued that the external environment is not influenced or changed by the way the person perceives it. Thus it is not perception but sense that becomes important. The key question here is: Is man better understood as a subjective experiencing being, with his own reality being fundamental? Or as an objective person who lives in an environment which can be tangibly observed and studied?

ACTIVITY

Here the focus is on understanding human nature in the context of activity and initiative. In one approach, the environment provides the stimulus that elicits reactions from the person. This approach gives supremacy to the environment around the person. However, it does not acknowledge man's capacity to engage with the world around him, explore, be curious and experiment. Such affects suggest a proactive approach where the behaviour is initiated by the person and not by the environment around him or her. The fundamental question here is: Can man initiate action and behaviour on his own or does he only react to forces outside of him?

STABILITY

Stability represents adjustment and tension release. This leads to the notion of a mentally healthy person who is well-adjusted and in control of the situation. Such equilibrium, however, does not promote growth. Dissonance and confusion creates a need for growth. In other words, disequilibrium may not be threatening to mental health and is considered by some as essential for development. This debate may also be stated as: Is adjustment and personality development better represented by equilibrium (homeostasis) or by constructive dissonance and disequilibrium (heterostasis)?

In the context of the discussion on assumptions about human nature, the subsequent paragraphs attempt to present a picture of how a person is understood in the three forces of psychology. Freud, Skinner and Rogers have been taken as the representative theorists the forces relied upon.

FREUDIAN MAN

Freud's view of human nature was somewhat pessimistic. His focus was on repressed desires and thoughts and not on productive actions. He reduced all human actions, thoughts, feelings and aspirations to instincts. Instincts in turn have sexual and aggressive overtones that paint a picture of a frustrated person. In some ways, he equates man and animal by the unidimensional understanding of man with reference to instincts and drives. He highlights irrationality of human beings. He also emphasised that human beings are driven by pleasure (id) much more than they are driven by rationality (ego). He emphasised the relevance of childhood experiences and the influence that they have on later life. In fact, he has often been seen to adhere to absolute childhood determinism. He propounded that basic personality is formed early in life and persists unaltered into the adult years. Man's personal world is best understood mainly in terms of the traumas, anxieties, repression and hostilities stored in the unconscious, which forms the core of man's being. Unconscious is also the reservoir of all one's hidden desires. His view of the unconscious is thus negative, and implies that man is 'innately evil' and 'innately destructive'.

SKINNERIAN MAN

Skinner viewed personality and human nature as a collection of behaviour patterns which are observable. The self has no place in a scientific analysis of behaviour. Notions of human freedom, autonomous man, dignity and creativity are explanatory functions that serve to analyse and understand behaviour. Skinner felt that humans must be known by what they do. In other words, what a person 'does' is an indicator of what a person 'is'. Persons can be better understood by turning to environmental explanations rather than to inner states or activities since environmental processes are objective and subject to scientific validation. People understand themselves and manage themselves much more effectively when they understand the relevant contingencies in which they are placed. Shaping, modelling, training, conditioning, moulding and casting are effective ways in which behaviour can be modified.

ROGERIAN MAN

The Rogerian view is a model of hope and optimism. All humans have a natural tendency to move in the direction of independence, social responsibility, creativity and maturity. He believed that they have unlimited potential to develop in self-fulfilling ways. Every person must be understood as a function of his/her own unique perception of the environment in which he/she lives. This includes experiences, personal constructions of meaning and phenomenological reality. When people are bitter, revengeful and antisocial in their behaviour, they are displaying signs of not being in harmony with their inner nature. There probably has been curtailment of their freedom to experience and satisfy their inner nature. They may have experienced conditional regard and worth, an absence of empathy and a sense of being controlled by external forces. Rogers viewed man as an integrated whole. He believed that man is basically rational. Irrationality arises only when he is out of tune with his true inner nature. Man is purposive, forward moving and oriented towards the future. He has an inherent capacity and tendency for self-actualisation and has creative potential. The actualising tendency in man thrives on tension increase and not tension reduction. Man has to be understood in a past–present–future perspective.

CONCEPTUALISING A MENTALLY HEALTHY PERSONALITY

The perspectives discussed above highlight the need to understand the notion of a mentally health personality from the lens of various theories that have been discussed above and in the earlier chapters. Chapter 1 discussed the notion of sound mental health. To reiterate briefly, the concept of sound mental health extends beyond the absence of illness. A person is regarded as mentally healthy when he/she understands himself/herself and his/her own motivations, his/her wishes, desires and drives. The person should be able to accept himself/herself completely—with both his/her strengths and weaknesses. It is also important that the person's self-image be rationally constructed and be rooted in reality. A positive self-image will not be a healthy notion of self, if it is not rooted in reality.

The term 'personality' has been derived from the word 'persona' which means mask. For a sound, mentally healthy personality, it is important that the person be able to use the right 'persona' at the right time. The larger goal of life can be to shed these personas and live an authentic life, true to oneself. Fixation of identity in a particular persona leads to an unhealthy state of being. Psychological well-being is important, not only for smooth functioning of life, but also for growth of the individual. In addition, all of us live in a social network. Therefore, it is of utmost importance that we are socially well adjusted and in harmony with the physical and social environment around us. Psychological well-being is thus represented by a sense of calm within and without.

Different theorists have put forth different ideas about personality from which their notions of a mentally healthy personality can be culled out. The paragraphs that follow discuss these notions for some of the key thinkers in psychology.

Behaviourism

All behaviourists explain human activity without recourse to terms referring to consciousness. Behaviour according to them is 'shaped' into skills or patterned habits by the use of reinforcers. Healthy personality according to a behaviouristic view calls for competence and self-control—the ability to suppress action that no longer yields positive reinforcers. Emphasis is on learning behaviour that helps in attaining the material progress. Adaptability requires that the human being possess the ability to discern contingencies. Needs are gratified and dangers averted according to the rules implicit in nature and in society. Gratification of needs and aversion of dangers serve as aims of life. Human beings are visualised as devoid of innate motivation for growth, agency and free will.

Sigmund Freud (1855–1939)

According to Freud, psychic life can be represented at three levels of consciousness: the conscious (consisting of sensation and experiences), the pre-conscious (a bridge between the conscious and unconscious regions of the mind) and the unconscious (stores primitive instinctual drives and repressed emotions and memories). Freud believed that the significant aspects of human behaviour are shaped and directed by impulses and drives which are totally unconscious. Any experience or emotion which the conscious found threatening was pushed into the unconscious. Freud felt that in this manner, the unconscious would therefore continue to expand. This imbalance would lead to a break down. And therefore, for a mentally healthy person it was important to have frequent cathartic experiences to give vent to the unconscious.

Freud gave three basic structures to personality: the id, which refers to the primitive, instinctive and inherited aspects of personality. It functions entirely in the unconscious and is linked to instinctual, biological urges that energise our behaviour. The id operates on the pleasure principle. The ego is the decision-making component which seeks to gratify the desires of the id in accordance with the constraints of society (superego). The ego operates on the reality principle. The superego represents an internalised version of society's norms and standards of behaviour.

The individual experiences frequent intra-psychic conflict. The id is always seeking gratification of instincts and the superego always imposes a moral code. The ego has to negotiate between the two and arrive at a decision. This intra-psychic conflict is essential. Without this conflict, growth of the individual cannot take place. But high ego strength is also necessary. This would ensure that the person remains rooted in reality and works rationally. Also, high ego strength is necessary to ensure that neither id nor superego dominates the person's behaviour which might lead to narcissism (id domination) or self-righteousness (superego domination).

However, this does not mean that id and superego are to be completely suppressed. Both id and superego should be allowed expression because as much as pleasure is essential for a person to be happy, conforming to the society is also important. Whenever the ego feels threatened, the person starts to feel anxious. Threat to the ego comes from three sources: external environment (realistic anxiety), the id (neurotic anxiety) and the superego (moral anxiety). While a little bit of realistic anxiety is acceptable and even necessary for a person to function in a mentally healthy manner; high moral anxiety and high neurotic anxiety are unhealthy. High moral anxiety also leads to social anxiety (fear of exclusions from peer group membership). In case of moral anxiety, the person loses complete touch with reality. In case of neurotic anxiety, the person remains in touch with reality but becomes highly irrational. Therefore, a mentally healthy person would be one with a dominant ego and the ability to reach a balance between id, ego and superego.

In order to relieve anxiety, the ego often uses defence mechanisms such as rationalisation, repression, reaction formation and sublimation. These may be integrative or disintegrative. Integrative defence mechanisms help in dealing with anxiety, while disintegrative distort reality for the individual. A mentally healthy person is one who is able to use more, though not only, of integrative defence mechanisms.

Freud maintained that all human activity is determined by instincts. Instincts, he said, represent innate bodily states of excitations that seek expression and tension release. All actions serve to reduce these tensions. Freud divided all instincts into two broad groups: the life instincts and the death instincts. Life instincts are forces that serve to maintain vital life processes and propagation of the species. The sex instincts were identified by Freud as the most significant life instincts. All forms of cruelty, aggression, suicide and murder are seen to stem out of death instincts. At a given point of time, in an individual, either life instincts or the death instincts are dominant. A mentally healthy individual is one who has dominant life instincts.

Freud also proposed five stages of psychosexual development with areas of libidinal focus. The five stages were: oral, anal, phallic, latency and genital. For any individual, it is important that each stage provides optimum gratification so that transition to the next higher stage is smooth. Also during the phallic stage, boys face the Oedipus complex and girls face the Electra complex. Resolving these complexes is of utmost importance. Otherwise, the individual may face problems in adult sexual relationships. A mentally healthy person would, therefore, be one who is able to attain optimum gratification level at each psychosexual stage of development and who is successfully able to resolve his Oedipus and Electra complexes.

Since Freud's whole theory focused on childhood years, for a mentally healthy person, healthy and happy childhood experiences are important.

Erik Erikson (1902–1994)

Erikson insisted that his ideas are only a systematic extension of Freud's conceptions. However, unlike Freud, Erikson's theory focused on ego development. He believed that the ego is an autonomous system that deals with reality through perception, thinking, attention and memory. He emphasised the adaptive function of the ego. Therefore, a well-developed ego is the first sign of a mentally healthy person.

Erikson stressed on the historical setting in which the child's ego is moulded. He laid emphasis on the influence of nature of social institutions and value systems on the development of ego. Therefore, a sound mental health, through sound ego, may be developed through providing an appropriate environment and opportunities.

Erikson believed that human development is characterised by a series of eight stages that are universal to human kind. These are: oral, anal, genital, latency, adolescence, early adulthood, middle adulthood and late adulthood. Each stage in the life cycle has an optimal time or critical period, in which it is dominant and hence emerges. A fully functioning personality emerges only when all stages unfold according to the plan.

Also, each psychosocial stage is accompanied by a crisis that is the turning point in life. Each psychosocial crisis includes both a positive and a negative component. If the conflict is resolved satisfactorily, the positive component is absorbed into the emerging ego and a healthy development is assured. If the conflict persists or is resolved unsatisfactorily, the developing ego is damaged. The person must adequately resolve each crisis in order to move to the next stage with maturity. Therefore, resolution of conflict appropriately becomes important for sound mental health.

Carl Jung (1875–1971)

Jung theorised that the psyche or personality is composed of three separate but interacting structures: the ego, the personal unconscious and the collective unconscious.

The ego is the centre of the conscious mind. It represents our thoughts, feelings, memories and perceptions. He linked conscious behaviour with two attitudes: introversion and extraversion. He believed that either one of these attitudes remained consistently dominant in a person. Further, he proposed four functions linked with these attitudes: thinking, feeling, sensing and intuiting. In every person, all four exist, but at a given point of time only one remains dominant. As long as a person is able to balance his rational (thinking and feeling) functions with the irrational (sensing and intuiting) the person is mentally healthy. Also, a balance needs to be maintained between, say, thinking and feeling, so that the person remains well-adjusted to himself and the environment.

The personal unconscious houses conflicts and memories (positive as well as negative) that the conscious has repressed and forgotten. The collective unconscious refers to a common evolutionary, hereditary pool that each individual inherits. On the basis of the contents of the unconscious, he proposed certain archetypes, which all of us inherit. Some of these are person, anima, animus, shadow and the self. While persona refers to the mask we wear to get along in the society, the shadow represents the negative side which we usually suppress. However, Jung saw the shadow as the source of vitality, spontaneity and creativity. An overemphasis on persona leads to a shallow existence and locking of emotions. Therefore, adequate expression of persona as well as shadow are important for sound mental health.

Anima represents the feminine side of man and animus represents the masculine side of women. In order for a person to be self-realised and not develop a lopsided personality, both anima and animus must be expressed in proper balance. The self is the core of personality around which all other elements are organised and unified. The development of self is the ultimate goals of life. The degree of adjustment of one's personality depends on the extent to which one is successful in actualising oneself. Balance between the archetypes represents harmony between conscious and unconscious.

According to Jung, failure to maintain or achieve reconciliation between one's conscious and unconscious behaviour leads to maladaptive behaviour and mental illness. When one's conscious is not in tune with the unconscious or when the unconscious turns hostile on account of being not properly understood by the conscious, imbalances are created which lead to hostility towards oneself and one's environment.

Jung refers to the process of individuation as important in the process of personality development. A mentally healthy person would be the one who would be moving towards becoming an individuated person. In Chapter 14 the characteristics of an individuated person have been discussed.

Alfred Adler (1870–1937)

Adler believed that each individual is born with some kind of subjective feelings of inferiorities that arise from psychological or social disabilities. The individual tries to compensate for these inferiorities. If these attempts at compensation are unsuccessful, the person develops inferiority complexes. Overcompensation leads to superiority complexes.

The first indication of sound mental health therefore is the ability to adequately compensate for inferiority feelings. To overcome inferiorities and strive for superiority (over self) therefore becomes the prime motive for life. This goal of superiority can take either a negative or a positive direction. A negative or destructive direction is seen in people who strive for superiority through selfishness at the expense of others. This is an indication of maladjustment. Well-adjusted people express striving positively, through a concern for welfare of others. Adler portrayed human beings as living in sync with their social world but perpetually striving to create a better world.

Adler also proposed the concept of each person's unique style of life. The style of life encompasses the unique pattern of traits, behaviours and habits of a person. He believed that the style of life is shaped by creative power. Linking to these life style attitudes, Adler gave four personality types: the Ruling, the Getting, the Avoiding and the Socially Useful type. According to Adler, a mentally healthy, mature person would be the socially useful type. With social orientation, such a person will be able to express genuine concern for others and will live in communion with those around him. Such a person embodies both a high degree of activity and social interest.

Adler considered the potential for social interest to be innate. Adler believed that an individual's life has value only to the extent that he adds values to others. People who are mentally healthy are genuinely concerned about others. Their goal of superiority is thus social, encompassing the well-being of all. Maladjusted or unhealthy people lack social interest.

Erich Fromm (1900–1980)

Fromm said that human existence is marked by loneliness, isolation and alienation. He believed that men and women today are caught in a painful dilemma between freedom and security. There is freedom from rigid social, political, economic and religious constraints. This freedom has led to a decline in a security and sense of belonging. People need power and choice but also need to be connected to others.

He described a number of strategies, which he termed as escape mechanisms, to cope with the dilemmas such as authoritarianism, destructiveness and automaton conformity. He suggested a healthy alternative to the above: positive freedom. He believed that people can be separate and unique beings without losing their sense of unity with others and social reality.

A mentally healthy person would use positive freedom rather than escape mechanisms to cope with the dilemma. Fromm emphasised that love and work are the key components to developing positive freedom through the process of spontaneous activity. These are important towards becoming fully functioning.

Further, he said that this dilemma has created five existential needs in man. The need for relatedness, transcendence, rootedness, identity and a frame of orientation and devotion. He also suggested the optimum ways of resolving these needs—

- 'productive love' which enables people to work together and at the same time maintain their individuality;
- creativity;
- maintaining symbolic ties with parents, home and community; and
- developing an objective and rational view of the natural and social world.

He said that a rational perspective is absolutely necessary for maintaining sound mental health. A mentally healthy person would also have an overall goal or God or object of devotion to which he would attribute meaning of life.

Fromm also suggested five social character types, which he grouped into productive and non-productive classes. He said that none of these types exist in purity but blend together in different proportions in different people. Receptive types believe that the source of everything good in life lies outside them. Exploitative types take whatever they desire from others through force. Hoarding types accumulate material possessions, power and love and they avoid sharing their possessions. Marketing types only value their self as a commodity to be sold or exchanged for success. Non-productive types are considered unhealthy. The productive type represents the ultimate goal in human development. It encompasses the human capacity to productive reasoning, love and work (creative self-expression). In general, the mental health of a particular type depends on the ratio of positive or negative traits manifested by the individual.

Abraham Maslow (1908–1970)

One of the most fundamental themes of Maslow's theory is that each person must be studied as an integrated, unique, organised whole. He also believed that human nature is essentially good. The evil forces within people result from frustration and thwarting of basic needs. He also saw creativity as an inherent, universal human function which leads to all forms of self-expression.

He believed that people are motivated to seek personal goals and make their lives meaningful. He proposed a hierarchy of needs. Man is a wanting organism. As soon as one need is fulfilled, another need arises. He also believed that a lower order need must at least partially be satisfied in order for a higher order need to become active. However, he agreed that in some people higher order needs would be more active. His hierarchy from lower to higher was physiological needs, safety and security needs, love and belongingness needs, self-esteem needs and self-actualisation needs. He said that the farther up the hierarchy the person is able to go, the more individuality, humanness and psychological health he/she will demonstrate.

He believed that self-actualisation was the ultimate aim of life, but very few people were able to achieve it. But, he said that the need to be the kind of person one is capable of becoming is present in everyone. A self-actualised person represents his ideal psychological self. He also gave two broad categories of human motives: deficit motives and growth motives. Deficit or D-motives refer to lower order needs in the needs hierarchy. On the other hand, growth or meta-needs or Being or B-motives are distant goals associated with the urge to actualise potentials. Deficit motives aim at repairing deficit states. Growth motives aim at expansion of horizons. Meta-motivation is not possible until the person has satisfied lower order needs. However, both are important for sound mental health.

Maslow said that meta-living was the ideal way of living. A person who is living in deficit state would only be a reactor. He would be bored, empty and half alive. Therefore, he would be psychologically dissatisfied. A mentally healthy person would therefore have a meta-life.

Carl Rogers (1902–1987)

Rogers regarded the person as an active force of energy oriented towards future goals and self-directed purposes, and not as a creature controlled by external forces. He believed that people were positive and rational, in harmony with self and others when they were functioning fully. When they occasionally expressed bitter and anti-social feelings, they were not in touch with their true self. He also believed that all humans have a tendency to be independent, socially responsible, creative and mature. Also, human beings have unlimited potential to develop.

Rogers hypothesised that all behaviour is guided and energised by a unitary motive called actualising tendency. Other needs such as hunger (for maintenance), sex (for enhancement), achievement and so on are ancillary to this actualising tendency. This tendency is the essence of all life. The person's need to develop and improve was therefore the ultimate goal of a mentally healthy person. A healthy person wants to achieve something that makes the person's life more enriching and satisfying.

Rogers used the term 'organismic valuing process' to evaluate all experiences in the context of how well they serve the actualising tendency. People therefore assigned a positive value to experiences that promoted and enhanced the self. Those experiences perceived as negating or hindering actualisation of the self are valued negatively. A sound mental health requires that the person has more positive experiences and is able to avoid the negative experiences successfully.

Rogers emphasised that a person's relationship to the environment must be understood in his/her perception of it. Similarly, past experiences affect behaviour in how the person presently interprets or perceives them. Past experiences also exert an influence on the meanings of present experiences. Therefore, a mentally healthy person would be the one who is able to perceive past and present reality positively and correctly.

Rogers said that the self was a significant element in human experience and people strived to become their real self. The self-concept includes our perceptions of what we are and what we think we ought to be. Along with this, what we would like to be. This he called the ideal self.

A mentally healthy person must have a positive self-concept. For this it is important that the person receive unconditional, positive regard. The person should feel accepted and loved unconditionally. Behaviour of a person is mostly consistent with his/her self-concept. Therefore, positive experiences are allowed to enter into awareness and are accurately perceived. Negative experiences are blocked out of awareness. Whenever the person feels that an experience is an incongruent with self-concept. The behavioural response of the organism to threat is called the process of defence. The goal of defence is maintenance of the wholeness or integrity of the self.

A mentally healthy person would have a strong defence and would be able to maintain himself/herself. For the process of defence, he suggested two defence mechanisms: perceptual distortion and denial. A mentally healthy person would use both of these mechanisms but only in moderation. A mentally ill person would be the one whose defences become inoperable due to significant degree of incongruence between the self and ongoing experiences. In such a defenceless state, the person's self gets shattered.

The ideal psychological state is achieved by the fully functioning person. Such individuals use their capacities and talents in realising their potentials. The characteristics of a fully functioning person have been discussed in Chapter 16.

Since Rogers assumed that man is inherently good, he stressed that violent actions were a result of a person who was not in touch with his true self. A mentally healthy person would recognise his true self and always remain in touch with his true nature.

Eric Berne (1910–1970)

Berne had a positive view of human nature. He believed that a healthy person would be the one who would be happy and at peace with himself/herself. At the same time, he/she would be at peace with others around him/her. A healthy person is reality oriented and has a built-in drive for sound physical and mental health.

In a mentally healthy person, the dominant ego state, either adult or child or parent, would correspond with his/her role in life. Communication would be complementary with the ego states. The need to be stroked would be gratified which would in turn satisfy stimulus, recognition and structure hungers. The state of a person's mental health may be inferred from one's life positions and life script. A typical mentally healthy person would assume the life stance 'I'm OK, you're OK!' and would be relatively game free.

ON A CONCLUDING NOTE

Theoretical perspectives discussed in the earlier chapters have provided the base for understanding human nature. The discussion on the various facets of human nature is facilitative towards comprehending theories. The assumptions about human nature vary across theorists. It is in this light that the notion of a mentally healthy personality is developed. This in turn is also helpful towards developing one's own perspective towards human nature and a mentally healthy personality.

BIBLIOGRAPHY

Addlakha, R. 2008. *Deconstructing Mental Illness: An Ethnography of Psychiatry, Women and the Family*. New Delhi: Zubaan.

Agochiya, D. 2010. *Life Competencies for Adolescents: Training Manual for Facilitators, Teachers and Parents*. New Delhi: SAGE Publications.

Archer, S. L., ed. 1994. *Interventions for Adolescent Identity Development*. Thousand Oaks, CA: SAGE Publications.

Axline, V. M. 1969. *Play Therapy: The Inner Dynamics of Childhood*. New York, NY: Ballantine Books.

———. 1974. *Play Therapy*. New York, NY: Ballentine Books.

Baron, R. A., Branscombe, N. A., Byrne, D., and Bhardwaj, G. 2009. *Social Psychology*, 12th ed. Delhi: Pearson.

Bharat, S. 2003. 'Women, Work and Family in Urban India: Towards New Families?' In *Psychology in Human and Social Development: Lessons from Diverse Cultures*, edited by J. W. Berry, R. C. Mishra, and R. C. Tripathi, 155–169. New Delhi: SAGE Publications.

Berne, E. 1966. *Principles of Group Treatment*. New York, NY: Grove Press.

Bichu, M. V. 2015. *Right Parenting: New Age Parenting and Child-health Handbook*. Mumbai: Popular Prakashan.

Bronfenbrenner, U. 1990. 'Alienation and the Four Worlds of Childhood'. In *Adolescent Behavior and Society*, edited by R. E. Muuss, 4th ed, 123–139. New York, NY: McGraw Hill.

Capuzzi, D., and Gross, D. R. 1997. *Introduction to the Counseling Profession*. Boston, MA: Allyn and Bacon.

Chaudhary, N. 2004. *Listening to Culture: Constructing Reality from Everyday Talk*. New Delhi: SAGE Publications.

Chib, M. 2011. *One Little Finger*. New Delhi: SAGE Publications.

Children's Society. 2008. *The Good Childhood Inquiry: Health Research Evidence*. London: Children's Society.

Choudhary, G. B. 2014. *Adolescence Education*. New Delhi: Prentice Hall.

Corey, G. 2012. *Theory and Practice of Group Counselling*, 8th ed. Belmont, CA: Cengage.

Dasen, P. R. 2003. 'Theoretical Frameworks in Cross Cultural Developmental Psychology: An Attempt at Integration'. In *Cross Cultural Perspectives in Human Development: Theory, Research and Applications*, edited by T. S. Saraswathi, 128–165. New Delhi: SAGE Publications.

Dobson, K. S., ed. 2009. *Handbook of Cognitive Therapies*, 3rd ed. New York, NY: Guilford Press.

Frager, R., and Fadiman, J. 1984. *Personality and Personal Growth*, 2nd ed. New York, NY: Harper Collins.

Garvey, C. 1990. *Play*. New York, NY: Harvard.

Gergen, K. J. 2011. 'The Self as Social Construction'. *Psychological Studies* 56 (1): 108–116.

Gilliland, B. E., James, R. K., and Bowman, J. T. 1989. *Theories and Strategies in Counselling and Psychotherapy*, 2nd ed. Boston, MA: Allyn and Bacon.

Ginsburg, K. R. 2007. 'The Importance of Play in Healthy Child Development and Maintaining Strong Parent–Child Bonds'. *Pediatrics* 119 (1): 182–191.

Goleman, D. 1995. *Emotional Intelligence*. New York, NY: Bantam Books.

Government of India. 2014. 'Rights of Persons with Disabilities Bill, 2014'. Accessed on 31 October 2016. http://www.prsindia.org/uploads/media/Person%20with%20Disabilities/The%20Right%20of%20Persons%20with%20Disabilities%20Bill.pdf

Graham, A. M., Fisher, P. A., and Pfeifer, J. H. 2013. 'What Sleeping Babies Hear: A Functional MRI Study of Interparental Conflict and Infants' Emotion Processing'. *Psychological Science* 24 (5): 782–789. doi:10.1177/095679761245880

Grover, S., Dutt, A., and Avasthi, A. 2010. 'An Overview of Indian Research in Depression'. *Indian Journal of Psychiatry* 52 (7): 178–188.

Gupta, A. 2012. 'Understanding Children's Play at Pre-primary Level: A Psychosocial Perspective'. In *Education for Mental Health: Rethinking Issues in Guidance and Counselling*, edited by N. Ranganathan, 50–72. New Delhi: SAGE Publications.

Gupta, L. 2008. 'Growing Up Hindu and Muslim: How Early Does It Happen?' *Economic and Political Weekly* 43 (6): 35–41.

Harre, R. 2006. *Key Thinkers in Psychology*. London: SAGE Publications.

Hjelle, L. A., and Ziegler, D. J. 1992. *Personality Theories: Basic Assumptions, Research and Applications*, 3rd ed. New York, NY: McGraw Hill.

Jenkins, R. 2008. *Social Identity*, 3rd ed. London: Routledge.

Kakar, S. 1995. *The Colors of Violence: Cultural Identities, Religion and Conflict*. New Delhi: Viking.

———. 2005. *The Inner World: A Psychoanalytic Study of Childhood and Society in India*, 2nd ed. New Delhi: Oxford India Paperbacks.

———. 2007. 'Family Matters'. *India International Centre Quarterly* 33 (3, 4): 214–221.

Kumar, A., Pathak, A., Kumar, S., Rastogi, P., and Rastogi, P. 2012. 'The Problem of Child Sexual Abuse in India. Laws, Legal Lacuna and the Bill-PCSOB-2011'. *Journal of Indian Academy of Forensic Medicine* 34 (2): 170–175.

Kumar, K. 1992. *What is Worth Teaching?* New Delhi: Orient Longman.

Larson, R., Verma, S., and Dworkin, J. 2003. 'Adolescence without Family Disengagement: The Daily Family Lives of Indian Middle Class Teenagers'. In *Cross-cultural Perspectives in Human Development: Theory, Research and Applications*, edited by T. S. Saraswathi, 258–286. New Delhi: SAGE Publications.

Marcia, J. E. 1966. 'Development and Validation of Ego Identity Status'. *Journal of Personality and Social Psychology*. 3(5): 551–558.

Maslow, A. 1971. *The Farther Reaches of Human Nature*. New York, NY: Viking.

Maslow, A. H. 1943. 'A Theory of Human Motivation'. *Psychological Review* 50 (4): 370–396.

McLeod, S. A. 2015. 'Humanism'. Accessed on 25 November 2016. www.simplypsychology.org/humanistic.html

Ministry of Human Resource and Development. 2009. *Right of Children to Free and Compulsory Act, 2009*. New Delhi: Government of India.

Ministry of Social Justice and Empowerment. 1995. *Persons with Disabilities (Equal Opportunities, Protection of Rights and Full Participation) Act, 1995*. New Delhi: Government of India.

Ministry of Women and Child Development. 2012. *The Protection of Children from Sexual Offences Act, 2012*. New Delhi: Government of India.

National Scientific Council on the Developing Child. 2004. 'Young Children Develop in an Environment of Relationships'. Working Paper 1. Accessed on 5 October 2016. www.developingchild.net

Patel, V., and Thara, R., eds. 2003. *Meeting the Mental Health Needs of Developing Countries: NGO Innovations in India*. New Delhi: SAGE Publications.

Ranganathan, N. 2008. *Changing Contours of Family Dynamics in India. National Conference on Indian in the 21st Century*. Mumbai: University of Mumbai.

Ranganathan, N., and Wadhwa, T. 2014. 'Creating a School Environment Free from Trauma, Stress and Anxiety'. In *What is RTE? Some Ways of Making Education Accessible: A Handbook for Teachers*, edited by S. Sharma, 22–44. New Delhi: NCERT.

Repetti, R., Flook, L., and Sperling, J. 2011. Family Influences on Development Across the Life Span. In *Handbook of Life-span Development*, edited by K. L. Fingerman, C. A. Berg, J. Smith, and T. C. Antonucci, 745–775. New York, NY: Springer Publishing.

Rogers, C. R. 1946. 'Significant Aspects of Client-centered Therapy'. *American Psychologist* 1 (10): 415–422.

Sarason, I. G., and Sarason, B. R. 2005. *Abnormal Psychology: The Problem of Maladaptive Behavior*, 11th ed. New Delhi: Prentice Hall.

Saraswathi, T. S. 1999. 'Adult-child Continuity in India: Is Adolescence a Myth or an Emerging Reality? In *Culture, Socialization and Human Development: Theory, Research and Applications in India*, edited by T. S. Saraswathi, 213–232. New Delhi: SAGE Publications.

Sedikides, C., Gaertner, L., and O'Mara, E. M. 2011. 'Individual Self, Relational Self, Collective Self: Hierarchical Ordering of the Tripartite Self'. *Psychological Studies* 56 (1): 98–107.

Seligman, L., and Reichenberg, L. W. 2011. *Theories of Counselling and Psychotherapy: Systems, Strategies, and Skills*. New Delhi: Prentice Hall.

Sharma, N. 1990. 'Current Trends in Infant Care: An Indian Experience'. *Early Childhood Development and Care* 58 (1): 71–79.

Veereshwar, P. 2002. *Indian Systems of Psychotherapy*. New Delhi: Kalpaz Publications.

Verma, S., and Saraswathi, T. S. 2002. 'Adolescence in India: Street Urchins to Silicon Valley Millionaires? In *The World's Youth: Adolescence in Eight Regions of the Globe*, edited by B. Brown, R. Larson, and T. Saraswathi, 105–140. New York, NY: Cambridge University Press.

Wadhwa, T. 2013. 'Religious Commitments, Identity Development, and Family Life Experiences of Young Adults from Inter-Religious Families'. Unpublished Doctoral Dissertation, University of Delhi, Delhi.

Weiner, I. B., Stricker, G., and Widiger, T. A., ed. 2003. *Handbook of Psychology: Volume 8—Clinical Psychology*. Hoboken, NJ: John Wiley & Sons.

Whitebread, D. 2012. *The Importance of Play*. Belgium: Toy Industries of Europe.

Woolfolk, A. 2006. *Educational Psychology*, 9th ed. New Delhi: Pearson.

World Health Organisation. 2011. *Mental Health Atlas*. Geneva: WHO.

Young, J. E., Klosko, J. S., and Weishaar, M. E. 2003. *Schema Therapy: A Practitioner's Guide*. New York, NY: Guilford Press.

INDEX

Lightning Source UK Ltd.
Milton Keynes UK
UKHW030614121220
374995UK00005B/206